THE
STUDENT
JOURNALIST
GUIDE
SERIES

THE STUDENT JOURNALIST AND

21 KEYS TO NEWS REPORTING

by

HAZEL PRESSON

Poynter Institute for Media Studies
Library

JUN 27 '86

PUBLISHED BY
THE ROSEN
PUBLISHING GROUP, INC.
NEW YORK

Published in 1982, 1984 by The Rosen Publishing Group, Inc.
29 East 21st Street, New York, N.Y. 10010

Copyright 1982 by Hazel Presson

All rights reserved. No part of this book may be reproduced in any form without written permission from the publisher, except by a reviewer.

Second Printing

Library of Congress Cataloging in Publication Data

Presson, Hazel.
  21 keys to news reporting.

  (The Student journalist guide series)
    1. Journalism, School. 2. Reporters and reporting.
  I. Title. II. Title: Twenty-one keys to news reporting. III. Series.
  LB3620.P73   371.8'97   81-15767
  ISBN 0-8239-0519-5   AACR2

Manufactured in the United States of America

*The Student Journalist
and
21 KEYS
TO NEWS REPORTING*

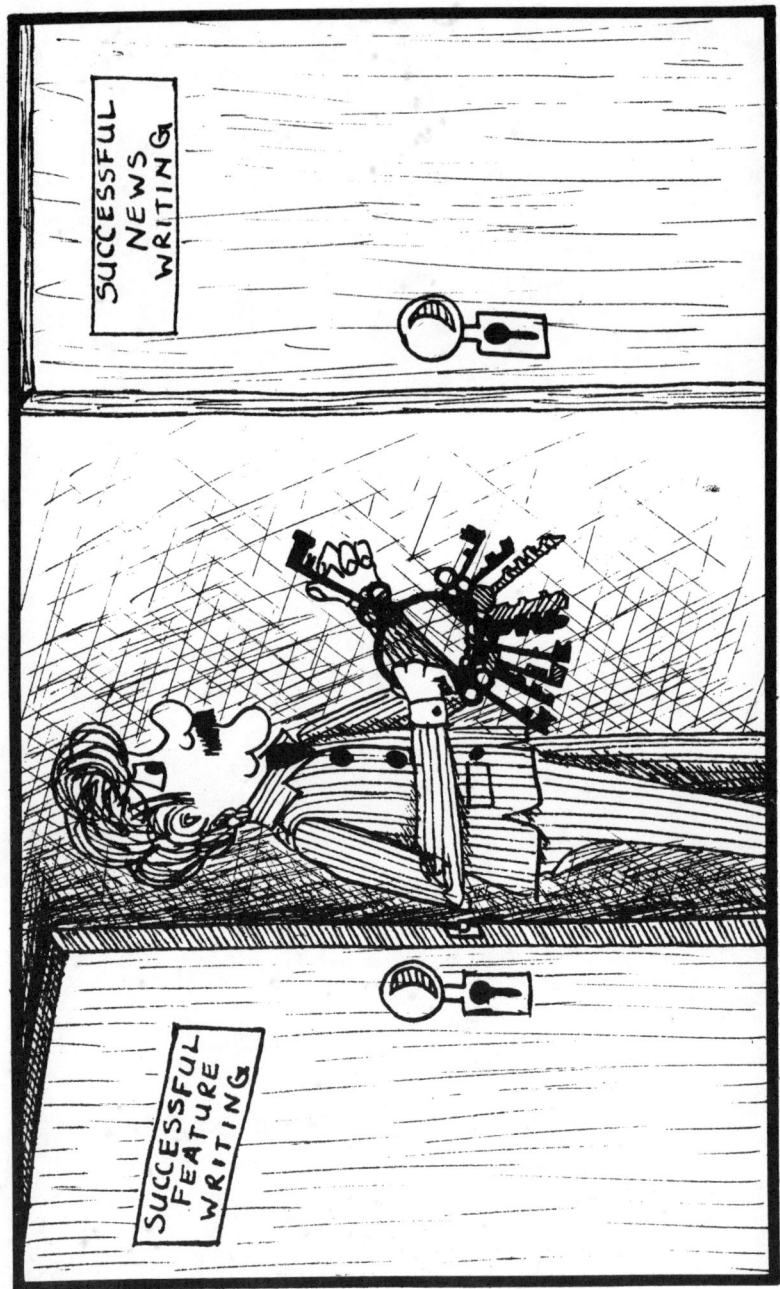

About the Author

Hazel Presson's experience as editor, teacher, adviser, and author dates from a "glorious hour," as she puts it, when she won a prize for a news story in junior high school competition.

That excitement has continued, for her activities have included editing a high school newspaper and college yearbook, teaching on the high school and college levels, and advising various publications that have earned top awards in national scholastic press competition.

With this, she has been interested in scholastic press associations and in a wide range of related activities. "Journalism is a rewarding way of life," she says. "It's interesting to know what's going on—and fun to pass the news along to others."

A member of Phi Beta Kappa, Miss Presson holds an MA degree from the University of Arkansas and has done additional work at Columbia University under a grant from Time-Life, at the University of Oklahoma as a Newspaper Fund Fellow, and at the University of Minnesota with a Jostens Award. Among honors she holds are the Gold Key and Golden Crown of the Columbia Scholastic Press Association, the Pioneer Award of the National Scholastic Press Association, and the Golden Quill of the University of Texas. A past president of the Columbia Scholastic Press Advisers Association, she now serves as executive secretary of the Ark-homa Regional Scholastic Press Association. She was recently named to the Future Journalists of America Hall of Fame.

In addition to serving as a judge and consultant in critical services, Miss Presson participates in conferences, workshops, and short courses. "It's exciting to work with young people interested in producing better publications," she says. "Most of us face the same basic problems and needs, so both students and advisers benefit from experiences we can share."

Miss Presson becomes the author in after-school hours, this interest dating back to *The Story of Arkansas,* adopted as a state text. It was followed by three volumes in the Student Journalist series: *The Student Journalist and News Reporting, The Student Journalist and Interviewing,* and *The Student Journalist and Layout.* When time permits, she "relaxes" by working on a historical novel.

Contents

About This Book	ix
Acknowledgments	xi
The 21 Keys	
Key #1—*Understand Your Responsibility as a Journalist*	3
Key #2—*Develop a Sense of the Newsworthy*	13
Key #3—*Ask Questions, Think Questions*	25
Key #4—*Cover the Story*	35
Key #5—*Know the Rules*	41
Key #6—*Recognize the Various Kinds of News Stories*	51
Key #7—*Look for Feature and Sidebar Stories*	85
Key #8—*Report in Depth*	97
Key #9—*Seek Background Material*	105
Key #10—*Achieve Skill in Interviewing*	113
Key #11—*Remember: "Accuracy Always"*	125
Key #12—*Organize Your Story*	133
Key #13—*Be Thorough—Be Complete*	145
Key #14—*Consider the Lead*	157
Key #15—*Be Specific*	175
Key #16—*Learn to Use the Language*	183
Key #17—*Cultivate an Effective Writing Style*	193
Key #18—*Employ Effective Work Habits*	203
Key #19—*Develop Confidence*	211
Key #20—*Learn by Seeing What Others Do*	217
Key #21—*Report in Pictures, Too*	229
Associations Offer Aids	243

About This Book

The plan for this book has grown from a long-expressed need for a very simple approach to a very complex subject—the reporting of news. Specifically here, that means reporting news for the school paper, but it is to be hoped that in the stating of basics, even those reporters with experience will find something helpful.

Reporting is both a craft and an art. The craft can be learned, and this book is designed to be a help in that learning. But the art of reporting lies with the writer himself, and a book like this can only hope to stimulate and encourage him to his best efforts.

News reporting as a career is providing meaningful lives for professional journalists the world over. News reporting on a school paper is providing meaningful school activity for many students every year. Working on a school paper is work, sometimes tedious and tiring, with all the problems that can arise—but it is also work that is stimulating and affords many students an experience that enriches their lives in many ways.

This explains why staffs spend many hours beyond class time working on the paper. It explains why busy teachers take on additional duties to sponsor a publication. It explains why books are written about news reporting.

Because this book is designed primarily for students and advisers who have had little or no experience in writing for the school paper, it is informally written. It has seemed to me all through this writing as if we might be a small group of students and advisers discussing these points across a table. Both the organization and the contents are in answer to what students and advisers across the country have said they need.

The illustrative material is taken from school papers that have received top ratings from scholastic press associations and from the broadcast and print media.

It is hoped that both the "Keys" and the illustrations will be helpful in developing competence in news reporting. Although there is no one way to write, there are certain principles and practices to follow as guides. Every beginning reporter is on his own, launched on the tide of his enthusiasm and capacity for self-discipline. With a pencil and some paper he sets himself up in business. Where else can he be so much an individual? Where else can he have such an opportunity to make a place for himself by his own efforts?

If this book helps you increase your understanding and sharpens your skills, you may find that it shows you the way to an interesting and rewarding future. It is my hope that it will help you see more of what is interesting around you and help you tell it with more pleasure.

Hazel Presson

Acknowledgments

In thinking back over all those who have had a part in some way in the making of this book, I am reminded anew that in a work like this, one owes a great deal to a great many people. There are close friends and associates, professionals who said a word or set an example that has been unforgettable, colleagues who have been inspiring and who have supplied material or other aid, and certainly the students with whom I have been associated. Their eagerness, their excitement, their problems and needs, the wonderfully wise comments they make when least expected, and the insight they show—all are so much a part of a work like this. I am most grateful to all. To Colonel Joseph M. Murphy, J. F. Paschal, Paul S. Swensson, Don Carter, Becky Meeks, Cristy Foley, John and Debbie Cutsinger, Ruth and Richard Rosen, and Jack Moseley, a special word of appreciation. I am indebted to Mr. Moseley, editor of the *Southwest Times Record*, for permission so freely given to use material published in that newspaper.

About the Illustrations

Cristy Foley, a 1980 graduating senior, created the reporter character and illustrated each of the 21 keys. A three-year high school journalist at Van Buren High School, Van Buren, Arkansas, she served during her senior year as editor of "on the pointer trail." She has won numerous individual awards in art and copywriting and has been published both locally and regionally. The paper has won top honors in state and national competition.

Adviser of "on the pointer trail" is John Cutsinger. Formerly active in the Oklahoma Interscholastic Press Association, he now serves as president of the Ark-homa Regional Scholastic Press Association. As adviser of award-winning publications, Mr. Cutsinger is popular as speaker and teacher in journalism conferences and workshops.

*The Student Journalist
and
21 KEYS
TO NEWS REPORTING*

Key #  # Understand Your Responsibility as a Journalist

... A writer is a very special kind of person because he deals with ideas, ideas expressed in words—and a journalist is a very special kind of writer because he tries to picture and interpret for others the world as he sees it.

Because people tend to believe what they read in print, the journalist becomes a person with power.

Even the student journalist must remember this, for with every word of his printed in the school paper, there is some effect. If he writes trivia or rubbish or inaccuracies or half-truths, he is guilty of wasting his readers' time, if not of actually doing them a wrong.

From coverage of debates in the United Nations to fashion tips for teens, from guerrilla warfare to club socials, the reader goes to his newspaper for information.

Whether the journalist's words are printed or broadcast, his responsibility is to his readers, his listeners.

As a student journalist, decide to the best of your ability what is important or interesting to the reader, cover the story fully, dedicate yourself to seeing that *every item is correct,* and endeavor constantly to improve your writing skills so your copy will be not only clear but interesting.

First School Paper

Some two hundred years ago when Samuel Fox produced what is considered the first school paper in this country, he started something that has attracted thousands of students down through the years.

(Entitled *The Students' Gazette,* and "containing Advices both Foreign and Domestic," this little sheet was published at the Francis Latin School, now the William Penn Charter School, in Philadelphia, on June 11, 1777.)

That basic urge to report what is happening and to comment thereon is still strong among thinking students. It is evidenced in many forms, from the newsletter in purple ditto, to the neat printed newssheet, to the news magazine sophisticated in concept and content.

Since the publication of that little handwritten sheet, the story of the scholastic press and the role of the student journalist have become increasingly important. Over the years, courses in journalism with qualified teachers have been established as a respected part of the academic program in thousands of schools.

Those who plan curriculum have become more and more aware of the importance of the newspaper in a democratic society, and thus the need to train students to produce quality publications. With this understanding of the need for a free press and an enlightened public, there has also developed a need to emphasize an understanding of the role of the journalist and his responsibility to society.

Definitions

Responsibility: At a time when much emphasis is put on "rights," it is easy to overlook or underestimate the meaning of "responsibility."

Journalist: And at a time when the public is deluged with tons of newspapers and bombarded with sound waves from radio and television newsrooms, the meaning of the word "journalist" is generally vaguely understood.

But to the beginning journalist, both words are of special importance. Unless he understands his position and his purpose, he will merely drift along. One of the most important aspects of this understanding of responsibility as a journalist is a sharp distinction in the difference between news reporting and news commentary.

There is widespread misunderstanding—or lack of understanding—as to these terms, not only among student journalists but among readers as well. Many adult readers who are aware of the difference between the news pages and the editorial page of a newspaper seem never to hear the word "commentary" that so often accompanies a newscast.

For example, John Chancellor on the NBC evening news may give twenty minutes to reporting the events of the day, his statements being fact after fact. Then he says, "Now to David Brinkley in Washington with a commentary on the day's news."

Brinkley then discusses some facet of the day's happenings. He attempts to help the listener understand what the facts mean. He evaluates and voices an editorial opinion, justifying his statements with facts.

Purposes Differ

The purpose of the news reporting is to give the reader or the listener the facts concerning the event or situation, as fully as possible. The purpose of the news commentary is to help the reader or listener understand what the news means, understand what is happening, give him insight. The news commentator, obviously, must have a background of information so that he can put the news into perspective. This combination of news reporting and news commentary has become increasingly popular as the news has become increasingly complex.

In a democratic society in an enlightened age, everyone needs to understand as much as possible about himself, about the world around him, and about his place there—how he fits into it. Furthermore, he needs to know what is going on and what it means, both in general and to him specifically.

Whereas once the "right of the public to know" was construed to mean chiefly knowing about what was going on in government, now even more than that is important to him.

The journalist is the person to provide this information. Sadly, we find that even with our great abundance of newspapers, radios, and television sets, there are not only many Johnnies who can't read, there are many Johnnies who aren't informed.

Power in Print

Although most students working on school papers and calling themselves student journalists are not serious about going into journalism as a career, it is important that they, too, realize what power they have when what they write appears in print.

Many of the 16,400 school papers in this country carry prestige because over the years one staff after another has met the standards of good journalism and like the great professional dailies and weeklies has met its responsibilities to its readers.

In many other schools this is not so. Sometimes the administration does not take the paper seriously as a valuable feature of the academic program and as a training ground for young journalists. In many cases, then, the paper becomes a plaything operated on an "anything goes" basis. Sometimes the staff considers the paper principally as a mouthpiece for whatever they want to say.

As a former adviser said, when the paper she had advised won a major conflict with the administration recently: "We have won the case, but our school paper and our journalism program has suffered irreparable loss in prestige. Our students have been so embroiled over our 'rights' that we have lost sight of our 'responsibilities.'

"The excitement of seeing one's words in print carries some of us into false pride. We become careless and thoughtless of the reader and his rights. Not only that, we suddenly discover that with words in print often comes attention—or notoriety—and we consider ourselves crusaders who are always right, not only in our cause but in how we pursue it."

WANTED: PEOPLE WHO CARE

Suppose you are the editor, newly appointed, of the school paper. You have dreams of the Great Year you are going to have. You launch upon it with enthusiasm—and suddenly discover that you need help to get the work done.

At once you begin to rely on other students, only to find that the word "responsibility" is not in the vocabulary of some of your so-called reporters. You also learn, with the first copy turned in, that some of your staff members also do not understand what the word "journalist" means.

One editor, speaking of this situation, said: "I suddenly realized that there are some basic needs if you want to produce a good school paper. First, of course, is people who really care, who want to give their best to the paper. There just wasn't room in our columns for the 3F stuff—flighty, flimsy, foolish. Second, is people who are concerned with what will be informational, meaningful, and interesting to the reader. Some of our would-be reporters, I observed, really wanted to be soapbox orators.

Key # 1 *Understand Your Responsibility as a Journalist*

"Putting out a school paper is work, but it is work that can be fun. There's nothing like the excitement of seeing in print the story that you have spent so much time on. But nothing appears in print unless the staff members have gone out to get the news, have written—and rewritten—the story to be sure it is clear and correct, and have done all this BEFORE THE DEADLINE."

EDITOR DEFINES RESPONSIBILITY

The responsibility of the newspaper to the community is evidenced in many ways, and continuously. Occasionally an editor appears in the columns of his paper with a definitive statement. Such is the case in the following story written by Jack Moseley, editor of the *Southwest Times Record:*

> With its successes and its failures—Lord knows, we all have both—a newspaper speaks for itself with each edition. But if you ever wondered what a newspaper is all about, last Monday's *SWTR* provided the answer.
>
> When you put down that paper, you had a comprehensive understanding of what had happened at Fort Chaffee.
>
> You held the pictures in your hands. Pictures taken from 20 yards in front of the shrieking mob. Pictures taken from the air. Pictures taken as state and area lawmen quelled a rampage. Pictures of the rioters leaping over fences and returning to the fort. The appeals for reason. The violent confrontations. The shattered windshields and rock-pelted police units. The subdued Cubans in handcuffs.
>
> The accompanying stories, written by *SWTR* staffers who were eyewitnesses to what they wrote, told you of the good, the bad, the ugly, the acts of courage, the senseless acts of destruction spawned by agitators, fear within and without the military reservation, those who acted and those who stood by in frustration, the governor's battle for more troops and the use of "necessary force" to save the lives of Americans and Cubans. The involvement of the White House, the Army, area hospitals.
>
> In your hands, you held as complete a picture as any newspaper ever gave of a sudden violent event that happened here to us, but made headlines around the world.
>
> Some of the local broadcast coverage of the riot and related events was outstanding, but because of the very nature of radio and television, it was fragmented and did not convey the comprehensive picture presented by the newspaper, in my admittedly biased opinion. Some local broadcasters do deserve credit for correcting false reports that originated with the networks in New York.
>
> Yes, I'm bragging, but the credit for Monday's *SWTR* is not mine. That goes to the young professionals who staff this newspaper, who had to be called in on a Sunday afternoon, who went 24 hours without sleep to get

the pictures and stories, write, edit and lay them out in the comprehensive package that was delivered to your home.

That belongs to people like managing editor Leroy Fry, metropolitan editor Richard Break, news editor Kenneth Fry, and the reporters and photographers who worked with, not for, them. The staff was working for someone, however. It was working to get the story for YOU.

The staff also was doing something else. It was working with the Associated Press, which had its own people here doing an outstanding job. When the riot came, the *SWTR* staff and the AP staff became a total team with the responsibility to accurately report what was happening to the rest of the world. The AP moved our pictures and stories, along with those of regular AP staffers, over news and picture wires around the globe.

Because of that teamwork, a truthful picture of the situation and the people of this region was presented. Of all the thousands of words and dozens of pictures transmitted by AP from Fort Smith, not one word by either an *SWTR* reporter or an AP staffer had to be corrected by the wire service because of inaccurate information.

With other national news organizations, that was not true. Those news agencies ended up retracting false reports they had wrongly circulated to newspapers, radio, and television stations all over this country. That was a disservice to journalism and to the people who live around Fort Chaffee. Such sensational reports may have sounded exciting, but they just did not happen.

Since last Sunday, more than 500 journalists from America's leading newspapers have come to Fort Smith to report on the Cubans at Fort Chaffee and the people of this area.

Most began their assignments by reading the *SWTR* Monday edition. In many cases, *SWTR* stories provided the basis for their follow-up reports that put our region and our people in honest, positive focus for millions of Americans.

In the days ahead, you will be seeing *SWTR* pictures from the Chaffee incidents in national news magazines.

I hope you share my pride in the people who produce your newspaper. They are second to nobody. They're pros.

That does not mean they will never make a mistake. They're human and certainly will have their share of foulups. But Sunday night and Monday morning, they were tested and found not lacking.

By the way, last Monday's newspaper was increased in size to provide space not only for the Fort Chaffee coverage, but to assure that none of the normal news and features had to be left out. You still got the weddings, the Old Fort Days Rodeo results, Dear Abby, comics, sports, and all the rest.

A True Story

The big newspaper plant had settled into the hush that falls when the newsroom is suddenly deserted and before the big presses begin

Key # 1 *Understand Your Responsibility as a Journalist* 9

to stir into action. The newly appointed editor—a youngish man, with more experience than you would think could have been crowded into his short professional career—stood at the door of the conference room as the visitors were shown in.

There were six of them, editors from small high schools in the area who had asked to tour the remodeled plant to see the latest equipment that had just been installed.

He smiled. "I'm your tour guide tonight. You know why? Because when I learned that you young journalists were coming, I wanted the opportunity to meet you and to hear what you have to say. Hopefully, too, to give you some understanding of the role of the journalist in today's society."

Telling about this later, one of the students said, "We were impressed. He was so frank and so serious-minded about what comes out in newspapers, and well, too, what news readers get from television and radio. He was interested in us, we all felt this, but what he really was concerned about in journalism is what's important to the readers.

"He showed us all through the plant—the hushed newsroom, the quietly busy composing room, and we even waited for the presses to run so we could see it all—but what I remember most is what he said as we sat around the table in informal conversation. He asked us some questions I've never forgotten:

1. Did you know that people tend to believe what they read in print?
2. Have you ever stopped to think how many readers never question whether the writer is completely accurate and trustworthy or whether the 'facts' are authentic?
3. Does your staff plan every issue to try to serve the best interests of the reader, or do staff members consider the paper a sounding board for their own enthusiasms?
4. Is your news covereage complete? That is, campus-wide with thought also given to student interest in matters off-campus?
5. Have your reporters covered the stories fully so the reader will have as much information—reliable information—as possible?
6. Have the stories been written so they are not only correct but clear, easy for the reader to follow? (Many times readers have incorrect information because the writer was ambiguous, misleading, or confusing.)
7. Is your editorial copy clearly indicated so the reader will know he is reading fact rather than opinion?"

This editor is typical of numerous editors across the country who are dedicated to meeting young people and helping to encourage and train them to be defenders of the rights of the public.

They consider the responsibility of the journalist so important to the good of society that they are providing scholarships, offering internships, conducting seminars, making speeches, and working with journalism educators to bring to the news media, print or electronic, the best possible reporters and writers.

CONTINUING CHALLENGES

As would be expected, members of the American Newspaper Publishers Association, at their recent 95th convention, discussed the challenges facing today's newspapers. These include "credibility," "a compelling need for presentation of the kind of detailed information not suited to broadcast journalism," and "concern for the First Amendment."

The chairman of the Washington Post Company referred to the story recently revealed as a hoax after it had won a Pulitzer prize, saying that this had "for the moment" an impact on how readers judge newspapers. She then pointed out that there is a danger in drawing the wrong conclusions from the *Post*'s problems with the reporter who fabricated the story of an eight-year-old heroin addict. (The *Post* returned the prize after the hoax was admitted.)

One real danger, she said, is "that we will become so nervous we will go to the other extreme, and not do the job that a free press is supposed to do. Most of all, this unhappy episode must not be allowed to result in any curtailment of the First Amendment in other forums."

Key #2 Develop a Sense of the Newsworthy

. . . A good news reporter is a person intensely alive and keenly aware of the world around him, rather like a little bug skittering along the sidewalk with its feelers out. He is one who dashes up with "Hey, what's going on?" He enjoys passing this on to anyone who will listen: "Guess what I just saw!" or "Wait 'til you hear this!"

Not gossip-mongering, not curiosity about the private affairs of others, but an eye and an ear for action, with its causes, its effects, its meanings. Of course, much that happens is merely that, a happening. To be newsworthy an event or situation must be related to readers or in some way be of concern to them.

"When anything happens anywhere in the world, we'll be there with on-the-scene coverage." That is the way the Columbia Broadcasting System speaks of its news teams.

The school "world" is not so vast, but the meaning of newsworthy is the same in both areas. This implies being ready, being so well informed and having sufficient background that you know where to expect to go for what may happen. Art Buchwald wrote in a piece about prominent journalists and their "nose for news" . . . "But Barbara Walters didn't wait to ask anyone for permission to go, she was already on the plane."

"Idea" vs. "Subject"

Some reporters seem to have a continuing supply of story ideas that turn into interesting copy. Others are always looking for something to write about. You hear them say, "I'd like to write a story for the paper if you will give me a suggestion or a subject."

Also, it seems, the first kind of reporter turns out a longer, more interesting story than the second does—and he has more fun doing it.

This supply of ideas has much to do with the production of full, newsy, readable stories. There is more to a story than the choice of a subject. Perhaps the difference lies in the distinction between the words "idea" and "subject."

When a reporter finds—or "sees"—a story idea, he has already brought to it an enthusiasm and a feeling that are going to provide momentum when he begins to find background material, gather information, and plan and organize his story.

On the other hand, the reporter who depends on someone else for an idea goes to his subject "cold." If he is to do a good story, he must generate for himself enough enthusiasm to get him started and enough feeling for the story to cover it fully and to write it as well as he can.

Obviously, when reporters operate on the beat system or special assignment, they have learned—or must learn—how to generate this self-help. It is not impossible to do this; it is not even difficult. The secret is caring enough about your story to work at it.

(And here let us not define "work" as merely devoting so many minutes to the effort. "Work" means careful, thoughtful effort at every step of the process.)

Solution for Editor

Many high school editors find themselves with "reporters" who can think of nothing to report. Fortunately this is a situation that can be improved:

1. The editor can conduct staff meetings at which he teaches the members how to find story ideas and recognize news subjects.
2. He can organize a complete beat system (trying to match the reporter with a beat that seems to interest him) and then suggest his own special assignment ideas.

3. He can combat the general comment that "Nobody is interested in this old stuff" by pointing out that usually the lack of interest is first in the writer's mind, not the reader's. (Many a reporter has moaned, "Nothing interesting ever happens in this school." In fact, many schools have very poor school papers—or no paper at all—because any would-be staff members have that idea.)

FINDING STORY IDEAS

Question: So then, how do we learn to see story ideas that will interest the reader?
Answer: Develop a sense of the newsworthy:

1. Study people to see what they respond to and what their interests are.
2. Study the work of journalists whom you consider successful, to try to understand their selection of subjects and their approach to coverage.
3. Observe what students read in the daily papers, listen to their general conversation, note what attracts their attention, holds their interest.
4. Observe what the professional papers do to try to put something of interest to every reader in every issue.

ROLE OF SCHOOL PAPER

Experienced staff members have at least a general understanding of the role of the paper. They know that a paper is expected to reflect campus activities, from academic to extracurricular, and that every issue should in some way appeal to every reader.

They know that the purpose of the school paper is (1) to inform students about what is going on, (2) to interpret the various activities and situations, and (3) to entertain with both light and more substantial feature material.

Established papers have built up a kind of personality on the campus. However, with inexperienced staff members and on campuses where newspapers are being set up, this is not the case.

Therefore this point should be made and emphasized. Not only should the paper serve the stated purposes, but also it is expected to interest its readers in doing so.

In order to impress that word *interest* on staff members, a kind of acrostic might be worked out at a staff meeting to serve as a guide in deciding what to include in the paper.

The following old favorite is proposed:

I—information about activities on the campus.
N—names of people who are doing things.
T—timely events.
E—experiences of students and teachers.
R—readability in all copy.
E—entertainment features.
S—school-wide coverage of activities.
T—tailored to fit this particular campus.

If you draw this up as a poster for the bulletin board, it will continue to serve as a reminder and guide. It can also serve as a checklist.

Reporter Is Key Man

A school paper is not a newspaper in the sense that a big daily is. It is more like the local weekly, a community paper. There is not too much emphasis on the big story that may break, because most of school life is routine. Occasionally there is an unusual story such as a fire, a robbery, or a scholarship winner, but most of the "news" can be more or less anticipated.

If you and your staff are bright-eyed and enterprising, you will gain skill as you gain experience. By looking ahead, you can anticipate a story in time to do advance coverage. If your issues are too far apart to allow for an advance story, you can recognize the importance of the event by covering it for the record in a follow-up story. Usually, also, there are feature and sidebar story possibilities.

There is no substitute for an active mind. As Bob Letts, California news analyst, put it: "A reporter should be as full of ideas as a watermelon is of seeds."

The main strength of the school paper, as of any newspaper, lies in reporting the news and reporting it well.

"This means that the key person on the newspaper staff is the reporter," said R. V. Peterson at a meeting of the Oklahoma Interscholastic Press Association. "The success or failure of a newspaper is in proportion to its news coverage and the quality of news writing."

So What Is News?

"Okay," you say, "and so what is news?"

Key # 2 *Develop a Sense of the Newsworthy*

That question is answered in a number of ways.

Horace Greeley, editor of the New York *Tribune* more than a hundred years ago, suggested this to his beginning reporters: "Begin with the clear conception that the subject of deepest interest to the average human being is himself. Next to that, he is most interested in his neighbors."

This, of course, is still true. Readers are more likely to be interested in what touches their lives than in what doesn't.

Your next football game certainly is no earth-shaking event, but it goes into the school paper. The war in Asia doesn't, unless you see there some idea that has a bearing on student life on your campus.

News is not just any information. It is information that has a meaning for a certain set of readers. That's why the writer must have an understanding of people—so he knows about meanings.

Students want to read about other students and what they are doing of consequence. Several factors enter here:

1. Well-known students will interest more readers than unknown students will.
2. Yet an unknown student may be doing something very unusual or very dramatic, and therefore the story is important.
3. In a humorous occurrence or in a human interest story, it does not matter particularly who the person is, as the emotion is stronger than the identity of the person involved.
4. Stories with names are always important, even though the activity or event is not especially noteworthy. People read lists of names if their own or their friends' names are included.
5. Stories of success, conflict, or suspense appeal to readers.

All news is relative. It must be considered with reference to the place, the time of printing, and the readers.

MEASURING NEWS VALUES

There are certain basic elements of news evaluation that even beginning reporters soon learn to use as measuring sticks. These are the elements that attract attention and determine the appeal of the information.

In deciding whether a piece of information has news value, ask yourself the following questions:

1. Does this concern people the reader knows? How many people? How important are they to him? Are they interesting to him in some special way? Are they prominent?

2. Is this humorous? Does it have other human interest or emotional overtones?
3. Is there some unusualness about it?
4. Is it timely?
5. Is it dramatic? Is there some conflict? Suspense?
6. How important is it to the reader? What will be the consequences?
7. Is the locality important? Does it mean something to the reader?

Answering these questions thoughtfully will help you decide how long the story should be and how to handle it.

If you keep these questions in mind as you observe what goes on around your school, you will develop what has long been called a "nose for news."

This "nose for news" means:

1. The ability to recognize that a piece of information will interest readers or that it can be made to interest them;
2. The ability to recognize clues that might lead to other stories;
3. The ability to recognize the relative importance of a number of facts concerning the same general subject; and
4. The ability to recognize the possibility of other news related to the particular information at hand.

The term "educated nose for news" is used by Neale Copple, of the University of Nebraska. "A liberal education," he says, "should provide a reporter with an educated nose for news—which means a platform from which he can (1) spot the significance of a story, (2) ask intelligent questions of the real experts, and (3) then research, organize, and write his story."

"Important Difference"

A "new look at news" is offered by Carol Griffee, of the *Arkansas Gazette,* in the following definitions:

Mass communication and education have knocked newspaperdom from its pedestal as the "kingmaker" of public opinion in the United States. More than ever before, newspapers *reflect* the societies in which they operate and are experiencing less and less influence in molding these societies.

Thus, "society" in the broad sense of the term—be it a school, a rural Midwestern community, or a large coastal city—sets the standard of what is news.

News is *anything* that makes "an important difference" in the way a society functions. Because societies vary and their standards of "normalcy" can be expected to change over a period of time and circumstances, there can be no rigid definition of what is news. News always must be viewed in relation to where one is, in terms of both society and time.

For example: A dance sponsored as a fund-raising and social event by a group is generally so normal in a larger society that it rates but a bare mention, if even that, in newspapers operating in that society. However, does the student council choose to sponsor a dance open to all pupils every Friday night? Not normally. Thus when a council does decide to sponsor such a dance, it is news because it is not normal and it makes an "important difference" in the routine functioning of the society which, in this case, is the school.

Unfortunately, the larger and more complex our societies become, the more the individual and thus the "who" loses out in importance to the "what" in terms of news. News can be thought of in terms of someone who is different from or at variance with—performing either above or below—the standard of "normalcy" set by society.

It is still not the individual who is news, however. Rather, it is what he has done differently from the standard of "normalcy."

News also can be thought of in terms of someone who makes an "important difference" in the way a society functions. Here again it is not usually the who but what he has done that makes an "important difference" which is news.

The "who" involved has its greatest impact as the gauge to determine how newsworthy a "what" is.

Who a person is may determine if what he does is news.

For instance: A number of students ride bicycles to school, so when a healthy junior boy decides to join the bike riders, it is not news. But one morning the principal rides to work on a bike for the first time. This is news because of who he is. The mind already knows who and what, where and when, and so it should wonder "why?" If it does, we have a story in the making.

Thus, to summarize, news is a judgment based on three fundamental questions:

1. Is it normal, as normalcy is defined by a given society?
2. If not, how different from the normal is it—that is, does it make an "important difference"?
3. Who is involved?

"Find" and "Recognize"

A reporter's job is not only to "find" news but to "recognize" it. What good does it do if a reporter writes down all the facts of a situation but does not recognize their importance?

For instance: A reporter covers a meeting of the city council at which an ordinance is adopted. The reporter writes down what the ordinance concerns and what the vote was, including some comments made by the councilmen.

He does all this simply because it is happening. It may be a far-reaching ordinance that will make an "important difference" in the functioning of that particular city. But the story may never be written because the reporter failed to recognize its importance. He "found" the news, but he failed to "recognize" it.

Developing "Story Sense"

Equally important as "news sense" is "story sense."

This "sense" begins to develop when one realizes that there are few if any newsworthy events that stand by and of themselves, suspended in time and space. Something or many things led up to or produced the newsworthy event, and something may result from it.

A story about a news event must be viewed as a whole, designed to give the reader all the important aspects he should know and to answer all the logical questions he might have.

Some readers always will be satisfied with only the basics—the who, what, where, and when. As the educational level in the United States continues to rise, however, fewer and fewer readers will be satisfied by four W's.

They will and do want six W's including "why" and "worth." Why did this event occur? Why was this policy adopted? What is its worth to me? What is its worth to the normal functioning of the society about me?

Take these points into consideration when writing a story about a new policy adopted by the student council. In addition to the who, where, and when, tell the reader the following:

1. Exactly *what* the new policy is, if possible using quotes from the persons involved to explain it.
2. *Why* the policy was adopted, that is, what made it necessary or desirable.
3. *What* are the expected implications—what is its expected worth to the individual student, the school, AND the community (if

Key # 2 *Develop a Sense of the Newsworthy*   21

affected). What is the policy's perspective? Here again, the reporter may wish to rely on quotes from persons involved in the policy's adoption.
4. *Who*, exactly, were the persons instrumental in getting the new policy? Do *not* neglect to cite or quote the "whys" of those who were opposed, if there was controversy. If there was no controversy, say that it was unanimous.

The "why" and "worth" of a news event normally are not the most important aspects, and that is why leads most often rely on "what" and "who." Sometimes, however, the "why" or "worth" are important enough to share the lead.
For instance:

> *Three fatal auto accidents involving teenagers recently, today prompted the Fairfax County School Board to forbid students to drive to school.*
> *The new policy, which goes into effect October 1, is expected to affect about 15,000 student drivers attending the county's 15 high schools.*

Or:

> *A policy adopted today by the Fairfax County School Board is expected to stop more than 15,000 students from driving cars to school.*
> *Three fatal auto accidents involving teenagers this month prompted the school board's action.*
> *Under the new policy . . .*

Sometimes one event or one story will be the genesis for future related events to become what this writer calls a "running story."
For example:
A story reveals that several justices of the peace have earned more fees than the state law allows and have not turned the excess over to the local treasury as required.
A second story reveals that several justices of the peace failed to file required reports of their earnings.
A third story reveals that one justice filed an incomplete report by failing to include half of his income which, in full, put him over the legal limit.
The first story laid the groundwork for the others, and together they have produced or can be expected to produce these subsequent articles:

1. The county attorney states that he will investigate.
2. The state attorney general says that he will investigate.

3. The state files charges against the justices.
4. The justices answer the charges brought against them.
5. The results of a meeting held by the area's legislative representatives to consider changes in the law.
6. Trial on the charges.
7. Jury's decision.
8. County states that it will sue to collect "excess" fees.
9. County files its suit.
10. Trial.
11. Judge's decision.
12. Collection of the money.

In each article, it is incumbent upon the writer to say immediately what this particular story is about, what led up to it, and what the next expected step is. This is a "running story."

These preceding definitions by Carol Griffee, of the *Arkansas Gazette*, indicate how professional reporters see news.

However, the definitions in themselves are not sufficient.

A good news writer develops for himself an understanding of what news is. This understanding comes only with an active interest in searching for news stories and covering stories that are assigned.

INTEREST IN PEOPLE

Definitions will help you only if you are responsive to the world around you.

Are you interested in people? Yes? No?

If your answer is no, then you might just as well go join the chemists or the band or the office machines class. Even the historians would not want you if you aren't interested in people.

But if your answer is yes, then that is your starting place. Watch people, listen to them, talk with them (*with*, not merely *to* them).

Observe what people are doing, how they are doing it, why, what the consequences are. What do they talk about, work at, think about, like, dislike, want, reject? What makes them tick?

A perceptive journalist emphasizes this point in a comment on how to learn to write news stories:

"The things that make for a well-written book on journalism don't tell a person how to write the news. How can you teach a person to be genuinely interested in human beings?"

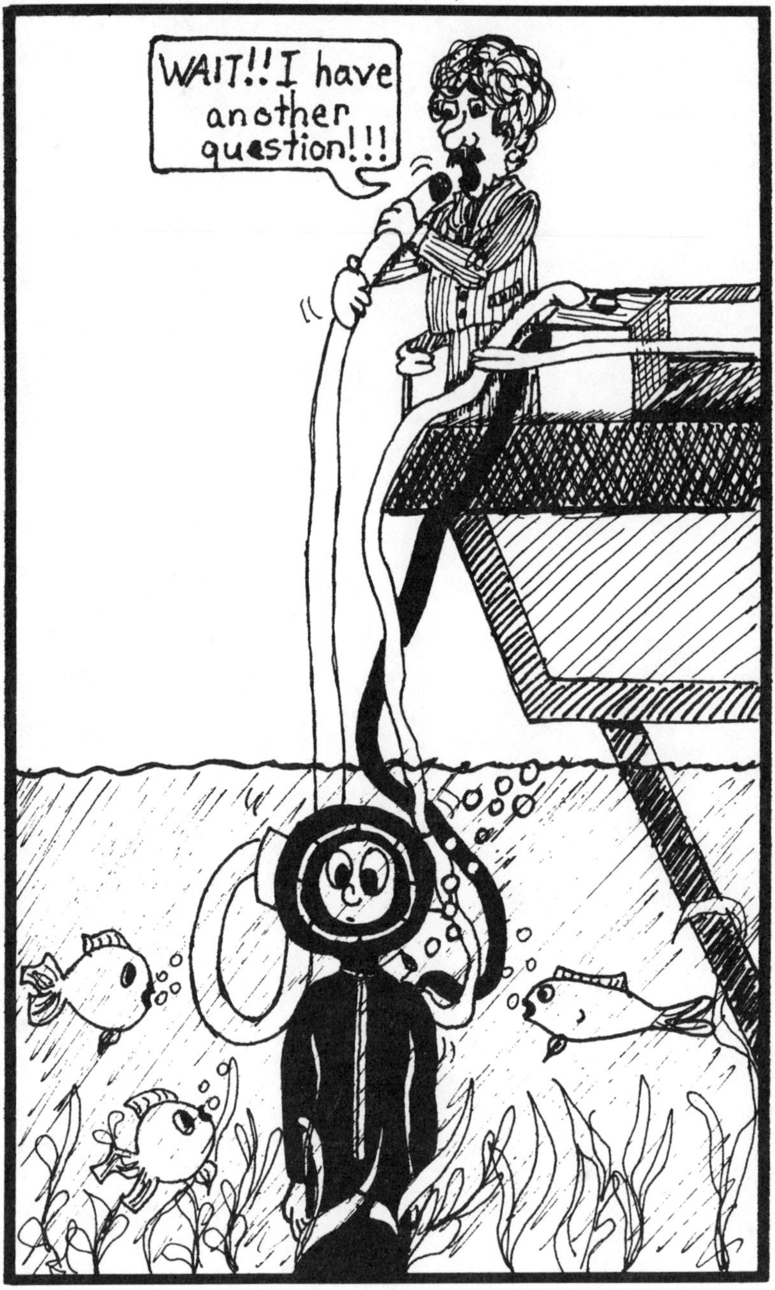
WAIT!! I have another question!!!

Key # 3   *Ask Questions, Think Questions*

... "I know I have some good ideas for stories, but I just don't have the courage to go up to anybody and get the information." If this is your problem, you are one among many beginning journalists.

Helpful Hint #1—Don't worry about asking questions yet. Begin by just *thinking* questions. Think to yourself all the good questions you would ask if you were the Great Reporter. Imagine yourself a Tom Hart or Jane Pauley. Then list all those questions you have thought of, pretend you are your favorite professional journalist, and set off briskly to cover your story. (Suggestion: Since probably you won't want anyone to know how you are pretending, don't tell anyone your secret.)

Helpful Hint #2—A few basic questions will serve as a general outline that will help you get started on stories. Revise these as necessary after you have done your research and have background material for each specific situation:

(1) What is going on here now? (2) What has been going on prior to this? (3) Who is involved? For what reason? (4) How has this come about? (5) When did it begin? Why? Where? (6) What is likely to happen next? (7) What results and consequences can be expected? (8) How important is this? (9) Can you tell me anything more?

An Inquiring Mind

Of all the qualities a reporter needs, none is more important than an inquiring mind. The Happy Reporter lives with a question mark in his eye or on his tongue. No matter when, no matter where, he is alive to what is going on and to the people who are involved.

Question: Can one develop this quality?

Answer: Yes—but it must be admitted that some people really have an enthusiasm that is an advantage here.

How to develop this inquiring mind?

One experienced reporter suggested this to a beginner who was feeling inadequate:

"Don't try to start too ambitiously—(1) merely play a game with yourself by making it a point to look at as many *people* as possible around you at any one time.

"Conditions will vary, and your attention will be diverted often, but ask yourself with every individual: What is he really like? What makes him tick? What is different about him? Is he doing something unusual, or does he look as if he might do something unusual?

"And then to vary the game, (2) some days look for *things,* study *things* as well as *people*—and (3) some days look for signs of *action.*"

These "setting-up exercises," of course, are only that, but such definite effort on your part to try to develop a questioning mind will make it easier to *ask* questions—and, more important, to *think* of questions.

And these questions are what lead the reporter to find story ideas for himself.

People + Action = Stories

Any school, every school is a great source of news, but a news source is like a gold mine—nothing comes out by itself. The gold lies hidden and unclaimed until a gold-seeking miner comes along.

So with news stories. Many interesting articles about school lie unseen and untold until an enthusiastic reporter comes along looking for "gold."

Where there are people, there is action, and where there is action, there are stories.

Some school papers, issue after issue, overlook many of the possibilities that would interest readers. How do you find these good stories?

Some reporters, both beginners and those with experience, have the proverbial "nose for news." They are enviable people who always seem to be bubbling over with bright ideas.

Key # 3 *Ask Questions, Think Questions* 27

This quality—or talent—comes with an intense excitement about life. Some people, it should be said in fairness to the rest of us, just naturally see stories everywhere. And they not only see these stories, they always seem to know how to tell them well.

But here is a word of comfort to everyone else. There are ways to find good story ideas. And you can learn to write well, if you work at writing. Conscientious practice has paved many a road to success.

Assignments and Beats

These ways to find stories for newspapers are summed up in two words: "assignments" and "beats."

On a school paper as on professional papers, the editor keeps an assignment sheet. Various reporters are given stories to cover. These special assignments include such items as important visitors, results of play tryouts, announcement of holiday activities.

In order to keep his assignment sheet timely and complete, the editor must be in touch with the entire school scene. It is his responsibility to see that every issue of the paper covers the entire school, or at least that all phases of school life are covered fairly and in proportion to their importance in the school program.

For this purpose he keeps his calendar up to date—a large wall calendar is practical—and he keeps his futures file current.

Important as the special assignments are, the beat system is the backbone of news coverage.

Several variations can be worked out, but essentially the plan is this: all the areas of activity, known as news sources, are listed, and a reporter is assigned to each. It is his responsibility to visit each news source periodically to see what is going on. Some beats should be visited every day, some less often, perhaps once a week.

Visit Sources Regularly

If all news sources are listed and all reporters cover their beats, the school paper will indeed reflect campus life completely. Should there be a failure anywhere along the line of beats, the coverage for that issue is not adequate.

By visiting the same news source regularly, a reporter can build up a background of information and understanding so that his stories take on an interpretive tone. His background gives his writing depth.

Furthermore, advance stories can often be picked up by the beat reporter. For instance, a reporter whose beat is the guidance office may hear a chance remark about an expected visitor. Being acquainted with the beat, he senses a meaning and asks questions—to learn that a nationally known architect will probably be the school's guest speaker for Career Day.

Beats should include the following:

1. Areas of special interest—the band, choral groups, dramatic groups, classes, student council.
2. The athletic program—varsity sports, intramural sports and games, boys' and girls' physical education.
3. Clubs and organizations.
4. The academic program—all departments, all faculty members, library.
5. Offices—guidance, business, administrative, especially the principal's office, dean's office, board of education.
6. School-community activities—booster clubs, band parents, civic programs.
7. Miscellaneous—cafeteria, maintenance.

Classroom Stories

As you cover your beat, watch for signs of activity. Remember: where there's action, there's likely to be a story.

Every classroom should at one time or another be good for a story. Stories on these subjects have appeared in school papers:

In the *art department*—ceramics, leathercraft, poster contest, visit to art center, visiting sculptor, art auction, exhibit, demonstration of clay molds, stained glass demonstration.

Vocational classes—book racks, desks, cedar chest made in woodworking, repairing a boat, printing stationery, office forms, course catalogues, school magazine, drawing house plans, making model house, repairing a car, field trips to local industries.

Commercial department—guest speaker on salesmanship, employer-employee relations, income tax study, state tests, banking, demonstration of newest office machines.

English—construction of Globe Theatre model, literary maps, panel discussions, visiting author, old European Yule log ceremony.

Social studies—visit to courthouse, visit to local historical sites, economic survey, family living projects, teenage surveys, studies in finance, naturalization ceremony, visit with case workers in special services.

Science and math—class and outside experiments, special research, new equipment and aids used, field trips, models for study, group interviews with professional people in related careers.

Key # 3 Ask Questions, Think Questions

Language—language labs, exhibits, programs, special studies, guest speakers, "travel" parties, group trips to Europe.

Home economics—cutting garments, style show, making hats, refinishing and upholstering furniture, making peanut brittle, staging a luncheon for teachers, planning and staging a mock wedding, a baby visitor with mother in home nursing study.

Journalism—trip to local newspaper plant and graphic arts studio, demonstrations in photography, results in advertising survey, guest speakers, visit to nearby nuclear plant.

General—testing program, enrollment figures, system of scheduling, overall look at the curriculum and trends in education, comparison of today's textbooks and visual aids with materials used when the school was first opened, school regulations, policies, first school building in city now being razed, furor in city because of condemnation of residences to make room for a new school building and campus.

Community—employment opportunities for teenagers now, later, how to plan to train yourself for specific careers, grants for special study, loans available for continuing or special education, legal rights of teenagers, how to set up a professional or vocational plan for yourself, how to file income tax returns, teenage interest in political careers, what teenagers should know as voters, what you should know about credit, loans, savings plans, handling your finances, business affairs.

(Stories of this kind are found in regular visits to such sources of information as the local employment offices, courthouse, federal programs offices, government offices, community centers, various industries. This list of sources can be as long as you want to make it.)

GUIDELINES SUGGESTED

A set of guidelines is often helpful to an editor or reporter in covering the academic program. Although others can be added in specific situations, the following list is basic:

1. Are there going to be, or have there been, visitors or speakers in any of the classrooms?
2. Is anything new or unusual going on in any classroom?
3. What experiments are in progress in the science labs?
4. Are any panel discussions or special programs being planned in any department?
5. Are any objects being made, as in art and home economics or in English or math as a special project?
6. Are any field trips being planned, or have any been made?
7. Is there a picture idea here? If so, there's probably a story with it.

Pictures add interest to classroom stories. There are many possibilities. Because these stories are action stories, it is easy to get good pictures—a boy bent over his wood carving, a debater making his point, a group staging a closed-circuit television program, a chemistry class unpacking glassware, the foods class making apple butter.

Three-Way Approach

As a triple check, approach coverage of campus activities from three angles: (1) people, (2) activities, and (3) organizations.

For example:

If you do not know to approach Miss Nancy Stewart about future plans of the scholarship committee, of which she is chairman, she will never think to tell you about them.

If you do not know that the testing program is being expanded, no one will think to give you the story about what this means.

If you do not know that the Library Club always undertakes a special service project in the spring, you will miss the story about their installing a bookshelf in one of the elementary schools.

Teachers and administrators and students generally want to be helpful. The fact is, they usually *do not realize* that what they are doing is news.

Look, Listen, Visit

It is up to you, with your "news sense" and your "story sense," to discover these story possibilities as you look around, listen, and then check them out.

Suggestions that will pay off:

1. Make friends with the principal and with the teachers on your beat.
2. Gradually teach everyone you meet what news is so that each will understand and help you find stories.
3. Study the general calendar of school events in the office and general bulletin boards for tips on future happenings.
4. Keep an eye on the future. Educate everyone you meet on your beat about the importance of knowing in advance.

5. Try to get more and more pictures of activities on your beat. These will "sell" your point that there is news all about. (Incidentally, you might be able to sell extra prints of these or of related

shots not run in the paper to persons pictured and thus help pay for the cost of running the pictures.)

Surprisingly, people on your beat will recognize a news *picture* idea in what they are doing sooner than they will a news *story* idea. Therefore, if you encourage everyone to help you find news pictures, you are teaching them about news story ideas at the same time.

6. Get a list of all heads of departments, all faculty committees, PTA officers, Band Parents officers and so on. Call on them.

7. Develop a happy, pleasant outlook and manner so that you enjoy meeting people and they enjoy you.
8. Consider your appearance and your manners. Forego chewing gum when covering assignments.
9. The more often you visit the persons on your beat, the more you will learn, and the more *they* will learn about what is news.
10. Encourage everyone to suggest news stories and continue to explain what news is. Cover your beats at least once a week. Even if your paper is a monthly, you will get better stories if you keep current. To be a successful news writer you must know what is going on.

   Keep this information you acquire and file it in readable notes to build up a background for reference.
11. Look for humor in classrooms. Study bulletin boards. Ask for amusing test answers, coincidences, interesting projects. Look around. You will probably see something that excites your imagination or arouses your attention, perhaps even appeals to your emotions.

12. Don't let anyone on the staff have a beat or an assignment in which he is not interested if you can prevent it. If he thinks it is dull, his story will be dull, and no one will read it. No reader is going to be any more interested in the story than the writer was.

To Summarize

Most readers are not aware that what takes place in the classroom is often newsworthy. Therefore, if the reporter drops in and asks, "Do you have any news today?" the teacher will probably say, "No."

The successful reporter looks around to see for himself what seems to be going on and then asks questions to get the facts.

Today's successful reporter goes even further than that.

"What is going on?" he asks.

Then he looks around again and asks other questions that today's readers want answered: "Why?" "What does this mean?" "How does this work?" "What will the consequences be?"

Similarly, the rounds of off-campus sources will provide ideas for stories of interest to your student readers. A visit to the local employment office, for example, might afford material for such stories as how to apply for a job, how to keep a job, what employers expect, how to help yourself succeed in the job market.

Note well: Any activity in which teenagers are interested, or in which they might be interested, is a possible subject for a story.

Your school paper is primarily intended for your campus readers, but the interest of your campus readers is not limited by campus boundaries.

To repeat: People + Action = Stories. The inquiring mind makes the difference.

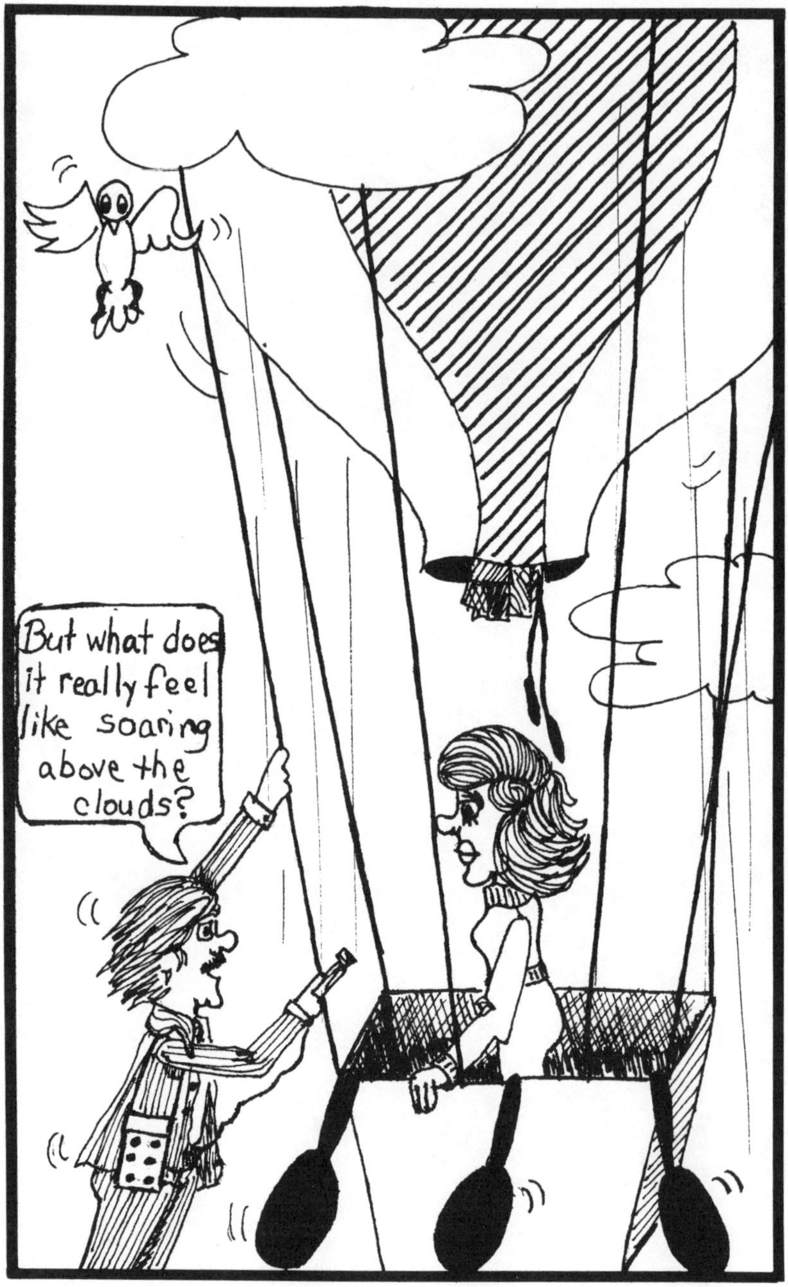
But what does it really feel like soaring above the clouds?

Key # 4 Cover the Story

... "A good reporter wears out more shoes than pants." This old saying is still true. It means that the reporter is going to serve as a medium between the reader and an event or situation—like a camera, in many respects, and a sound track.

With a little experience, you soon find that "wearing out shoes" refers to more than getting to the action or to the persons to be interviewed. Sometimes when you arrive, you find the sources of information are indifferent or uncooperative.

"Nobody would think that's interesting," they may say. Or, "Oh, I really don't know much about it."

Question: What do you do? Answer: Have plenty of "shoes."

Try these "shoes": (1) Enthusiasm, so you can say, "Well, *I'm* interested—and I can tell this to my readers so they will be!" (2) Poise, so you won't be discomfited by indifference. (3) Preparation, so you can ask specific questions you want answered. (4) Background, so you can begin by discussing the subject, rather than by asking questions, if necessary. (5) Determination, so they don't cause you to fail to cover the story properly. (6) Understanding of people, so you enjoy the challenges. (7) Sense of humor, so you can survive happily to go on to the next assignment.

Ringside Seat

Although most news stories are obtained entirely or partially through interviewing one or more persons, some stories are of events that occur or situations that exist.

A reporter assigned to such a story thus has a ringside seat at a newsworthy event, and he also has an opportunity to build up a reader following by writing an interesting account of what he saw or the situation as he comprehended it.

The procedure in covering this kind of story is somewhat different from the procedures in interviewing, although success in both kinds of coverage is based on the reporter's enthusiasm for the assignment.

Steps to Follow

Generally speaking, the reporter who is going to cover a story by firsthand experience will follow several steps. As a beginner, you will want to follow these:

1. Prepare yourself in advance as much as possible by checking on known facts, getting background of the event or situation, reading about it, interviewing persons who might have information on the subject.
2. Find out in advance what persons to see for information at the event.
3. Arrive with pencil and wits sharpened and all five senses ready to fill in all the parts of the total picture.
4. Arrive early and get a good vantage point, making sure that you can see and hear all that goes on.
5. Make notes that will serve for background information for your story. That is, note details of the setting so you can give your reader an idea of where the event took place as well as of what happened and who the participants were.

    Make a practice of looking at everything carefully so you can relay the scene to your reader. Pause to see what your five senses are telling you as the event progresses. Give your reader something to look at, something to hear—even feel, smell, taste.
6. Make careful notes as the events progress, remembering that your purpose is to "see all, hear all, tell all."
7. Study the reactions of other persons present, listen to comments made, hoping to find sidebar stories and tips for other stories.

8. Immediately after the event, get off by yourself for a few minutes and compose a quick summary of what happened, jotting it down in incomplete sentences, perhaps, just to be sure that you get the main ideas condensed in your thinking as a kind of focal point.
9. Then, as soon as possible, write your story. Write it fully and with as much detail as you possibly can. Then, go back to trim, condense, and reshape it to fit the space required.

LOOK FOR RELATIONSHIPS

You must make every effort to see how this single event is related to other things going on. Very few events are isolated, complete in themselves.

As a reporter you are responsible to your readers for checking to see how this event is related to others and what this relationship means. Begin by conferring with your teacher.

For example:

Suppose you are assigned to cover an open school board meeting at which a new high school building is to be discussed. In listening to what is said, remember that this meeting is but one in a series.

The subject may be new to you, but it is not new to the board. In order to present a clear picture of this meeting to your readers, you must find out what has gone before and tell about this meeting in the light of that information.

FIRSTHAND INFORMATION

Another example:

You are assigned to cover a forthcoming open house. You check with the president and find that it is the eleventh such annual event held by the Parent-Teacher Association, the schedule is to be the same as last year, teachers are urged to set up exhibits, displays, and demonstrations. Having checked the files, you find that the stories have been short, merely reports that the open house was held, the number attending, and the like.

You attend the open house, finding that the classrooms look entirely different by night, brightly lighted and with parents following the class schedule with some difficulty in finding rooms, making their way through the crowded halls, getting to "class" before the tardy bell rings, and so on.

Souvenir cards are being given away in the print shop, the French club is serving refreshments at a "sidewalk cafe," the art department is conducting an auction of originals by students, popcorn balls are being served as the girls make them in the foods lab, science students are working on a science fair project, something with flashing lights that spell out w-e-l-c-o-m-e, the first-aid class is bandaging a "victim."

The parents seem to be enjoying this, and they are getting an idea of what school is like. The students in the classrooms to help with the program seem to be enjoying it, too—a different kind of "school day."

Is this a successful activity? "Yes," several parents and teachers are heard to comment. Is it worthwhile? Yes, several parents and teachers say so. Students say they think it gives parents a better understanding of the school program.

You can write a story on this because you were there, you were interested. There were people, there was action, the subject is one that concerns the entire student body, for all are students there and all have parents.

NEWS AND SIDEBARS

Another example:

The Key Club sponsors an annual banquet honoring club sponsors and presidents. You are assigned to cover it. You attend. The tables are gaily decorated with clubs' insignia, little pennants for place cards, purple asters and yellow candles. Key Club boys are serving the plates, sporting their traditional yellow vests. You learn that the boys and their sponsor prepared the entire meal. (For a human interest story, ask them what went on in the kitchen.)

The program is presented by a local doctor, demonstrating some of the principles of hypnotism, using one of the Key Club members as a volunteer "patient." The program is tremendously popular with the guests. Others volunteer to be "hypnotized." The meeting lasts twice as long as was expected.

You write an interesting story because you were there and you were interested. You can tell the readers all about it. Also, you have a sidebar story on hypnotism, to be written after you have time to do some reading on your own and interview the doctor.

Another example:

The fire alarm sounds, and you fall in line and leave the building as in the usual fire drill. Then you discover that there are fire trucks clanging around the corner and grinding to a halt at the gym entrance.

Since you have made a reputation for yourself as a reliable reporter, the teacher gives you permission to cover the story. You discover that there is more smoke than fire, that something is smoldering in the boys' dressing room, that hand-operated fire extinguishers are being used, but that five trucks are on hand.

You move around the campus and discover that some students still do not know there is a fire. Some have left the cafeteria with their trays in hand and are lined up along the walk finishing their lunch. You have an interesting story because you were interested in what was going on.

After interviewing the principal, you have a story on the fire. You have a story on how students behave in an emergency, with human interest overtones, perhaps—and you have at least one editorial based on the importance of fire drills and fire prevention.

THE READER WAS THERE

Students will be interested in reading your stories because they, too, were there, and they will compare their ideas and their impressions with yours.

They will want to see what you saw that they did not see, or what they noted that you missed.

Also, they will be interested in HOW *you* saw what *they* saw. It is important to remember this: Readers are interested in reading about things that are familiar to them if they think the writer saw these things in a fresh, original way.

Stories of this kind require a great deal of work, because from a wealth of information and ideas you must write a story that is comparatively short and concise. This means that you must decide exactly what your story is going to say and then make every word count.

The object is to crowd as much as possible into your space. That is, you do not trim off important ideas, you merely use fewer words to convey more ideas, thoughts, facts. Obviously, however, you would disregard facts that do not contribute directly to the story as you see it shaping up in your mind.

The excitement of covering the news firsthand is one of the sustaining forces in a newsman's life.

I'd like to know who these reporters think theyare! Now they'll get everything right!!
I'd like to welcome all of you fine active journalists...
LIBEL

Key # 5   *Know the Rules*

... "When all else fails, read the directions." We laugh at this old joke, but we know the advice is good. From electronic baseball to chess, from tennis to barrel racing, you want to know the rules of the game before you begin.

In journalism the no-no's are few. But sad is he who discovers too late that one little oversight can cause staggering problems.

No matter what the publication or what the school community, the student journalist should understand that there are guidelines. It is his responsibility to know what these are and to follow them. He is expected to uphold the honor and traditions of the paper.

Every staff should remember that every publication is unique and therefore should set up its own statement of policy. Obviously, the guidelines followed in a small church academy might not be suitable for a large metropolitan high school. For one thing, the concept of the administration varies regarding the place of the school paper in the total school program.

The basics do not vary. They include "taboo" and "libel." Freedom of speech and press does not permit the publication of libel, blasphemous or other indecent articles, or other publication injurious to morals or private reputation.

Statement of Policy

A school newspaper is an important part of campus life just as a daily or weekly is an important part of the community it serves. Study your paper's traditions and policies carefully so that you and your staff will know what role your paper is expected to fill.

If your paper does not have a formal statement of policy—that is, "the rules"—then the staff and adviser should work one out. Give every staff member a copy, file a copy in the journalism office, and file one with the principal.

Battles occasionally shape up over what to print or not to print. In such struggles, the statement of the paper's policy is a guideline.

Can the school paper print anything it wants to print?

This question has long been argued with considerable heat. It should be settled for your paper by your statement of policy. You print what fits in with your policy. You do not print what doesn't.

It should be said that any school paper that can print anything any student wants to write is about as safe as a match in a keg of gunpowder. School papers can be sued, the school board can be sued, the adviser can be sued, the student writing the article can be sued.

Since the early sixties school papers have been involved in innumerable court cases over what appeared in print. In fact, a $1,000,000 libel suit filed in 1962 in Long Island was in the courts some fifteen years. The suit charged that, in the yearbook, a quotation printed beside the picture of a former girl student was "false, scandalous and defamatory." Defendants were the board of education of the high school district involved, the principal, and the printer of the yearbook.

Editorial comment appearing in *Scholastic Editor* made this point: "This goes for newspapers as well as yearbooks. This libel suit might easily have been filed against the persons responsible for some of the vicious items in the student gossip columns we have seen."

Example of Statement

Although statements of policy may be drawn up in various ways, the following is a good example. It is called "The Code of Ethics for Student Publications of the Denver Public Schools." It is given here in full because it has been widely used as a guide.

> School publications in the United States, both from the standpoint of authorship and readership, must be a training ground for American democracy.
> Since freedom cannot survive nationally with a controlled press, we must

Key # 5 *Know the Rules*

take care not to rear a generation of journalists who take censorship for granted, nor readers who are accustomed to getting only controlled news.

The school publication must be aware of its responsibility as a living part of the American journalistic tradition; it must not live in timidity or apathy.

Any publication should cooperate with the faculty and administration, but it should not sacrifice its inherent rights and obligations to the school to observe, to probe, to question, to report, to entertain, to educate, to evaluate, to interpret, to initiate, to recommend, to encourage, to criticize and to commend.

We, the staffs and sponsors of the student publications of the Denver Public Schools, believe that the following principles should apply to all publications for which we are responsible:

To fulfill its responsibilities to the individual reader, *a publication should—*
. . . *respect the privacy and dignity of the individual.*
. . . *respect the right of the individual to express his opinions.*
. . . *be concerned with affairs within the realm of student interest.*

To fulfill its responsibilities to the school and to the community, *a publication should—*
. . . *serve as a fearless and concerned spokesman and service organization for the school which it represents, yet not abuse its freedom of the press.*
. . . *act as a sounding board for student opinion on matters pertaining to the school; it should be free to initiate responsible thought and to guide action intended to improve situations in the school; it should be a communication link between administration and student body through presentation of facts and interpretation of them.*
. . . *use wisely the right to offer constructive criticism of a topic after conscientious gathering and evaluation of the facts.*
. . . *acknowledge any significant factual error, and correct it, if it is feasible to do so.*
. . . *practice good sportsmanship, good taste, and decency at all times in the material presented to the public.*

To fulfill its responsibilities to the journalistic profession, *a publication should—*
. . . *strive to maintain the highest modern standards of good journalistic practice.*
. . . *be sure that news items are accurate, factual, and objective.*
. . . *be sure that editorial materials are supported by facts, logical reasoning, or expert opinion.*
. . . *be sure that good taste is exercised in the choice of feature materials, especially regarding objectionable personal items as defined by professional organizations such as National Scholastic Press Association and Columbia Scholastic Press Association.*
. . . *strive for balance in the amount of emphasis given to each phase of student activities.*
. . . *give full credit for all material that is not original or that is professionally produced.*
. . . *maintain an efficient and responsible organization that does not abuse any of its journalistic rights and privileges for private advantage.*

... *recognize the significance of journalism as a means of maintaining the highest principles of democracy in a free society.*

GOOD TASTE

Taboo and *libel* are two terms that beginning journalists should understand, for both refer to what the paper does not print.

Taboo is the term for the inside censorship that a publication observes to insure fair play and good taste in its own columns. Every publication draws its own lines. Usually the smaller the group of readers, the stricter the paper.

"Good taste is good sense," says Carl Warren in *Modern News Reporting*. "Your newspaper is a guest in the homes of its readers."

Generally taboo items for school papers include disagreeable words and subjects, bodily functions, unpleasantness, gruesomeness, and facetious treatment of subjects of respect.

The rule is, "When in doubt, don't print it."

Libel is defined briefly as written or printed defamation.

Defined more fully in legal language, Warren says, "It is any false and malicious representation which tends to hurt the reputation of a person, to expose him to hatred, ridicule, contempt, or obloquy, to injure him in his occupation; or which damages a firm financially. There are two types of libel: (1) Libel *per se* is libel on its face. (2) Libel *per quod* is not apparent on its face but is made so by the surrounding circumstances."

The First Amendment to the United States Constitution says, "Congress shall make no law . . . abridging freedom of speech, or of the press." The Fifth Amendment protects the right of each person to be protected against abuse by others.

An interpretation by the United States Supreme Court put it this way: "All men have a right to print and publish whatever they deem proper unless by so doing they infringe upon the rights of another. For any injury they may commit against the public or an individual, they may be punished. . . . The freedom of speech and press does not permit the publication of libels, blasphemous or other indecent articles or other publication injurious to morals or private reputation."

Freedom of the press, therefore, means that a newspaper can print anything it pleases, but thereafter can be held liable for it.

"Check and verify are the only procedures against ignorance and error," says Warren. Evidence is the sole criterion of the reliable reporter as he sifts fact from fiction.

As a final test, the reporter should ask himself: "How would this affect me if I were the person involved? Do I know this to be the truth? Is it fair and just for me to report this information for print?"

Maxine Wiseman, a teacher-adviser stressing this point, suggests this: "If a story is questionable, ask yourself this: 'Would my name look good in this story now?—and 10 years from now?'"

Again, the rule for school papers is, "When in doubt, don't print it."

SOME DO NOT SUCCEED

Important as the school paper is, it is unfortunate that occasionally a newspaper staff handles a situation in such a way that the administration suspends the publication and drops journalism from the curriculum.

In the last several years students have been actively interested in the total school program and have frequently voiced strong feelings in opposition to the administration. The question of censorship thus arises.

Feeling secure under the First Amendment, students are daring to express themselves, and the school administration in many situations views this as reason for censorship.

One school official says: "Many student newspapers are published by the school system, with students as working and learning journalists, the adviser a teacher in the system. Because it is in the curriculum, the journalism program is subject to administrative supervision."

On the other hand, censorship of the school paper is described as "interference in the free exchange of ideas as well as infringement on students' rights."

The following story in the *Southwest Times Record*, dated May 6, 1977, indicates what can happen—and does:

POCOLA MAGAZINE BURIED
Student Publication
Gagged to Death

POCOLA—*Approximately 50 Pocola High School students—some with "Freedom of the Press" emblazoned on their shirts—symbolically buried their school magazine Wednesday afternoon in a brief "funeral" at a Pocola cemetery.*

"Pocola People" staffers say the school administration cut off funds for the May edition and dismissed the journalism teacher.

"Because of our editorial comments on alleged open meetings violations by the Pocola School Board, this will be our last edition," according to an article in the April 18 issue.

A source close to the controversy indicated one reason journalism instructor-

assistant coach Larry Miller's teaching contract won't be renewed at the end of the school year is because the magazine was not submitted to Supt. Farmer Wann before publication. The source said censorship by Wann earlier was agreed upon by Miller.

Wann refused to discuss the matter in detail.

Wann did say, however, that Miller's contract was not renewed "in the best interests of the school." He said another journalism instructor will not be hired.

The fledgling magazine, which won first place in its class during competition at a recent Northeastern Oklahoma University, Tahlequah, Press Day, alleged in several stories violations of Oklahoma open meeting and open records laws.

However, minutes of school board meetings since March do not reveal any obvious violations.

The magazine alleged that student council members were asked to leave the March regular meeting while board members discussed its policy on allowing students to have a dance.

Under Oklahoma law the only items board members may discuss in an "executive" or closed session are employment, hiring, promotion, demotion, discipline or resignation of employees. Voting must be done in public.

The magazine also alleged that in one instance reporters were denied access to board minutes, but were later allowed to read them into a tape recorder.

President of the school board Arthur Moore said the students simply got up and left one meeting of their own accord.

"We gave the students all the time they needed, and when they got through, we asked them if they had anything left to say," Moore said. "Then they left."

In another incident March 16, Miller said he and his group were denied access to a meeting of board members to discuss the dance policy.

Miller said board members told him the meeting was for that purpose.

Wann said it was an executive session to discuss personnel matters. He added that only three board members showed up, and the meeting was called off.

Miller said he started sending magazine reporters to school board meetings after the first March meeting at which he alleged the students were asked to leave.

"Earlier, we were going to send student reporters as a training exercise, but we didn't get around to it until after the first March meeting," he said.

Miller, who is 23, said he has taken a job as a sports editor of the Seminole, (Okla.) Producer. That job will begin after his current contract expires.

Miller is a journalism-certified teacher and graduated from the University of Oklahoma. He has worked part-time for the Daily Oklahoman on the sports desk and as a proofreader for the Norman (Okla.) Transcript.

The school magazine, with a breezy, modern layout, during its six-issue existence, explored such areas as legalization of marijuana, crime in LeFlore County, the student drinking problem, and the married student.

The magazine also carried a feature on Pocola Coach Walter King, who

Key # 5 *Know the Rules* 47

allegedly threw mud at an official, leading to the school's forfeiture of the Pocola-Porum football game last October. The story was an exclusive on the coach's side of the incident.

A careful reading of this account shows what happens. The staff has an idea for a story. Something has happened that should be exposed. However, in covering the story, apparently sufficient care was not exercised. It appears that the coverage was not complete, or that the wording was inadequate.

Undoubtedly there is a good story here. But when a subject is controversial or when allegations are made, the reporter must protect himself by being thorough in coverage, accurate in reporting, exact and careful in wording.

When a subject is controversial or when a reporter wants to make allegations, he should ask himself what the heart of the story really is:

What does he expect to accomplish? Does he want to cover the complete story, giving both (or all) sides opportunity to speak? Does he want to embarrass the board? Does he want to call attention to misdoing? Does he want the wrong corrected? Is there really a wrong?

These questions may seem tedious, but the staff would have done well to answer them because now their voice is gone.

Can we afford to give up even one student publication, the students' right to express themselves, by poor reporting and inadequate care in covering a story? If we are going to venture into these areas of controversy and allegation, we must be careful how we do it. Otherwise all may be lost.

Jack Moseley, editor of the *Southwest Times Record,* makes the following comment on editorial policy for school publications:

> *If there are subjects that are not to be reported or discussed in editorials in the school paper, the student reporters and editors should be clearly informed at the outset, not after they have expended time and effort on something that will not be printed.*
>
> *I contend that there is no subject that a newspaper cannot report, provided it is handled correctly. The key words always are* accuracy *and* fairness.
>
> *I have never seen any issue or object that had only one side. That contradicts the laws of nature. The reporter may see only the good, or right side from his perspective, but he has a responsibility to seek out and at least afford the other side an opportunity to air its views.*
>
> *A teacher can be extremely effective in developing fairness-conscious reporters.*

Take the case of the long-haired radical who worked for me in the 1960s. Although he was opposed to the war in Vietnam, I sent him to cover the annual stockholder meeting of one of the largest defense contractors in America. Tight private security surrounded the meeting. The young reporter was "arrested" and searched four times while getting the story.

When he returned to the office, he was furious and prepared to write a story about police-state tactics and ungodly merchants of misery.

I told the young man about other corporate meetings at which bombs had exploded and at which student radicals had disrupted proceedings.

I asked him if he didn't think it was funny that he had been mistaken for a bomber or a disruptive radical four times in one day. He cooled down a bit and wrote a first-person story about his experience. It was highly readable, fair, accurate, and honest. The chairman of the board of the defense firm personally called the young man and apologized for the inconvenience created by the security forces. The New York Times picked up the reporter's story and published it.

The young man was very proud of that story and later told me that once I helped him detach his fiery emotions from his work, he was able to do the job he had been trained to do. That young man, by the way, today is a major writer for one of the national wire services.

You can write about anything as long as you write it right. And for me, right means correct facts coupled with fairness.

That editor thinks he knows everything! All news stories are alike... Just like these Paperdolls!
?

Key # 6   *Recognize the Various Kinds of News Stories*

. . . Not long after a beginning reporter learns about the "nose for news," he makes a significant discovery: not all news stories are alike.

Fortunately, there are guidelines and patterns that make it easy to plan and write full coverage stories with the emphasis in the proper places. Stanley Campbell, of the Oklahoma School of Professional Writing, advised his students to search constantly for stories they considered well done and then clip them to use as "patterns."

He suggested that any writer, from beginner to professional, could find help by keeping a clipping file of good ideas—such as possible feature stories—and of good examples of all kinds of writing.

"This serves as a kind of self-inspiration for ideas as well as a guide for story patterns," he said. "Not only this, to clip passages that you consider good writing will help you develop a more effective writing style."

Would this be a kind of plagiarism? "No," he replied, "because in news writing your subject is always changing. The purpose of your 'pattern' is to show you the how-to-do-it."

Recognizing quickly the kind of story you are doing—coverage of a situation (as a fire), meeting story, speech story, result of a poll—will help you plan your story as you take notes.

SIMILAR THOUGH DIFFERENT

Since school activities are generally similar in many respects, it is not surprising that stories appearing in school papers are similar.

Though just beginning to work on a school paper, you will soon be writing one or more of the following: (1) meeting story, (2) speech story, (3) honors or awards story, (4) play story, program or similar activity, (5) special events and situations story, (6) classroom activities story, (7) sports story.

As a beginning reporter, you should understand that no one story is isolated from all others. No one story is a complete unit in itself. Everything that happens is the result of something that went before and also has relationship to other situations and events.

Furthermore, every event or situation leads to something else. That is, it has consequences. It is important that you bear this in mind at all times. You must be aware that *there is a before–now–after* to each of your assignments.

You can write about the present event or situation only if you know about and understand what has gone before and are aware of what the consequences may be.

MEETING STORY

The meeting story is one of the most common of all school news stories. It varies from the short announcement of a coming meeting to an extensive report of what happened at the meeting and its results, often running into a series of stories.

Though this is one of the simplest kinds of assignments on the school paper, you can gain valuable experience with it.

If you cover the meeting by attending, you have time to look for sidebar stories and suggestions for features. Also, you have time to consider various ways to approach the story when you are ready to write and thus can sit down at your typewriter with a lead already in mind. Developing this ability is one of the best ways you can help yourself.

Information for a meeting story can be obtained by attending the meeting or by getting the information from the presiding officer, the secretary, or someone else who has not only accurate information but all the facts needed for a complete story. This information may be supplemented by interviews with the officers, the speakers, or others who may have certain information that would round out the story.

You will always find out more if you attend the meeting than if

Key # 6 *Recognize the Various Kinds of News Stories*

you rely on someone else to tell you what happened. For routine and relatively unimportant meetings, as far as the paper is concerned, it is usually sufficient to get the story from the president or the sponsor of the organization.

However, if you are there—and alert—you will probably see much to interest you. Usually you will see additional stories. If nothing more, you will gain background information and understanding about the particular organization.

Remember, since officers and sponsors of an organization do not always know what is newsworthy, they often overlook interesting story possibilities.

It is the reporter's business to seek out those items that will interest his readers. The alert reporter will soon discover that *where there are people, there is action*—and that *where there is action, there is reaction.* Both of these make good copy.

To say this in different words: The action makes good straight news copy. The reaction makes good human interest copy. *Human interest stories never come secondhand. The only way to find a human interest story is to be there and see—and feel—it for yourself.*

There are several kinds of meeting story.

ROUTINE MEETING

The routine meeting is common among school organizations and usually only slightly newsworthy. However, the reporter who covers that organization should know what was said and done at the meeting so he can fit it into his complete coverage of that group.

For example:

The newly organized Boys Pep Club held their weekly meeting and spent the entire time discussing what kind of uniform to adopt.

There is very little here to print for a story in the paper a week later, especially as the deadline for copy is tomorrow. But the enterprising reporter will find out all he can about it and include the information in another story later, saying merely that the decision about uniforms finally adopted was made after several weeks of discussions.

In some instances, however, the routine meeting does provide information for a news story, though it may be short. Suppose the Boys Pep Club decided definitely on a uniform at the meeting but made no decision as to what kind. The reporter then has an item for information to relay to his readers, something they did not know and in which most will be interested.

The story would have this information: *Who*—Boys Pep Club. *What*—have decided definitely that they will have a uniform this year. *When*—decided this yesterday at a routine meeting, will be ordered later, will be ready as soon as can be decided upon and ordered. *Where*—will wear these at all games and pep-making occasions. *Why*—to help boost school spirit and give the club prominence.

More than one good lead can be written for every news story, but usually the *who* or *what* is most important as an opening idea. In this case, the *why* is also suitable for the opening.

For a simple meeting story where the beginning reporter is assigned to see a sponsor regarding a club meeting, DeWitt Reddick, of the University of Texas, offers this suggestion:

What questions would you ask? Beginning reporters should make a list of essential questions before seeking an interview, so list some questions. It would be well to start with the five W's and H:

What—What is the name of the organization? What kind of association is it? What happened at the meeting?
Who—Who presided at the meeting? Who was on the program?
Why—Why was this meeting held? Was this purpose accomplished?
Where—Where was the place of meeting?
When—At what time was the meeting held?
How—Was there anything unusual in the way the meeting was conducted?

The answers to these questions will supply the basic outline of facts for a short news story. The lead should start with the most important element.

Never begin these stories with the *when* or the *where* unless that information is significant. In these simple routine items, when and where are not important.

If either when or where is important, the story will not be routine, and your lead will play up *whatever is unusual* at this meeting.

Unfortunately, far too many student reporters begin a routine meeting story thus: *At the March 11 meeting, held in the art room, the members of Alpha Rho Tau discussed the plans for the annual art auction in May, but no definite decision will be announced until next week.*

Better: *Alpha Rho Tau will announce plans next week for the annual May art auction, following discussion at the regular meeting March 11.*

Actually, there is more to be said here, for the word "annual" shows that this item has a background that the reporter can include if space is available.

Key # 6 *Recognize the Various Kinds of News Stories* 55

MEETING NOT ROUTINE

Frequently, however, the business meeting is not routine. In this instance, you have to use your judgment as to what to feature and how long the story should be. The significance and the consequence of the action taken dictate the length. Take care to get all the facts. Also, consider this carefully to determine the full significance and consequence.

Incompleteness is a kind of inaccuracy.

Poor lead in paper dated September 28:

> *A student council meeting was held September 19 principally to inform club presidents how the council plans to coordinate club activities according to the by-laws at present being drawn up by a special committee.*
>
> *Student council president Carl Moore said that according to the constitution adopted last year, no organization shall have any recognition by the student council unless it has been granted a club charter by the council.*

The reporter here has not looked for the most important item of interest. Actually, it is not a lead. It is merely a collection of words that are printed first. A lead has meaning. It is the reporter's effort to get the most important and interesting elements first in order to attract the reader's attention and hold his interest.

Better:

> *Club presidents have been informed that club activities are to be coordinated by the student council this year in accordance with by-laws at present being drawn up by a special committee.*
>
> *In a meeting held September 19 to explain this to club presidents, student council president Carl Moore pointed out that according to the constitution adopted last spring, the only organizations to be recognized by the student council will be those holding club charters.*

Sometimes a meeting that was expected to be a routine business meeting turns out to be unusual in some respect. If you cover the meeting by attending, you see this. However, if you merely interview the president or sponsor to get the information, you are likely to miss the interesting part.

The news source may say, "Well, really, we didn't accomplish much because we all got into a wrangle, so there's nothing to report."

Actually, the "wrangle" might be a very interesting story, if handled properly.

A "routine" student council meeting was recently reported in a school paper with this as the opening sentence: *A special student council meeting* was held January 21 for the purpose of appointing committees for special projects.

Naturally, the reader expects more about the committees. However, what really happened, as was told later in the story, was a spirited debate over an existing situation that was contrary to the newly adopted constitution and by-laws.

A better lead would have been this: *A special meeting of the student council, planned for the appointment of committees, turned into a heated debate over the constitutionality of the club program.* The date could have been given later.

Program Meeting

The program meeting is also very common among school organizations. In covering these stories, you will find that although the programs vary widely—from talks by visiting dignitaries to "funzies" and refreshments—your problem is always the same, namely, how to combine a number of activities into one well-organized story with a suitable lead.

The answer is simple, though carrying it out may require considerable thought and rewriting. Here the several-feature summary lead is the best solution.

In writing this multifeature lead, name the items in the order of their importance. Then in the body of the story tell about each in that order, adding details about each to complete the account.

Feature Meeting

The feature meeting is a meeting characterized by some outstanding or unusual item of interest or element of importance. In writing this kind of story, you naturally play up the feature, thus making use of the feature summary lead.

This will vary according to the event and the way you see the event, but the example shows how this kind of story is planned:

> *A bomb that didn't boom gave Science Club members a few anxious moments yesterday on the north campus.*
>
> *Gathered to see the results of some experiments in explosives, club members were advised by Dr. John Williams, sponsor, to stand back until reason for the failure could be determined.*

Pre-meeting Coverage

Pre-meeting stories afford an opportunity to see how much you can find out in advance about what is expected to take place. As every

Key # 6 *Recognize the Various Kinds of News Stories*

meeting is held for a purpose, this purpose should be the feature of the advance story. You find out the nature of the business to come up, the committees to report, speakers, entertainment, regular activities, special activities, and the like.

The pre-meeting write-up should give the name of the organization, the place, and a summary of the program planned. In the follow-up story, the place and hour are not given, though the date is.

The follow-up features the outcome or result of the meeting, with a look ahead for a future angle. For the follow-up story, find out about the disposition of each item of business that was to come up.

In a pre-meeting story mention your source of information. In a past-meeting story the reader assumes that the reporter gained his information by being present.

Always identify the organization in all meeting stories, unless the name is self-explanatory. Thus, *Quill and Scroll, international honor society for high school journalists,* but, *Future Journalists of America.*

Speech Story

The speech story, like the meeting story, is popular in school papers. Speakers covered range from visitors in the classroom to prominent lecturers appearing on special programs in the community. In either case, you get your story by being present and hearing the speech for yourself.

As a reporter on a school paper, you will find that assignments to cover speeches fall into two groups:

1. Frequently a celebrated or unusually interesting person is to appear for a lecture. In this case you have opportunity to make preparation in advance:
   a. You find out all you can about the speaker.
   b. You try to find out the subject of his speech, the exact title if possible.
   c. You obtain a copy of the speech in advance, if available.
   d. You try to find out why this particular person is speaking on this particular subject.
   e. You try to find out if there are other interesting items in connection with the speech, as other important persons to be present, reason for the meeting, background, attendant circumstances.
   f. You make sure that you know the exact time and place for the speech.
2. However, there are many occasions when visitors to the campus

make informal talks to classes or other small groups. These are frequently unpublicized, so you have little opportunity to do any preparation in advance. Many times you will discover the story for yourself before it ever gets to the assignment sheet.

LISTEN, TAKE NOTES

Practice and experience will help you meet this kind of occasion. The rule here is simple: Start listening and taking notes. You can do research later if not before.

Covering a speech story is a matter of *hearing what the speaker says* and then *communicating his message* as clearly and directly as possible to the reader.

The reader's enjoyment and understanding will be increased if you also give him some idea of why the speech was made, tell him something about the speaker and something about the occasion.

There are several ways in which you can help yourself:

1. Go early and get a seat where you can see and hear well.
2. Study the surroundings, general atmosphere, size of crowd, so you can bring this in as background if you want to.
3. Notice how the speaker looks, what he is wearing, his demeanor, any characteristic that would add flavor and color to your account.
4. Note the audience response.
5. Take plenty of notes but be sure to write so that you can read them later. All reporters have to work out some system of abbreviated writing unless they have learned shorthand or notehand. A reporter can write about 30 to 40 words per minute with a pencil—a speaker can say about 150 to 160 words in that time.
6. Listen for *thoughts,* and try to take down those thoughts rather than every word.
7. Cultivate the practice of trying to see the speaker's outline. This will help you discern his main points and see the relationship of subordinate points. Almost all effective speakers organize their talks according to a well-ordered outline.

    This outline generally falls into three parts—introduction, body (made up of two or more main points with varying subdivisions), and conclusion. Not only this, in order to make it easy for the listeners, the speaker gives clues as he goes along, with something like "The third and last point is this . . ." or "Now in conclusion, I would like to summarize . . ." Here the reporter takes care

Key # 6   *Recognize the Various Kinds of News Stories*   59

to get the summary down completely. Often this kind of summary can be quoted directly.
8. Get direct quotations to make your story more appealing to the reader—including summary ideas, effective statements, and colorful phrasing to provide character and personality. Be sure that in direct quotation you get the speaker's exact wording.
9. Cultivate the practice of forming in your mind a total impression of what was said. As soon as possible after leaving the speech, write this unified impression in a complete summary statement. This will force you to think actively about the speaker's main idea in a definite and effective way.
10. If there is opportunity, try to see the speaker after the speech, possibly to clarify some point you might not be sure about or to gain additional information. Any background material you can pick up will help round out your story. Occasionally you find a sidebar story this way.

Preparing to Write

How you write your story will be determined by how you listened to the speaker and how you took notes. The actual writing will be easier and your story will flow more smoothly if you accomplished these things while you listened:

1. Made a special effort to get main points as you listened.
2. Made notes of colorful phrases and characteristics to give your story personality.
3. Took down verbatim some especially effective or interesting passages to quote.
4. Made a special effort to summarize the main ideas.
5. Forced yourself to state the speaker's purpose in one complete, concise sentence.
6. Made notes of setting, audience, and the like to use as background.
7. Kept your story in mind as you listened to try to frame it partially before you got to your typewriter.

It is important to write any story as soon as possible after securing your information. This is especially true of speech reports because you want to take advantage of the closeness, the interest, the speaker's personality and your own reactions.

The longer the notes lie unused, the less you can read from them.

You write best when your mind is still occupied with your subject and before your attention is attracted elsewhere.

The one great rule is this: *write it now.* Every reporter would do well to letter that sentence in red and tape it on his typewriter.

Study Your Notes

You write the speech story as you would any straight news story. This means that you follow these steps:

1. Go over your notes carefully to get the complete story in mind. Be sure that you know the main points and their relationship.
2. List the facts in the order of descending importance. Always bear in mind that the end of your story may be cut if space is limited. Consider carefully what would be sacrificed first.
3. Write a complete sentence stating the speaker's specific purpose.
4. Find quotations in your notes supporting or illustrating this.
5. Summarize this purpose in some way for your lead. This may be a general summary, an indirect quotation, or a direct quotation if such a quotation is in your notes.
6. Consider the quotations carefully, making sure that they are not merely random thoughts. Every quotation, direct or indirect, should support the speaker's main purpose.
7. Study the possibilities for an effective lead. There is of course no one best lead for any story, for the way the story is written is determined by the way the writer viewed his information and his "feel" for the story. However, several kinds of leads can be written for speech stories.

Consider the Lead

If what the speaker said is especially interesting or significant, three kinds of lead are possible:

1. The general summary. As the term indicates, this is a carefully phrased statement of the speaker's main points presented so the reader understands the specific purpose of the speech.

    This is almost always a wise choice and lends itself to endless variety. Since every speech is different from every other, so would the leads differ. Also, this affords the writer an opportunity to show his skill and ingenuity in writing a lead that will attract the reader and keep his interest.
2. The direct quotation. Although few speakers state the general

Key # 6 *Recognize the Various Kinds of News Stories*   61

summary of their speech in a few effective phrases that could be quoted verbatim to produce an attractive lead, occasionally this does happen.

If the quotation is adequate, the lead is good. Sometimes the speaker makes a startling or significant statement as illustration for his general idea. This can be quoted directly and followed by a summary.

3. The indirect quotation. Often the speaker's exact wording is not suitable for a lead, and yet his general idea would make an effective opening for the story. In this case, the reporter uses his own words to give the speaker's thought.

This is especially effective when the speaker has made a significant or interesting statement that illustrates his general idea. It is more widely used than the direct quotation or the summary statement.

Other leads suitable for the speech story are determined by the situation:

Title of the speech. This is especially effective if the title is startling or an attention-getter. It is also used if the speech is not particularly important.

Name of the speaker. Occasionally the person who makes the speech is more interesting than the subject.

The occasion or unusual circumstances of the speech, if significant.

SPECIAL POINTS

Because the speech story is a special kind of news story, there are several points to remember:

1. Follow the lead by an explanation of the occasion or the setting of the speech. Include in this paragraph all the general lead information not already included in your opening.
2. Be sure to keep the speaker's main points in mind as you write. Be sure to give a fair and complete picture of what the speaker said, though the story may be brief.
3. In writing, follow *your* notes arranged in order of descending importance. This means that you do not follow the speaker's order.
4. Do not quote the speaker out of context, for this distorts his meaning.
5. Arrange paragraphs so that a paragraph quoted directly will be followed by a paragraph of indirect summary. Do not let quoted paragraphs follow one another.

6. Consider the meaning of the words you use. "Speech," "address," "talk" are not exactly the same. Other words that you use in place of "said" should be carefully selected. Words like "announced," "stated," "declared" have a specific meaning and should be used only when that particular meaning is required.
7. Give your story continuity and easy readability by making use of carefully selected connective and transitional devices in linking quotations and summary paragraphs. The following are examples:

    He explained also that . . .
    In pointing out specific instances, he noted also that . . .
    In further criticizing these tests, he named instances . . .
    Stressing the danger here, he warned that . . .
    As a consequence of this, he said, it will be necessary . . .
    Summarizing his points briefly, he concluded by saying . . .

Honors, Awards

The third group of stories common in school papers includes honors, awards, and the like. These stories follow the general structure of the fact story.

Because in most cases the information included is straight fact gained from a source interviewed, you list your facts in order of descending importance and write them in that order as the body of your story. In these stories the lead is generally thought out with care and phrased to attract reader interest.

The following examples show how such stories are handled when the subject is important but space is at a premium:

Couch Named AEA Candidate

A Jonesboro teacher—Mrs. Lou (Paul E.) Couch—has been named a candidate for vice-president and president-elect of the Arkansas Education Association.

Election to the office that Mrs. Couch seeks is the highest honor obtainable in the Arkansas education field. Too, the AEA is the largest and most powerful professional organization in Arkansas, wielding substantial political power from the county to state levels.

The more than 10,000 AEA members will vote for the vice-president president-elect February 7–8. Two candidates oppose Mrs. Couch—Mrs. Helen Henderson, a teacher at Imboden, and Mr. M. D. Forest, superintendent of schools at Wynne.

If Mrs. Couch should be elected to the position, she would automatically become AEA president next year, succeeding Mr. James Ahlf of Searcy.

Mrs. Couch, an elementary school teacher at West School for the past nine

Key # 6 *Recognize the Various Kinds of News Stories* 63

years, has received unanimous support of the Jonesboro Classroom Teachers Association and local school administrators. JHS teachers are actively campaigning for her election.

The main purpose of AEA is to work for the up-grading of education in Arkansas. The organization covers all problems in the school system, such as teachers' salaries, legislation and educational standards.

"If elected, I hope to devise the best educational program that Arkansas can afford to give her children," Mrs. Couch said. "It is my firm belief that every Arkansas boy and girl should be given the opportunity in education that will help them meet all changes in the world today. We teachers owe that to our children in Arkansas."

Mrs. Couch has received statewide recognition for her work in seeking a "fair share" of tax money for teachers' salaries. Her work in this field has gained respect for her from many Arkansas teachers and educators.

Holding bachelor's and master's degrees in elementary education from Arkansas State College, Mrs. Couch is a member of the National Education Association, Association of Childhood Education, Arkansas Elementary School Council, National Congress of Parents and Teachers, Delta Kappa Gamma, Kappa Delta Pi, and the American Association of University Women. (High Times, Jonesboro, Arkansas)

Ken Kloss Competes for $7,500

A senior boy with a genius for mathematics left for Washington, D.C., last Wednesday night after a send-off by classmates who had gathered at the Mansfield depot to wish him luck.

Kenneth Kloss received this all-expense-paid trip and a chance to compete for a $7,500 scholarship after being chosen one of the final 40 contestants in the Westinghouse Talent Search.

He wrote a 21-page report on his science project, a math computer, and he took a three-hour test to fulfill the original requirements of the talent search.

Only two other Ohioans join Kenny among the top 40 contestants.

In accordance with the contest rules, Kenny made the trip alone. The judges want to see how contestants react by themselves in Washington, and they believe students can learn more if they are unaccompanied.

As the final part of his test, Kenny will give a three-hour lecture before several thousand people and a group of judges. He will explain the complicated workings of "Alpha," the computer he designed and built.

Instead of shipping his 250-pound computer to Washington, Kenny took pictures of it. He will also display some operating equipment associated with the machine.

"I would have preferred to take the model because you can show its operation more clearly," explained Kenny. "But the computer would be hard to pack and bulky to handle on the train."

Before he left for his trip, the young scientist stated that he had received through the mail about three pounds of literature from Washington. In Washington he will stay at the Statler Hotel, where all of his expenses, including tips, will be paid.

"The only thing about this contest which worries me is that I will feel lost in Washington," he admitted.

He will return next Wednesday. (The Redbird, Loudonville, Ohio)

Plays, Programs

The fourth group—covering plays, programs, and similar activities—also follows the fact story structure pattern. However, as the following examples show, the wide variety of subject matter lends itself to more freedom on the part of the writer.

'Silver Whistle' Begins Tonight

Motivated by selfish interests at first, a tramp reverses his outlook on life and helps others to believe in dreams in the "Silver Whistle," this year's first major speech production. The three-act comedy written by Robert McEnroe will be presented at 8 tonight and tomorrow in the auditorium.

Centered around the theme that life can be as happy as one makes it, the play takes its name from the fable: "The dog crawled away to die and hid amid the thistle. There joy and youth came back to him on the note of a silver whistle!"

Leading the cast, Clarke Evans plays the role of Oliver Erwenter, a middle-aged tramp who pretends to be 70 so he can get free lodging in an old folks' home. One of the older residents of the home, Mr. Beebe (Carley Clark) has nothing on his mind but his funeral, which he hopes will be "very elaborate."

The "old crone" of the home, Mrs. Hammer (Vicki White) does nothing but complain about her need for an operation and Mrs. Sampler's giddiness. Mrs. Sampler is portrayed by Diana Fanning.

Other cast members include Janie Tripp, as Miss Hoadley; Cindy Sanders, as Miss Tripp; Johnny Ford, as Reverend Watson; Peggy Ferguson, as Mrs. Groves; Lamar Forrest, as Mrs. Cherry; Johnny Broome, as Emmett; Lance Wilson, as Bishop; Suzette O'Dear, as Mrs. Beach; Susan Woodruff, as Mrs. Reddy; Reed Lenti, as the policeman; and Tom Schaffer, as Father Shay.

Committee heads include Elata Ely, publicity; Sally Halley, props; and Dorian Clawson and Tim Daniels, set. The sixth period class will also help with the sets.

Tickets will be sold at the door, but activity cards will also be good. Price is 50 cents for students and 75 cents for adults. (The Westerner World, Lubbock, Texas)

Doernbecher Tea Slated for Dec. 5

The recipe: needles, thread and work in generous amounts, well blended. The yield: Dolls! Dolls! Dolls!

Key # 6 Recognize the Various Kinds of News Stories

With Christmas on the way, dolls and stuffed animals of every description are being created in the homes of South's girls as they plan for one of the major social events of the year, the Doernbecher Tea, sponsored by the Girls League.

All girls and their mothers are invited to attend the event Thursday, Dec. 5, from 3:00 to 5:00 p.m. in the cafeteria.

Purpose of the Christmas tea is to obtain dolls for holiday gifts to be given to children of Doernbecher Hospital and the Rehabilitation Center, Portland, and the Children's Hospital School and Pearl Buck School in Eugene.

Last year's tea featured a display of 101 Dalmatians created by Seniors Diana Brown and Janet Golden. The winning class award was the junior exhibit built around the theme of "The Seven Dwarfs and Their Cave."

At Sunday's tea dolls will be placed in class displays, each made up of at least 40 dolls.

Prizes will be awarded in these categories: most unusual doll, best workmanship, most complete display, and largest number of well-made dolls.

League hours will be given for each doll made, with double hours given to girls making the dolls in the winning class display. No doll may be over three feet in length.

Committee chairmen include Julie Taylor, refreshments; Daryl Stark, publicity; Mary Jean Heym, invitations; Terry Barid, hostesses; Laura Hollister, judges and prizes; Ann Martin, entertainment; and Gail Wolfe, display. (The Axe, Eugene, Oregon)

SPECIAL EVENTS

Stories of special events and situations may follow any one of the basic structural patterns. The following examples pass the test of a good news story. That is, they begin with a carefully planned lead. They then present the facts in the order of descending importance, tying the second paragraph in with the lead, including only facts presented in a straight news style, excluding any feature approach.

Original Name Returns to LHS

"Tom S." is dead!!!

After six years of being Tom S. Lubbock High School (more commonly known to the general public simply as "Tom S."), LHS had its original title restored at the last meeting of the school board, Jan. 16.

The action came as a result of a formal letter penned by the SC president Joe Murfee asking the board to drop the unwanted "Tom S." prefix.

When the announcement of the name change was made at Chapman Fieldhouse during the half-time of the Palo Duro basketball tilt, it was a moment no one attending could ever forget.

The air of game-time excitement became tense with anticipation as Prin. Howard Price walked to the microphone and uttered the simple words, "We are no longer Tom S." Then, after a split second of intense silence, the roof came down.

Almost as one, approximately 1,000 spectators jumped to their feet and let loose an earth-shaking roar that preceded several minutes of happy, rejoiceful yelling and singing of the fight song.

The next day, spirits rose even higher as the "body" of "Tom S." lay in state in front of the auditorium before his fifth-period funeral.

During homeroom period, the student body was called to the auditorium for the "solemn" burial ritual. As part of the service, Sara Cox and Nan Faulkner compared records of the school before and after the change.

Pallbearers George Fletcher, Barry McNeil, Johnnie Knowles, Leeroy Herron, Johnny Walker and Lonnie Dillard then transported "Tom S." to his final resting place in a small hole in a quiet corner of the open patio.

To conclude the service, Joe offered a stirring challenge to the future as Lubbock High School came to life again.

The original story of how Tom S. Lubbock High School was born is an interesting and often misquoted one. After hearing many varied versions of the truth, the Westerner staff dug back in the files of The Avalanche-Journal to find this information.

In October and November of 1954, before construction of the present Monterey High School had even begun, the school board appealed to the people of Lubbock to send in suggestions for new names for both schools to become effective the next year.

Citizens replied to the request with gusto and approximately 140 different suggestions came pouring in. (One little-known fact of this phase is that most people still favored leaving Lubbock High School with its original title.)

After consideration, the trustees, on November 23, 1954, decided to name the schools after the two original settlements of this area, Monterey and Lubbock. But more or less as an afterthought, since the city and county were both named in honor of Col. Tom S. Lubbock, the board thought that the school should bear his name also.

Names suggested for LHS included George F. Singer, Westerner, Sam Houston, Alamo, George Washington, Lone Star, Tech Senior High, and even Monterey.

Suggestions for Monterey included Chester Nimitz, Thomas Jefferson, Wrangler, Robert E. Lee, Quanah Parker and Buffalo Springs. (The Westerner World, Lubbock, Texas)

Key Club, NHS, FTA Spearhead Bread Sale;
Funds to Aid March of Dimes Campaign

"Bread for the March of Dimes!"

That slogan will be heard hundreds of times Sunday as families answer the ring of their doorbells from 2 to 5 p.m.

Armed with loaves of bread from one of Louisville's bakeries, students from

Key # 6 Recognize the Various Kinds of News Stories 67

Male and Presentation Academy will offer bread in exchange for donations to the March of Dimes.

"Since the bread will be large fresh loaves, we do hope it will be exchanged for large pieces of silver and fresh crisp bank notes," stated Mr. William G. Long, sponsor of the Key Club.

The Key Club, the National Honor Society, and the Future Teachers of America are sponsoring the campaign for the March of Dimes.

"We need 200 boys and girls to help us in this big drive Sunday," said Miss Willa Shaffer, sponsor of the National Honor Society. Students who will volunteer should see any member of these three clubs.

Jeff Wade, coordinator of the drive, expressed the hope that members of the band, the Brook 'n' Breck staff, glee club, debate team, athletes, and all other young people will volunteer.

Each school has a clearly defined area to cover. Male's territory is from Shelby and Oak north to the river on Shelby Street. It runs along the river to Algonquin Parkway to 7th Street Road. From 7th Street Road, it goes to Oak and up Oak to Shelby.

All doorbell ringers and bread carriers are to report to Male High as soon after 1 p.m. Sunday as possible.

Bread for the March of Dimes was first tried in Little Rock, Arkansas, by an All-Teens Drive. It netted $20,000. Teens from Presentation and from Male High are hoping to do their share in reaching this sum, Jeff said.

"Ring doorbells for all the crippled children in the United States!" urges Bill Bryan, of the Key Club.

The National Foundation—March of Dimes is the name of the fund-raising program for the treatment of children born with physical defects. There are at present 24 Birth Defect Treatment Centers in the United States, one of which is located at the University of Kentucky School of Medicine.

"The proposed plans call for the building of another center in Louisville," Mrs. Mary F. Heichelbech, secretary of the Western Kentucky area, informed the Brook 'n' Breck editor.

She further stated that a fourth of the money raised in Jefferson County will be used for research in allied fields, including polio.

"Our patient-costs are heavy in Louisville for the treatment of post-polio cases. We now pay all the costs for maintaining six respirator cases in this city," she said.

Mr. Howard Linker of Linker's Bakery stated that his company was honored by being chosen to provide the bread for the drive. (Brook 'n' Breck, *Louisville, Kentucky*)

Township Library May Be Possible within Six Months

In four to six months the Whitehall Township library board hopes to open a community library on a temporary basis if a building can be rented which meets the board's budget.

"We will then move into the township's new municipal building until we *find an establishment centrally located for everyone, possibly on the Seventh Street Extension," says the Rev. O. R. Fritze, president.*

The township library will not operate in conjunction with the school libraries because the state will not grant funds to any community library associated with schools.

Two weeks ago the Whitehall and Coplay library boards met to explore the possibilities of combining their libraries for mutual benefits. After the meeting it was announced that both units will remain independent of each other.

There may be some cataloguing and library reference work which may be used jointly when the Whitehall library gets under way.

But other than in these two fields Coplay's board definitely took a stand that it prefers to remain an independent unit.

"The initial cost of the library is great so we need all the help we can get from volunteers and donors," states Mrs. Edward Gross, treasurer.

Coplay started its library the same way, she pointed out, but they had a great deal of support when the Allentown Library's Bookmobile went out of operation and the books were circulated among libraries operating in the area.

Appointed to the library board by the board of education and township commissioners, other members include the Rev. Howard Laubach, vice-president; Mrs. Glen Miller, secretary; and Orville Pfeifer. (The Owl, Hokendauqua, Pennsylvania)

CLASSROOM ACTIVITIES

Classroom activities offer a wide range of subjects for news stories, plus an occasional sidebar feature story.

A beginning reporter might never think of the classroom as a source of interesting information to pass on to his readers. With some experience, however, he would realize that here as well as in extracurricular areas there are people and activities. And where there are people and activities, there is likely to be news.

Too few classroom stories appear in school papers. In fact, does your school paper give any indication, from issue to issue, that students go to class? Would a reader of your paper think that only extracurricular activities take place on your campus? Would a reader of your paper have any idea at all about the teaching methods practiced, the new techniques employed, the academic program?

A school paper should give the readership a true picture of campus life, and that means telling the complete story of campus life, inside the classroom as well as outside.

Note this, however: Classroom coverage does not mean merely telling what the various classes are studying. That may be information, but it is not news.

Key # 6 Recognize the Various Kinds of News Stories

To cover the academic front well, you not only find out what is going on in the various classrooms. You must seek out what has news value, and you must write it interestingly. A school paper should interpret the academic program for the readership.

The following stories are examples of classroom coverage.

Art Class Prints Calendar

Westerner calendars will be distributed to LHS faculty and the administrative staff of the Lubbock Public Schools as a Christmas greeting from the Graphic Arts 31 class.

The top of the pages indicate traditional activities of Lubbock High each month of the year. The sketches were designed and drawn by students in Miss Norma DePasqual's Graphic Arts class.

Tim Thompson was selected to coordinate the pictorial section, and Donna Simmons was calendar editor.

The calendars are printed in two colors by a silk screen process. Each student built his own printing frame, sketched the silk and cut film for his part of the design.

In order to print the 130, 13-page calendars before Christmas, Miss Mary Wilson and many students in Art 31 classes kept the printing processes running throughout the day.

Cartoon sketches of the class members are silhouetted in black across a gold band on the outside cover, with the message, "Greetings from Us, Graphic Arts 31."

The 11 students in Graphic Arts 31 are Sarah Arguio, David Colmer, Josie Flores, Wylie Hawthorne, Bob Herron, Diana Mitchell, Lewis Murdock, Donna Tim, Annette Tomek, Lila Sampson and Tommy Tubbs. (The Westerner World, *Lubbock, Texas*)

Earth Science Students Soon to Predict Weather

The earth science class will soon play "weathermen" with the use of their new weather station constructed in the field across from the girls' gym.

The station was built by Mr. Leonard Nolte's woodshop class.

"The weather station will house scientific instruments, such as barometers and thermometers," explained Mr. Donald Hully, earth science instructor.

The weather station was approved by the government so that weather forecasts will be valid. A meteorologist from Weir Cook Weather Station helped set up the equipment.

The earth science class will conduct experiments and tests in meteorology. By taking daily readings and keeping records of the weather, students will be able to make forecasts.

"The earth science class is considering broadcasting daily weather forecasts over radio station WHMS," Mr. Hully said. They are also planning to send the data to the Weir Cook Weather Station. (The Manual Booster, *Indianapolis, Indiana*)

'Scheduling Gimmick' Is Basis of New English TT

"The major problem of the senior English student is writing," said Mr. Robert Lumsden, senior English teacher. "That's why 4 English TT was established."

Mr. Lumsden and Mrs. Elizabeth White are teaching 240 seniors this year in English TT, which is not the same as other team teaching classes.

"The TT label is just the name of the course," Mr. Lumsden said. "If it stands for anything, it would probably represent 'tutorial.'"

4 English TT covers the same areas in literature, grammar and composition and uses the same books as a regular English class. In TT classes, however, the emphasis is placed on personal help with composition.

"The uniqueness of the course is the scheduling gimmick," Mr. Lumsden said. A TT student comes in contact with his teacher in three different ways: in the lecture room, in small groups and in individual conferences.

Seniors enrolled in the TT program meet as a class of 120 fifth or sixth periods only three times a week, on Monday, Wednesday and Friday. Lectures are given on these days by Mrs. White and Mr. Lumsden as well as other English teachers and outside speakers.

On Tuesday and Thursday, the TT student has no class. He may study individually or meet with six or seven other students in a discussion group with Mr. Lumsden or Mrs. White.

To supplement class lectures and discussion groups, students are expected to confer individually with their teachers during study periods for private, tutorial teaching, mostly to discuss writing.

Student problems with literature at ETHS are not severe, and most difficulties arise in writing, Mr. Lumsden said.

"You can't teach composition to a large group," he explained. "That is a personal thing. What we want to strive for is a one-to-one situation in which to teach the student. That would be ideal, and 4 English TT is about as close as we have come to that at Evanston."

Asked about the success of the course, Mr. Lumsden said, "Well, I think it's working out all right. Everyone seems to be reasonably happy, and we have had only a few dropouts. It is, however, too early to make a complete evaluation." (The Evanstonian, *Evanston, Illinois*)

Games, Dolls—an Assignment

Kindergarten or high school was the question asked by many students as they passed room 110 this week.

Colorful games, toys and dolls gave an illusion of childhood to the room. However, the articles were made by Mrs. Gladys Sherar's home decoration classes. This is an annual project to accompany the unit on color.

Each girl is required to turn in a project using the 12 basic colors. The items contain every color in the rainbow.

"These projects help the girls learn to identify the basic colors," stated Mrs. Sherar. "Mainly, the projects are made for children."

Many of the toys will be sent to hospitals, though some will be given to younger brothers and sisters. (The Mission, Merriam, Kansas)

Distortion, Syllogisms Bias Senior Minds

Don't walk down the hall saying, "Blondes are always dumb," or "It was a typical teacher's attitude," because you will be told that you are making rash generalizations.

Members of Miss Thressa Newell's senior classes have learned that such statements distort the truth.

At the end of a unit on distortion, each class member was required to do a project, topics to be related to school or school activities.

By using statistics, percentage, samples with built-in bias, indefinite words such as "average" and "typical," and by leaving out certain relevant facts, they were able to distort their basic statements. Most asked questions of a statistical nature.

Distorted statements such as these were used in the study: (1) "Student Congress does not accomplish a thing." (2) "The cafeteria food is below average health standards." (3) "Student teachers are a hindrance." (4) "Teachers in this district are overpaid." (5) "Music piped into classrooms would help students concentrate better."

"The purpose of the project was to learn to recognize distortion in our everyday life," explained Nancy Rogers, who worked on the supposition that boys and girls should have separate classes.

Fred Krebs stated he learned that everyone, no matter how prominent, uses distortion to convince people to believe the way he does.

"Learning about the methods of distortion and propaganda, I am able to construct better arguments for myself and also to spot the faults in the statements of others," said Carl Brainerd.

Television commercials frequently have no bearing on the quality of the product being advertised, he pointed out. (The Mission, Merriam, Kansas)

SPORTS STORY

The sports story in the school paper occupies a special position just as it does in the professional paper. Almost all schools have one or more of the spectator sports—football, basketball, baseball, and the like—in which a few participate and many watch.

Both participants and spectators enjoy reading about those events, whether in advance stories or in coverage of games and contests that they have already witnessed.

Because students who enjoy sports and who read the sports page in the school paper keep up with sports in the professional papers and on radio and television, the student journalist is necessarily in competition with skilled writers on every story.

His readers are interested, but they are also critical, for they read with knowledge and understanding and also with a feeling for the story as the professionals do it.

Therefore, the school reporter must know what he is doing and care about getting his story right. This means that he must dedicate himself to accuracy and earnestly try to develop skill.

"It looks easy, but it isn't," says Carl Warren in *Modern News Reporting*. "Everybody, it seems, envies a reporter at a sporting event. He carries a pass, occupies a front-row, ringside, or press-box seat, invades the dressing rooms, hobnobs with stars and coaches, and knows all the dope. Even among the newsmen the feeling persists that sports writing is a cinch. Imagine being paid for going to a ball game!"

However, sports writers have their problems. Others are in the stands for the fun of it, but the writer must be constantly on the watch, tabulating statistics, taking notes, keeping his mind on the story.

RESEARCH NECESSARY

In preparing to write the sports story, as in writing any story, the reporter must learn as much as possible about the background of the event. This means that he must visit the morgue for reference helps and background information.

It also means that he must find out who could supply information for this particular event and then make an appointment for an interview. For student reporters such sources would be the athletic office, the coaching staff, and the players themselves.

All information, of course, should be carefully checked for accuracy, for few readers are as particular and read with as critical an eye as the sports enthusiast.

BUILD UP A FILE

Sports writers, also, should diligently build up a file of their own, so that as much as possible they can rely on their own information, carefully collected and tabulated by themselves for themselves.

If each sports editor, for example, keeps complete records each season for each sport, in a short while incoming reporters will have a background of information readily accessible. With this information thus at hand, any number of statistical references and comparisons can be made.

At the beginning of track season, for example, make out a form on which you can tabulate complete results and full information regarding

Key # 6 *Recognize the Various Kinds of News Stories* 73

all events. By the time the second event is to be written up, you have background information of your own.

This is increasingly full and helpful as the season progresses. If you compile a season report from these sheets and then file both the sheets and the report, you are already able to do some advance stories for next year's track. In two years, your sports desk will have available a store of information that even the coaches could not so readily supply. Building up by the year, such reference is invaluable.

In addition to this information, sports writers should add as much other material to their reference files as possible. This is called a "sportswriter's kit" by DeWitt C. Reddick, of the University of Texas. It includes information about individual players, facts about other teams to be played, and clippings that have appeared in the papers.

Suggestion: At the beginning of the year set up a filing system that will be easy to keep and convenient to use. If you have a filing cabinet or a file box, you are fortunate. However, a sturdy cardboard box can be very satisfactory.

In either case, it is *how* you keep your material that is important. Some persons prefer to use folders, others prefer manila envelopes. Each should be labeled so that clippings and notes can be kept ready for quick reference. You will want folders for each of the other teams your school plays, your coaches, your players, records of preceding years, and so on.

If you want to get firsthand information from other schools about their teams, you can draw up a questionnaire and mail it either to the sports editors of the school papers or to the athletic offices of the schools. Generally, if you enclose a self-addressed, stamped envelope, the questionnaire will be filled in and returned to you.

By filing these and keeping them, you will eventually build up a substantial background of information.

BASIC REQUIREMENTS

What are the requirements for writing a good sports story?

"Hard facts, cold figures and a clear style"—that's the suggestion made by Carl Warren to professional sports writers.

If you are a beginning reporter, you should cover a sports story just as you would any other news event. The five W's and the inverted pyramid form are a reliable guide to at least reasonable success.

In preliminary research and at the contest, you must acquire the following information:

1. The score or outcome. Who won? What was the score? Was there any unusual circumstance connected with the result? Was there a tie? A disputed score? A fight—during, before, or after the game? Overtime? Played in snow or sleet? Or cut short by rain?
2. Significance of the outcome. Was this an important conference game? Between traditional rivals? Do team standings change? Is a championship at stake? If these teams have played before, what is the record?
3. Spectacular plays, significant moments in the game. What about fumbles, intercepted passes, long shots, overtime ties?
4. Comparison of teams. In what respects were the winners outstanding? Where were the losers weak? How did the size, height, weight, and training compare? How many returning lettermen did each team have? Were coaches specializing in certain strategy?
5. Individual stars. Who were the stars? How did they star? What is their background? Was this expected?
6. Weather conditions, in outdoor games. Rain, wind, heat, cold—even snow and ice—may be factors in the outcome.
7. Crowd and background of the event. Was this a special occasion? How large was the crowd? How did the spectators behave? Note colorful details, atmosphere. What "personality" did this event have?

This information plus statistics and notes made during the contest will provide the facts you need.

CONSIDER THE LEAD

What do you play up in the lead? As in all news stories, you use your judgment, for you have a choice.

If you are in doubt which of the above seven basic story items is the most important, then play safe and begin with the score. To this you then add whatever else seems most interesting or spectacular.

Remember, however, that the lead of every sports story of this kind—that is, coverage of a contest—should include (1) the names of the two teams, (2) the score, (3) the date of the game, and (4) the place.

Follow the lead with (1) a description of the scoring, (2) significant points of the game, (3) outstanding players on both teams, (4) running comment on statistics of the game, (5) summary of statistics, and (6) line-up of both teams or of home team only.

Somewhere in the account, include interesting and significant information you listed in your seven points.

To lengthen your story, include a play-by-play account of the game before the line-up. For a very short story, include only the lead and the significant points.

To vary this story plan, follow this pattern: (1) lead, (2) remainder of the seven items in next paragraphs, (3) additional paragraphs to desired length written according to the action story structure: tell–retell, giving more details; retell, giving yet more details.

TIMELINESS

The problem of timeliness concerns sports writers for school papers, because usually days if not weeks intervene between the event and the publication of the story.

Since school papers serve as a record as well as a medium for fresh news coverage, most staffs run stories of sports events in order to keep the record complete.

Generally, the older the story, the shorter it is. Some staffs include all previous games in one story, and all the information about coming games in another, so that the sports page consistently carries one past-game story and one pre-game story. (By doing this, the sports editor can have additional space on the page for other kinds of sports stories.)

In the past-games account, the lead is a summary of the team standing to date, with the games then written up in the order of newness; that is, the last game first, and so on back. In the pre-game story, also with a summary lead, the nearest game is mentioned first, and so on.

SPORTS SLANG

How much sports slang is considered good form?

The sports writer enjoys more freedom in language than do most other news writers, for two reasons: (1) the reader of sports stories uses and is acquainted with a certain vocabulary associated with sports, and (2) accounts of sports events would be monotonously similar without the colorful words the sports writer can employ to give variety to his copy.

A word of caution to the beginner: Do not make up silly phrases such as "banged the apple" or "lammed the pill" or employ such triteness as "dribble derby."

Study the vocabulary of professional sports writers and use only the terms that they use. In this way you will build up a vocabulary of terms that not only are colorful but have an accepted meaning.

76   The Student Journalist and 21 Keys to News Reporting

Effective sports writing is "clear and colorful, factual and fresh, right and racy."

The following examples are typical of past-game and future-game coverage in school papers:

Topeka's Offense Sluggish;
Half Rally Saves Homecoming

The Topeka Trojans, relying strictly on a strong defense, scored their second straight Sunflower League victory over the Washington Wildcats, October 6. The Trojans trailed through the first half, but rallied with two TD's in the third period for a 13–6 Homecoming win.

Topeka compiled a 215-yard total offense to only 100 for the Wildcats. The Trojan passing attack, which was an instrumental factor in the Lawrence victory earlier, was held to only three completions in 19 attempts.

The so far winless Wildcats scored a surprise touchdown in the early second quarter on a 50-yard run with a Topeka fumble, and led the Trojans 6–0 at the half.

Troy's offense was more powerful in the second half, driving for their first tally in 10 plays.

Trojan quarterback Bill Williams swept to the Washington end for 14 yards to the five. After four plays, Joel Lawson scored the touchdown on a one-foot plunge with 7:51 minutes left in the quarter.

Topeka's second counter came with 1:49 left in the quarter, when junior center John Stinson recovered a Washington fumble on the Wildcat 34.

After four plays, junior left-half Andrew Williams scooted 14 yards after receiving a pass from Gale Howard. Richard Carmen added the extra point for the winning score, 13–6.

Topeka's game statistics are as follows:

Rushing: Howard, 46 yards in 13 attempts; Bill Williams, 42 yards in eight attempts; Loyce Bailey, 27 yards in five attempts; Andrew Williams, 22 yards in six attempts.

Passing: Bill Williams, one completion in nine attempts for 12 yards; Howard, two completions in nine attempts for 28 yards.

Pass receiving: Andrew Williams, 28 yards with two catches; Duke Jones, 12 yards with one catch.

Punts: Bill Williams, five kicks for an average of 31.2; Howard, two kicks for 31.5. (The World, *Topeka, Kansas*)

Trojans to Meet Chargers
In First Game

Tonight the Topeka High gridmen face a long-awaited game against Troy's newest cross-town rival, the Topeka West Chargers.

Most of the members of the West football squad are former Trojans, and the game will kick off the first athletic event between the two schools.

Key # 6 Recognize the Various Kinds of News Stories

West's newness to the Sunflower League is one of the deciding factors in their mediocre opening season, combined with the Chargers' very inexperienced backfield and a lack of depth. Coach Gene Smith has been forced to fill in his backfield with inexperienced sophomores.

The Chargers do have two of Topeka High School's best linemen in All-City Tackle, 6' 4", 210-pound John Caril and senior end Dan McJunkin.

West tied their first game of the season, 6–6, with Seaman, losing to Shawnee Mission East, 25–0, and to Wyandotte, 27–7.

So far the Chargers have been hampered with injuries and a lack of depth. Starter Larry Frost is out with a dislocated elbow, and junior Lee Wright received a broken leg in the Wyandotte loss. (The World, Topeka, Kansas)

Lubbock Cagers End Season as Co-Champions

The District 3-4A basketball race came to an abrupt end last Friday night for the Lubbock Westerners when Plainview's Bulldogs closed the door on Lubbock's state title hopes with a narrow 72–71 overtime win.

Trailing most of the night, the Westerners fought back from a 44–36 halftime deficit to knot the score at 68-all with 41 seconds remaining in the game on a three-point play by Gary Washington. Neither team scored again and regulation play ended.

In the overtime stanza, Lubbock jumped to a seemingly safe three-point lead, 71–68. Plainview's Paul Aday popped in two points to narrow the count to 71–70 with 48 seconds remaining, but still the Lubbock lead seemed enough.

But then tragedy struck. With seven seconds showing on the clock, the Westerners took the ball out near mid-court.

Doriam Clawson threw the ball in to Larry Doyle, who in turn tossed to Joe Dobbs. But before the tall senior could get it, Phil Stevenson intercepted and passed the ball to Aday, who scored the decisive points on a lay-up.

No more time remained, and Plainview had won the right to advance to bi-district.

Even though Plainview beat Lubbock last Friday, in the final district standings both will enter the record books as co-champions. Each finished regular conference competition with 12–4 records. Monterey was third with an 11–5 mark. Pampa, Tascosa, Palo Duro and Borger came next with 8–8 slates. Amarillo High was next to last with a 5–11 record, while winless Caprock ended in the cellar.

Buddy Fulgham led Lubbock in scoring and placed third in district with 258 points and a 16.1 average for 16 conference outings. Washington ranked eighth with 206 points and a 12.9 mean, while Dobbs tied for tenth with 196 and a 12.3 average.

In the playoff game, Washington hit 16 to lead Lubbock, while Doyle had 15, David Mulburn 14 and Fulgham 12.

The Bulldogs scored 1,114 points during the campaign to emerge as the district's highest scoring team. Lubbock scored 1,035 to rank third in that category.

Leading the defensive department, Monterey allowed only 779 points to district opponents. The Westerners were second in this division, giving up 875 points.

Plainview's success was a short one, however, as the Bulldogs lost to Haltom City in the bi-district tilt 88–82 in two overtimes. The Fort Worth school held Ronnie Peret, District 3-4A's leading scorer, to a scant 12 points. In district play, the Plainview junior had averaged over 21 points per game.

Doyle, who was the only other Westerner averaging in double figures, earned a 10.9, and overall scored 174 points. As a team, Lubbock averaged 64.7 points per game. (The Westerner World, Lubbock, Texas)

Complete sports coverage includes many other kinds of stories. However, if a reporter understands the news story structure in general and can cover games as in the preceding examples, he will be able to handle any story he wants to write.

Follow-up Story

Since some stories run over a period of weeks, coverage appears in more than one issue of the paper. By checking news sources well in advance and by careful planning, you can find out what is going to happen in time to get an advance story for your paper. Enterprising staffs on many school papers are successful in this, for they make the effort to have their front pages carry "new news."

Printing shop deadlines may pose several problems here, but generally a printer will hold a space for a last-minute story if he knows he can count on the staff to have the copy in at the time agreed upon.

Two words of caution: (1) be careful not to prophesy; (2) make no assumptions. Write your story so carefully that it will be accurate regardless of the turn of events after you go to press.

For example: You will come out Thursday morning. There is to be a band concert Wednesday evening. You have the program, which was printed last week, so you run a story about the concert as held. Surprise! There is an ice storm on Wednesday morning, so severe that classes are cancelled for the day. No concert.

You can protect yourself to some degree by careful use of tense. If the story is to occur soon after the paper comes out, or even before, use such verb forms as "were to be," "was planned," "was to be offered," "is scheduled for," "is expected," "faces" (as "The school board faces a debate tonight when . . .")

The following lead illustrates this point:

> Lamplighters have scheduled a field trip for tomorrow to the University of California Medical Center in San Francisco.

Key # 6   *Recognize the Various Kinds of News Stories*

> *The 48 students planning to make the trip hope to see the nursing, physical therapy and dentistry departments as well as a demonstration of the manufacturing of pills.* (Haypress, Haywood, California)

NEW DEVELOPMENTS

After the first story has run, often one or more stories follow as events develop.

Ordinarily one reporter handles the same story as long as it produces live copy. Thus he becomes familiar with the background, is able to recognize fresh developments instantly, is prepared for quick summary of what has gone before.

These follow-ups may include (1) new information, (2) causes not included in the first story, (3) developments, results, consequences, and (4) opinions regarding the event, with proper authority, of course.

This new information is carefully studied in relation to the former story. Then you (1) write a new lead giving special attention to the latest information, (2) work in the tie-in with former information, (3) give details of new developments, and (4) add other details.

Caution: Consider tie-in material carefully. Avoid too much tie-in, but also remember that the reader may not have read the previous story.

As you plan the follow-up, assume that some of your readers have not seen the previous account, or accounts. Your tie-in is merely a quick summary of what has gone before. Sometimes the tie-in is a sentence, sometimes a paragraph or more. In brief stories it may be included in the lead idea.

This keeping up with new developments is illustrated in the following series of stories from the *Locust Log,* Flora, Illinois:

First story:

> *Teen-town interested adults and students met in study hall last Tuesday night to question Mrs. Esther Childress, district representative of the Illinois Youth Commission, about the functions, cost and organization of a possible teen center in Flora . . .*

Second story:

> *For the second let's-get-going meeting of a possible teen town, about 100 students and adults congregated in the study hall January 16 to rehash the purpose and cost of a youth center in Flora . . .*

Third story:

> After a lag that threatened to close the teen town project, enthusiasm has picked up among the students, and everything is "go" once more.
> With a total of $25 in the treasury, students met . . .

Fourth story:

> Students on the teen town committee have methodically organized themselves, and under the steam of John Buckley, David Riggle, Ridge Case and Lee Eaton, have raised $110.24.
> But they need $2,889.76 to reach their goal of $3,000 . . .

The following series of stories appeared in *The Moor*, Alhambra, California:

November 19

Faculty, Varsity Cagers to Vie For Benefit of AFS Program

> With high hopes of "Taming the Teachers" and "Stewing the Students," the varsity and faculty cage teams will take to the hardwoods Nov. 27 for the AFS varsity-faculty basketball game, to be staged at the San Gabriel High School gym.
> The annual event, sponsored by the AHS chapter of American Field Service, will raise the needed money to bring foreign exchange students to AHS.
> Beginning at 8 p.m., the star faculty cagers will make their entrance and warm up for their fourth tilt with the students.
> Hoping to avenge last year's 54–39 loss and to even the record at 2–2, the faculty starting line-up will include Robert Damewood, Bill Higgins, Phil Heathley, Steven Kneeland and Tom McCulloch.
> Other faculty members to see action are Emmett Monasco, Jack Mount, David Rhone, Allie Schaff, Edward Sowers, Gilbert Strother and Richard Yerby. Chuck Weise is serving as faculty coach.
> Sideline activities provided by the faculty are under the direction of a special committee, made up of Miss Sharon Henrickson, Miss Elizabeth Burl, Mrs. Helen McGarry, Miss Jeannine Halet and Miss Gay Horchner.
> Male performers will be Alfredo Chavez, Claude Miller and Leland Mills.
> The varsity opposition is composed of Rex Bonnell, Steve Ebey, Bill Gibson, Alan Hale, Dal Jones, Kent Kasten, Jim Peterson, Jack Nestor, Min Chao and Richard Whorton.
> At half time, Coach McFate's gymnasts will give an exhibition and the faculty will present a drill routine.

November 26

Faculty, Varsity Cagers Ready for AFS Benefit

> The combination of fierce varsity-faculty roundball rivalry, hilarious half-

Key # 6 Recognize the Various Kinds of News Stories

time entertainment and a swinging sock-hop will headline tomorrow night's American Field Service benefit basketball game and dance. Scene of the annual event is the San Gabriel High School gymnasium.

Beginning at 8 p.m., the game will feature "veteran" athletes, a faculty "Pep Squad" and "Drill Team" and a number of specialty stunts. Half-time entertainment will be furnished by Miss Sharon Henrickson, head of the faculty committee.

Heading the faculty cagers, the starting line-up includes Robert Damewood, Bill Higgins, Phil Heathley, Steven Kneeland and Tom McCulloch.

The favored varsity team includes Rex Bonnell, Steve Ebey, Bill Gibson, Alan Hale, Dal Jones, Kent Kasten, Jim Peterson and Jack Nestor. Starting line-up has not yet been named.

Admission will be one dollar, all proceeds to be used to bring two more AFS students to Alhambra next fall.

Last year the varsity "upset" the faculty, 54–39.

December 3

Faculty 'Stews Students,' Wins AFS Benefit Titanic

Take one varsity basketball team, stir up and let stand flat-footed for 30 minutes. This was the recipe the Alhambra faculty used last Wednesday night to "stew the students" 64–61 at the San Gabriel High School gym.

Playing before a packed house of about 1,000 fans, the fired-up faculty came from behind late in first quarter to take a 14–13 lead, which they relinquished only twice for a few seconds.

The AFS-sponsored tilt, the fourth such game to be played, netted about $950 toward bringing at least one foreign exchange student to AHS next year.

Faculty cagers, attired in everything from a Tarzan outfit to a jailbird's suit, made their grand entrance at the stroke of 8, marking the beginning of a spectacular exhibition.

"Veteran" stars who scored for the teachers were Head Coach Emmett Monasco, Jack Mount, Bill Higgins, Allie Schaff, Steve Lawhorn, Steve Kneeland, Chuck Wiese and Dick Jensen. The latter was top scorer for the faculty with 13 points.

Top-scoring cagers for the varsity were Richard Whorton, with 17 markers, Steve Ebey 12 and Jim Peterson 9.

During the half time, the faculty drill team, composed of Miss Sharon Henrickson, Miss Gay Horchner, Miss Jeannine Halet, Miss Elizabeth Burl, Mrs. Helen McGarry, Miss Mary Louise Hood, Kurt Lesner, Oran Cousand and Claude Miller, performed a difficult but well-executed routine.

Drum major Gilbert Strother was leader for the formation.

Yell leaders for the students were this year's foreign exchange students, Angie Wanacek from Austria and Redamis Yacoub from Egypt.

Head yell leader for the faculty was Miss Horchner, who was dressed in six yellow pompons.

Following the tilt, the Cordons, with Cecil and Duane Allen, supplied the musical accompaniment for a sock-hop.

NEWS FEATURE

The term "news feature" appears in any extended discussion of news writing. This term is commonly used and should be understood, yet it is difficult to define.

The word "feature" has a dozen different meanings. That fact, in itself, makes definition a problem.

A news feature is a finished product—an end product. Yet writing a news feature is more an understanding of approach and method than it is of what the result should be.

In this book we have been speaking of what is generally known as straight news. The news story structure has been explained as the pyramid form.

The process of writing this kind of story is a matter of logically following logical steps.

A "feature news story" is merely a different approach to recounting the facts. Some people give "feature news" the name "warm news." Others say "human interest elements present." Some say "featurize" the news, or "humanize" the news.

Briefly, the purpose of the news feature is to bring the story home to the reader. The news feature is the recounting of the news in such a way that the reader can see it as a story of real human beings in a setting that he understands.

MOTION—EMOTION

A straight news story has *motion,* we say. A feature news story has *emotion.*

A straight news story tells about *action.* A feature news story tells that action in such a way as to gain a *reaction* from the reader, a response.

The straight news is aimed principally at the mind. The feature news tries to touch the heart.

The writer of a feature news story sees his facts with imagination. He can arouse the reader's emotions because his own emotions have been aroused.

When the writer smiles at his own story, the reader will smile. When the writer wipes away a tear, the reader will.

The experienced writer understands the meanings and implications

Key # 6 *Recognize the Various Kinds of News Stories*

of that word "feature." He can distinguish between straight news and feature, and he knows which way to handle a given story.

To the beginning writer this advice: Learn well the steps for writing straight news. Master the pyramid form.

Then, when and as you find a story that appeals to you, to your emotions, sit down and write it as you see it. Forget the rules. Simply dramatize your story as the characters play across your imagination.

Stick with facts, but write those facts as you *see* them, *hear* them, *feel* them.

If your story fails, you can always try again. If it succeeds, you can go on to others. Either way, if you *feel* the story and really work at trying to recount it so your reader sees and feels it, too—then you're bound to win.

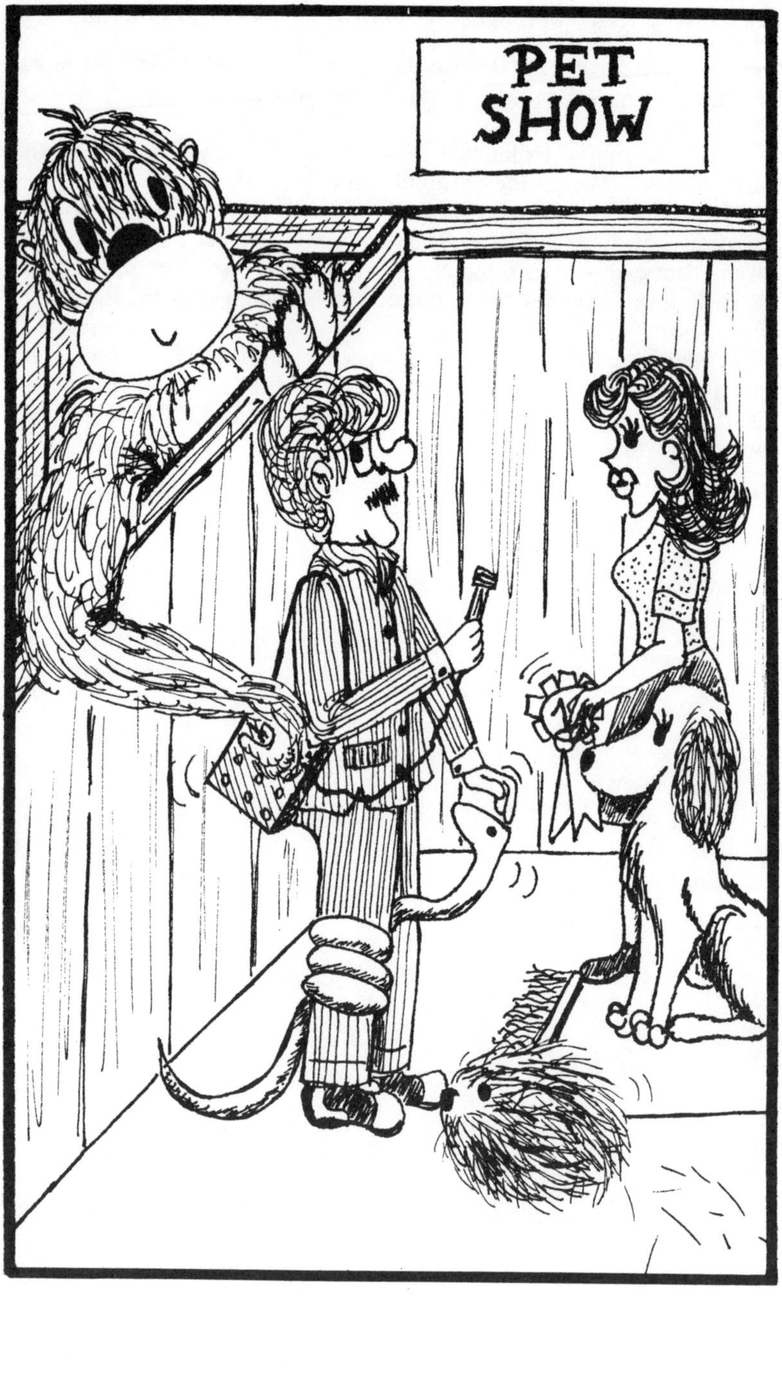
PET
SHOW

Key # *7* *Look for Feature and Sidebar Stories*

. . . "The school paper isn't interesting, just always the same old dull things." Sound familiar?

Readers are aware—sometimes before writers are—that news facts are merely the skeleton of a whole story. Readers like to know about the "body"—alive and in action. At best the news reporter can give only this skeleton. The feature and sidebar writer can tell about the "body" and how it behaves, what it says, how it is dressed.

This "body," of course, varies from story to story, but it's always there. For example: Fire drills—dull. Story on Fire Prevention Week—probably dull, too.

But at a fire drill a poodle bounded over to visit with the math group. And when the fire truck clanged into sight, the school photographer ran back into the building to get his camera (and the principal had words with him later!). And one of the girls in the foods class shared a pocketful of cookies just out of the oven.

Not earth-shaking, but "dress" for the "body." Obviously this kind of reporting requires constant alertness to the warmth and heart of everyday living. It requires awareness of what the reader will find significant. It's human interest in the news. Color. The "people look."

There's Something More

So much is said to the beginning reporter about basic news values that he ventures out fortified with determination to cover the who-what-when-where-why of campus activities. The assumption is that this coverage will tell the complete story of student life.

Soon he makes an amazing discovery: *There's something more.*

More? Yes, much more. All kinds of interesting things are obvious. They don't seem to fit any W-plan, but they're surely worth writing about.

For one example: It's an hour after school but the French teacher is standing by her car in the parking lot talking to three of the youngsters from across the street. Second look—the windshield is shattered. Interesting, but not a news story. Ideas: (1) What does one do when he discovers damage to his car? (2) How do parents react to this kind of situation? (3) Does anyone ever tell the story as the offending child sees it? (4) The grim thought of child abuse comes to mind. (5) Are teenagers victims of child abuse? (6) Guilty of it?

The interesting thing here is not just that the children's football broke the windshield. There are associated ideas that are significant and that can be written to be both informative and interesting to the reader, for they are related to everyday life.

Other examples: (1) Local high school boys volunteer to help fight a brush fire in the nearby mountains veering toward a village. (2) The Student Council participates in the Annual Great Raft Race to raise money in the current United Fund campaign. (The SC raft was first to sink. Why? What happened then? What safety precautions are required? Were there other sinkings? rescues?)

"Creative Looking"

"The facts, man, get the facts"—as always, the reporter's slogan. Now, if you are well prepared to cover a news story, in search of facts, you are in a position to do some "creative looking" as you visit your news source or sources. The term "creative looking" is coined to refer to the awareness that you can bring to any occasion.

Obviously, if you are on a mad dash to snatch a few words from a news source or if you have only a hazy idea about a news event, you will be in no position to look around to see what interesting ideas you can add to the factual information.

Every story has a setting whether you see it or not, whether you

Key # 7—*Look for Feature and Sidebar Stories*

write it into your account or not. Every story has characters. Every story has continuity of some kind. The news writer could well take lessons from the dramatist.

As you take notes, jot down pertinent observations about the setting, information that you derive through paying attention to your five senses: What do you see? What do you hear? What do you feel? Do you smell anything? Taste anything?

An example: A gas well located in a populated metropolitan area blew out. The story in the next day's paper not only gave information about the volume of the flow, the efforts to control the flow, damage, and injuries, but also told how the odor of gas covered the area, how the shouts of workmen rang out against the gushing gas, how the lights of the rig twinkled against the midnight blue of the sky, and how the flashing blue lights of police cars showed that the streets were being patrolled.

Suppose your beat is the band department. There has been an election of officers for the semester, so you plan to write this for the next issue. Being a junior, you know something about the activities of the band during the year, so you can assume that since this is the first month of school, nothing important is on schedule for some weeks yet.

Nevertheless, you look back through the files and find that the election story each year has been made up of names of the new officers and their duties, the date, and the director's name. Nothing more. So you make an appointment and visit the director in the band room after school. He has the list of new officers ready and hands it to you.

Is this to be all? No, definitely no, for you are going to see what your five senses can tell you about this visit.

What do you see? A group is gathered around the director at the piano. Incidentally, isn't that a new piano? Another student is dusting the shelves and sorting music, obviously new, for the paper wrapping is still on the floor. You can smell the dust he is stirring up, you can even taste it. He's humming to himself as he works. He doesn't even see you.

The group at the piano doesn't pay any attention to you either. They have an album of "Charlie Daniels' Band" on the piano. Idea: Could the band be planning a country music festival as their annual special program?

Something else: There's a different kind of uniform hanging on the door. It looks new. Idea: Could a change in uniform be likely?

And there's a note on the bulletin board: "Evening practice Thursday for Joe's combo. Been invited to play for the Rotary convention next week. BE THERE OR ELSE!!!!!" Idea: What a life these directors lead! Also: What is "OR ELSE?"? Obviously, your election story is only a part of the news about what is going on in the band.

WATCH FOR "ONIONS"

This could happen to you:

A new reporter in the sports department was trying to check some statistics for a track meet coming up that night. He had called the athletic office several times to try to locate the coaches. No answer. He went over to the athletic office to check. The door was locked.

When he told this to the sports editor, the editor looked puzzled. "They don't go home early on a day when there's a meet," he said. "And they don't lock the office, because Miss Poe's supposed to be there until four o'clock."

He started for the door. "Something out of the ordinary must be going on over there."

In five minutes he was back on a run. "Hey, get a photographer on the double! The coaches are barbecuing chicken in the stadium! Miss Poe's out there in a big apron telling them what to do. It's for the teams that are going to be here tonight."

The new reporter was aggrieved. "Looks like they would have told me they were planning a barbecue," he grumbled.

"Look, buster," the editor said pointedly, "on the newspaper nobody has to tell you anything. It's all up to you. You want to know what's going on? Okay, go find out."

"But how'm I supposed to find out all this?"

The editor shrugged. "If you'd looked in on them every day, you would have known about it. There's been a notice on the bulletin board—and Miss Poe said she'd had the onions in her office since yesterday. You've just got to watch for things like that."

He patted the new reporter comfortingly on the arm.

"Just remember this: If you see onions where you don't expect onions—figuratively speaking—well, there's a reason. It may mean a story—and in this case, it did."

THE LISTENING EAR

Another approach in gaining additional information for a story, or even another story, lies in a different kind of awareness when you visit a news source.

Key # 7—*Look for Feature and Sidebar Stories*

By developing a "listening ear," a kind of super-perceptiveness, you may get an inkling that there's a story you didn't know about or something that you hadn't prepared for.

In this event, be ready to switch your approach. Only practice will help you here. But it is important that you recognize the need to switch and that you develop skill in making the necessary changes in your approach.

For example:

You are to visit the dean to get a story on the new audiovisual equipment that has arrived. As you reach the door, you meet the secretary coming out with some papers and hear the dean say, "Please be sure that the truancy regulations come first in the revisions."

And so here is another tip for a story. Apparently there is a plan to revise school regulations, and apparently truancy is one of the important areas to be affected. This, of course, is a story you want to get for your readers as soon as possible, for it may really be news to them.

Two examples of this are described by a summer student at the University of Oklahoma:

> The first was an assignment to interview the head of the horticulture and landscape department at the University on the research being carried on in petunia growing.
>
> *"And so I read all about petunias and the horticulture department and checked the morgue to find out about him,"* the reporter said. *"But the story I came away with was a real scoop. He was leaving the next morning for the World's Fair and a special program there honoring him as the designer of the Oklahoma exhibit."*
>
> *The other story concerned a professor who had been compiling statistics relative to the economic progress of a community and the dropout rate in their high school.*
>
> *"I made the appointment to interview him,"* the reporter said, *"but from the first word, I knew that getting a good story was going to be difficult. The work was well known and carried considerable prestige, but his answers were perfunctory and he was indifferent.*
>
> *"At the end of ten minutes I was still searching my mind for a way to get him started talking. Then in connection with a statement about St. Louis, he parenthetically mentioned a school for exceptional children. Something about the tone of his voice was different.*
>
> *" 'Is this similar to the one in Houston?' I asked.*
>
> *" 'Why, yes,' he said, hitching his chair a little closer to the table. 'Have you seen the set-up? . . .'*
>
> *"Well, he opened up like a flower. I stayed an hour and came away with a story no one else had an inkling of. He was conducting a study of educational facilities for exceptional children. The first story? Yes, I got it, too."*

Too many people—even reporters—hear without listening.

Good reporters cultivate the art of listening. By listening, as well as by looking, they find a wealth of feature and sidebar story ideas—the feature and sidebar stories that give the straight news color, personality, human interest.

PROFESSIONAL COVERAGE

The coverage of the eruption of Mount St. Helens is an excellent example of the ability of professional journalists not only to present the usual news coverage but to give readers a broad understanding of the significance of the event. A glance at the wide range of subjects covered and a study of the stories written show how loosely we use the terms "feature" and "sidebar."

The following list of stories, for example, is far from complete:

Harry Truman and his Spirit Lake resort
A study of the ash content
Merchants offering packets of ash as souvenirs
History of earthquakes in this country, in the world
Tremors on neighboring Mount Margaret, in other areas
Smithsonian report on volcanoes
Photographer who just happened to get a picture of the first moment of eruption
Explanation of how airlifts looking for survivors were conducted
Diary of a nearby resident covering the eruption and effects for the next two days
Number and kinds of pets rescued
Effect of the ash on automobiles, machinery, etc.
Survey of volcanic history in the United States
Damaging effects on industry—agriculture, lumbering, fishing
Devastation of the streams, fishing, water supply
View of tourism in that area and the adverse effects now
Cost of the rescue missions, clean-up
Early closing of nearby colleges because of air pollution
Interviews with scientists regarding possible future volcanic activity in the area
Explanation of the drift of ash around the world and possibly into the stratosphere, effects
Description of Mount St. Helens three weeks later as viewed from a helicopter flying over the crater
Survey of logging operations in the area and timber clean-up.

Other Examples

The following stories from professional dailies show how reporters (these from the Associated Press) produce feature and sidebar copy based on timely events in the news:

Muhammad Ali Enters Men's Fashion Arena

NEW YORK—Three weeks after losing his world heavyweight title to Larry Holmes, Muhammad Ali has entered a new arena—that of men's sportswear.

Monday night at a fashion show and exhibition at Madison Square Garden's Felt Forum, Ali introduced the new line of clothes and commentated on them with Frank Shain, the boxing announcer.

Muhammad Ali Sportswear Ltd. is a line of "middle-to-upper-moderate" priced clothes including jeans and casual trousers ($30 to $40), knit tops ($15 to $30) and such active sportswear items as jogging suits, sweatshirts and shorts ($25 to $125). All of them bear Ali's signature "stinging bee" emblem and although Ali did not design them, he has final approval of all garments bearing his name.

Amid much fanfare—including appearances on the "Today Show," "Midday Live," a series of breakfasts for store buyers and presidents, and a scheduled campaign stop with President Carter at the Concord Baptist Church in Brooklyn—Ali, with characteristic overstatement, announced at a press conference at the New York Athletic Club:

"These will be the greatest clothes of all time! And they will be sold wherever people know the face and fame of Muhammad Ali. They will be a success! The other news is that I shall return, I will come back and take my crown!"

Despite his recent loss, which Ali called a "blessing," he evinced no sign of defeat or discouragement at the breakfast where he sat surrounded by bodyguards, members of W.O.R.L.D., which stands for the group he started called World Organization for Rights, Liberty and Dignity, and his new business partners. Ali was in remarkably good spirits, autographing eight-ounce boxing gloves, which, along with Rope-a-Dope jump ropes, were given to the retailers invited to the breakfast of scrambled eggs and bacon. These Ali would not touch, ordering corn flakes instead.

The principal in Ali's new venture is Larry Ashinoff, who is chairman of Coronet Casuals and owner of Forum Sportswear. Harold Schulman, founder and former chairman of Nik-Nik, another sportswear house, is president. And Ashinoff's daughter, Susan, is executive vice president.

Ashinoff said he had been approached over a year ago about the venture. "We thought it was a great idea since Ali has such tremendous drawing power," he explained. After much discussion, a contract between him and Ali was signed on July 4, 1979.

At that, Ali interrupted and said: "We're gonna go to Manila with these clothes, to Tel Aviv. We're gonna take them to China."

Ashinoff bent forward and said quietly into Ali's ear, "The best place to start is R. H. Macy. Once you get there, you get Harrods in London, the Galeries in Paris."

Ashinoff is, in fact, planning to merchandise the line all over the world, including Europe, Asia, South America, the Middle East and Australia. "What we've developed," continued Ashinoff, "is something called Ali's Corner, which we want in top stores, with a large picture of the champ." Neither Ashinoff nor his daughter, however, would say how much an investment they had made in the new company.

Ali said money was not the motivation behind his latest venture: "I've made $57 million in my life and I've got millions in bonds that I can't touch for 10 years. You ain't never gonna see me broke."

Most people, however, seemed more interested in Ali than in his clothes. Ali himself spoke freely about the future of his boxing career. "I'm gonna come back," he said. "And when I do, watch out. I've been written off. They're saying I'm through. But my legend is not through. The fight hasn't affected me. I've got more fans. More interviews. I'm a warrior. I've drunk the wine of success. I'm not just a little humdrum American Negro. I'm a world-great figure. The type character they make movies about. I'm the biggest draw in the whole history of the planet. I've got an emotional grip on the people. I know no failure. My attitude is my success. I'm determined. Positive. I'm where I'm at today because limitations do not stop me. There is a magic about me."

Teddy Bear Celebrates
His 75th Birthday

NEW YORK—Discarding more dire happenings, it has certainly been an eventful year.

It was the 75th anniversary of the Wright brothers' first flight and the World Series. The Space Age was 31 years old. The Academy Awards and Mickey Mouse were 50. Popeye neared 60, Monopoly was past 40, and Playboy turned 25.

Considering the things that have occupied Americans in their passage through life, it seems remiss not to mention one more.

Teddy Bear is 75.

Of course he never flew us to Paris or the moon. He never hit a home run with the bases loaded. He never had a fanfare or a fan club. He had no muscles, never owned Boardwalk and never owned or wanted a Playboy key.

Sure, his name was Teddy, but he was neither boy nor girl.

He was a friend.

For generations of children left in the dark, he was the guardian who kept watch while they slept.

Key # 7—*Look for Feature and Sidebar Stories*

He didn't weep or wet. He never said a word. But he soaked up tears and hid small faces from so many small embarrassments.

Probably no creature in history did so much by doing so little. He was true-blue. He served by only standing and waiting.

His face changed some over the years, but not his honey-color, not really his shoe-button nose and eyes. Funny that he was named for President Teddy Roosevelt.

Back in 1902, the president had gone to Mississippi to settle a boundary dispute. Afterward, he went on a hunting trip. He was very big on hunting. He wanted to bag a bear, a trophy.

But when a lean and lame bear was run down by the hunting party's dogs, the president balked. He would not allow it to be shot or tortured.

When the story got back to Washington, a newspaper cartoonist named Charles Berryman portrayed the president sparing the bear in The Washington Post *with the caption, "Drawing the line," which referred both to the act of mercy and to the president's refusal to go along with white supremacists in Mississippi.*

That led to all sorts of postcards, toys, books, buttons portraying the Roosevelt Bear.

Morris Michtom, a Russian Jewish immigrant who owned a candy store in Brooklyn, N.Y., designed a toy bear for his store window. Two of them, in fact. His wife did the sewing, stuffing them with excelsior and stitching the mouths with thread.

The day Michtom set the 2½-foot bears in his window, someone offered to buy them. That gave Michtom another idea. He sent a bear to the president and asked permission to call it a Teddy Bear.

Presidents had fewer constituents then, and no SALT talks or Middle East crises. Roosevelt didn't have to worry about oil or inflation, and Cuba was well in hand.

So he answered Michtom in his personal hand. "I doubt if my name will mean much in the bear business, but you may use it if you wish," he wrote, and he signed it T. R.

The original correspondence and the original bears have disappeared. But Michtom, selling the bears for $1.50 each, built an empire called the Ideal Toy Corporation. When he died in 1938, it was a multimillion-dollar business. He was producing over 100,000 Teddy Bears a year.

Today, Ideal produces all kinds of things. And it also produces the Teddy Bear, two pounds of fluff and dreams.

You see, the Teddy Bear is not so much what it is as what children for 75 years have given it. Bedroom companion, loyal friend, it has given a child its undivided attention, listened to stern lectures, bounced off walls during small rages, heard the apologies, forgiven.

It has over the years become frayed and soiled, lost an eye or a nose. But it never lost its faith. Because neither president nor seamstress, neither toy maker nor toy store gave it that.

A child did.

Atlantic, Gulf Hurricanes
Rank with Worst Disasters

Atlantic- and Gulf-spawned hurricanes—such as David which caused havoc in the Caribbean and threatened the South Florida coast Sunday, or Frederic, the latest hurricane of the season—rank among the world's worst disasters.

Such hurricanes have claimed thousands of lives, caused billions of dollars in damage and have subjugated at one time or another residents of practically every state along the coasts from Texas to Massachusetts.

In terms of lives lost, the most destructive hurricane struck at the United States on Sept. 8, 1900, from the Gulf of Mexico in the days before sophisticated warning systems. At least 6,000 residents of the Texas island city of Galveston died when a tidal wave built by the 85 mph winds inundated the city.

Hurricane Agnes, which moved across Maryland, the District of Columbia, Pennsylvania, and New York on June 21, 1972, was the most costly disaster in history in terms of property damage.

Agnes' rain caused rivers in those states to overflow, isolating cities along the James and Susquehanna rivers. Highways were cut, bridges collapsed and thousands of residents in river cities were isolated.

Agnes claimed 118 lives, ruined an estimated $132 million in crops and caused property damage estimated at more than $3 billion.

The so-called Eastern Seaboard Hurricane hit New York City, Long Island and most of New England on Sept. 21, 1938. It killed 600 persons and caused property damage estimated at $1 billion in Vermont, Massachusetts, Rhode Island, Connecticut and New York.

Hurricane Camille carried winds that the National Weather Service said reached 200 mph during gusts and raised tides 30 feet in the Gulf.

Camille struck at the coasts of Louisiana, Mississippi and Alabama on Aug. 17, 1969. Before it abated, 241 persons were killed.

The most recent storm to strike at South Florida was Hurricane Betsy—on Sept. 8, 1965.

Betsy raked Miami Beach, Miami and the Florida Keys and then moved across the peninsula to the Gulf and on to Louisiana. Seventy-five persons were killed, 58 of them in Louisiana. An estimated $1.4 billion in crop and property damage was caused by the storm.

That's a brother for you. If he keeps this up, he'll find my new dress and tell dad!

Key #8 *Report in Depth*

. . . Seek the story behind the story. Search for meanings.

Why did this event happen? What is the total situation? What has been going on before this? What can be expected to happen next? What will the results be? the effects? the consequences? (Note the difference.) What is the significance of this? Are there related events that might have seemed unrelated?

Depth does not mean length. A story may be very long and yet not be depth reporting. Depth means dimension.

Example: First you have a story idea, as opposed to a regular news assignment. Suppose you are to cover the Governor's speech at the Rotary luncheon: news, long perhaps, but straight news.

BUT—you hear him mention that 18-year-olds will have a chance to vote on the proposed new state constitution in the coming election. IDEA: How many are eligible in this school? How many of them will vote? What do they know about the constitution? How can we find out more about it? How is this going to affect 18-year-olds? What difference does it make? Why a new constitution? Etc., etc.

To construct a story like this, you begin by making an outline of all the questions that seem pertinent and then work the blocks of information you gather into a unified whole.

Newspapers Meet Need

Interpretive reporting is comparatively new in newspaperdom. Not new in the sense that something different might be welcomed to give newspapers a fresh look, but new because it has grown out of the needs of today's society.

No longer is it enough for newspapers to print spot news alone. A more meaningful kind of news writing has become necessary.

Over the past several decades this has been recognized as new terms were gradually introduced: "reporting in depth," "backgrounding the news," "explanatory writing," "research reporting," "interpretive writing."

Editors of even small papers today are proving that more than routine coverage can be afforded their readers. Readers are proving that they want to know more than just facts and more facts. They are seeking earnestly to know what the facts mean—specifically, what the facts mean to them.

Significance Emphasized

This interpretive reporting is not the same as editorial opinion.

"Interpretation is the deeper sense of the news," said one of the editors of the New York *Times* at a journalism conference. "It involves setting, sequence, and above all significance."

Depth reporting is more than increase in details. It gives the reader more than just facts and more facts. It helps him understand what is behind the news. It relates current events to the past and projects them into the future.

Depth reporting, in short, is telling the reader all the essential facts in a way that brings the story home to him.

How does the reporter accomplish this?

1. By explaining why the incident occurred.
2. By probing deeply into the background.
3. By developing the personalities of the principal persons involved.
4. By explaining what the incident means and attempting to see that no major questions are left unanswered in the reader's mind.

Qualities Needed

Interpretive reporters, it has been said, are "those who expand the horizons of the news."

Obviously, not all who call themselves reporters would qualify to work at reporting in depth.

If the interpretive reporter is to meet his responsibility, he must possess certain qualities and cultivate them earnestly:

1. He must have a mature understanding of his purposes.
2. He must be a keen and accurate observer.
3. He must have a broad background of knowledge to enable him to ask penetrating questions and understand the answers.
4. He must possess personality and tact, understanding of people.
5. He must be able to see trends, patterns, and relationships in the news.
6. He must be able to find meanings and then in well-chosen words communicate them to his readers.
7. He must be a man of ideas.

Depth Requires Time

Important as depth reporting is, a newspaper cannot run many depth stories. One reason is that no editor has enough reporters that he can spare them for depth assignments, because interpretive reporting takes time, much time.

For example, a reporter for the *Wall Street Journal* says that he took a month for an article on mine workers. Three weeks of this was for research and one week for writing.

Others working on depth assignments agree that time is necessary to gather information and then to sort it and write it. Obviously a story that requires much work cannot be done in a few hours.

In addition to being short of reporters, editors are short of space. They always have far more news than they can crowd into their columns and must continually decide what to run and what to omit. Depth stories require large amounts of space and consequently must be run at the expense of something else.

However, the newspaper's job today is something more than getting there first with the barest facts. There are rarely any "scoops." With radio and television, news happenings are flashed worldwide, often instantly.

Readers are now turning to newspapers for the content of the news story, looking for explanation and understanding. They want to know what this news means *to them.* Depth reporting is the answer.

Student Opportunities

The school paper affords student journalists an opportunity to try their hand at interpretive reporting. Undertaken by serious-minded students, this could be meaningful to all readers of the paper.

"A school newspaper can be just as informative as lessons in the classroom," says the director of the South Dakota High School Press Association. "Through interpretive reporting we can have a well-informed student body, as well as a well-rounded public relations medium."

Supposing that you decide to venture into this, where would you look for a subject?

A change in school policy? A change in student government? The testing program? The problem of students driving automobiles to school? A school-wide change in textbooks? A change in graduation requirements? Expansion of the summer school–evening school program?

This last suggestion is a good choice to consider for an example. For one reason, it means something to every student. For another, it means something to the community.

When you undertake reporting in depth, you become more than a chronicler of events—you become an interpreter. So you start with the five W's, but then you ask these questions:

1. What has happened? That is, what has taken place that tells the whole story about the establishment of an expanded program for summer school and evening school?
2. Why did this happen? That is, what is the explanation that lies behind it? What needs must be evident to the school board?
3. What does this mean? That is, how will it affect students? The community?
4. What next? Now that this has happened, what can we expect later?
5. What underlies this? That is, what are the trends that account for it? What general situation exists that might account for other such incidents as this announcement?

This is your starting point. Therefore, you must spend enough time and concentration on listing these questions to insure the proper scope of your story.

You must work out questions that will guide your research.

With these questions framed, you set out to give your story substance.

1. Fill in factual details. Visit the principal's office, interview the principal and deans, check the files. Interview students who have gone to summer school or evening school previously. What has summer school, or evening school, really been like? Describe this. Enrollment? Courses? Cost? Faculty? Purposes?

2. Seek explanations for the change. What causes underlie it? What is the background of the summer school and evening school program in this school? The city? How does this compare with other schools? Other cities?
3. What is the financial situation of the school system? How is this related to the summer school and evening school programs? Interview the superintendent, the school board. Visit the library. Read studies on the subject.
4. Work out an interpretation. Interview key persons. What significance do you see? How does this move compare with other moves made by the school board? What is the principal's part in this? What purposes are to be served? Why are these purposes sought?
5. Consider the consequences. What will the end result be?
6. Provide perspective for your study. What do students think about this? Faculty? Run a survey of both students and faculty. What trends seem to show up? What situation now exists? What has the summer school–evening school program achieved? What examples can you find to substantiate your findings?

Research means *digging for the facts*. The substance of your story comes through research. Research must be thorough. One of the greatest compliments that an editor can pay you is to say of you, "He can dig—dig and dig until he gets *all the facts.*"

GUIDELINE NEEDED

"Guideline" is a term that comes in here.

As you begin to think through this assignment, you will be guided by a basic idea of your purposes. This obviously contains an "educated opinion" based on the news.

As you gather the facts and sort the items of information in your mind, you will need to work out a complete sentence summarizing the main idea that is leading you through your research.

The "guideline" is similar to the "controlling purpose" that editorial writers use to insure unity of thought. It is a statement of the basic news reason for your doing the story.

A study of professional newspapers will afford a variety of helpful examples showing how trained reporters report a story in depth. The following are taken from papers across the country:

... "Long stretches of America's waterways are so shamefully dirty that it will take enormous, expensive effort to clean them up for necessary use."—Jean M. White, Washington Post.

... "What impact is the increase in teenage pregnancies having in this community?"—Bill McGiffin, Fort Smith Evening News.
... "Does the boom in licking and pasting trading stamps make economic sense?"—Louis B. Fleming, Los Angeles Times.
... "The so-called isolationist Midwest has become the front line of defense for the Western World."—Hal Brown, Nebraska Daily.

A more detailed guideline for a story in depth reporting is outlined in the following illustration by Carol Griffee of the *Arkansas Gazette:*

... To whom do the waters in Arkansas belong?
The answer used to be relatively clear-cut, but the water laws now are in a state of chaos as a result of three developments:
*An Arkansas Supreme Court decision that the Mulberry River is a navigable stream on ground not previously recognized in Arkansas law.
*A clash between the Grand Prairie landowners about whether water can be diverted from the White River for irrigation, and perhaps on the use of the subsurface water for municipal and industrial purposes.
*A court challenge to the Army Engineers who plan to build a new water supply on Cypress Creek for Conway, based in part on whether Arkansas law now prohibits transferring water to be sold commercially from one watershed to another.

Developing this guideline may take careful thought and may be more time-consuming than you like, but it is necessary, not only in research but later in your efforts to sort out what you are going to include in your story. Furthermore, your lead must make the point of the guideline, or get to it soon.

Putting the Parts Together

Once you have completed your research, what next? To answer that question the following suggestions are helpful:

1. Keep your guideline clearly in mind all the time. Refer to it often to be sure that your story has unity and that every item included is important to this unity.
2. Work on your lead idea until you are satisfied that it opens the story built on your guideline. Phrasing this lead idea as a lead that seems just right can come later.
3. List the important points that you must make. Consider the order.
4. Arrange and rearrange until you feel sure you have these points in the order to best develop your guideline. At all times think

of the reader. Can he follow your points easily in a meaningful sequence?
5. Decide on an ending for your story. Though it may be cut later if space is a problem, you will find that seeing your story as a whole will help you write smoothly. Our sense of order in our ideas is satisfied by proceeding from beginning to middle to end.
6. Review your story for interest. Find anecdotal material that will brighten the story and make good illustrations.
7. After this careful preparation, you are ready to begin the actual writing. By now the story should, as we like to say, "write itself."
8. Review your story as written for logical sequence of parts. This means to check for suitable transitions and connectives. Transitions and connectives clearly stated will help hold the reader's attention so he can follow your points.

To Summarize

The interpretive reporter must know how to add a personality to the *who,* a definition to the *what,* a dimension to the *when,* a location to the *where,* a cause to the *why,* and a reason to the *how.*

"There are almost as many definitions of depth reporting as there are people to define the term," says Paul Swensson, of the American Press Institute. "But all of them involve essentially the same elements: (1) expanded coverage, (2) more time to do the job, (3) the ability to organize facts and write well, and (4) the opportunity to help the reader understand a significant part of the news."

The student journalist who dreams of doing assignments in depth can begin now to develop in himself the qualities that will help him succeed. If you, the beginning writer, are ambitious for yourself, this is the place to start.

To illustrate: A news bulletin flashed on KFSM-TV dramatizes the basic approach to reporting an event in depth. A fledgling reporter on his first job was summarizing the brief information about a plane crash in the Ozark Mountains—the location of the wreckage, the names of the survivors, the time, the apparent cause. Then he added, "But until the investigation is completed, no one will know exactly what happened, nor why."

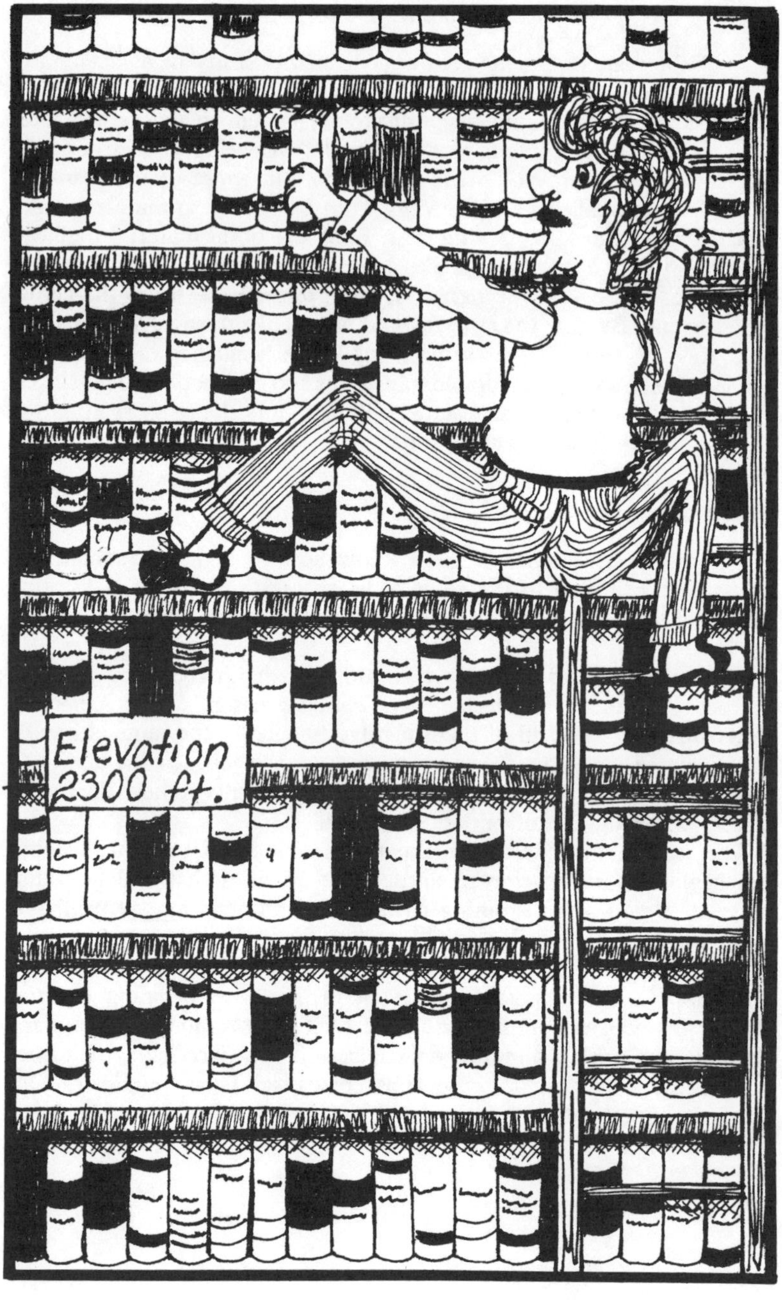
Elevation
2300 ft.

Key # *9* *Seek Background Material*

... Nothing will be of more help in performing well than being fully prepared for your assignment. Preparation begins with (1) knowing how to prepare and (2) doing it thoroughly.

Your sources of background information will be of several kinds: (1) reference materials, as files and records, both at school and elsewhere and (2) people who might be sources of general information.

Remember: When asking individuals for information, (1) be SURE to check the reliability of the source and (2) be SURE that you have factual material, not half-truth or opinion.

One editor's sad tale: "We intended to run a simple little story about co-ed gym classes next year. Instead of reading what had already been issued regarding the co-ed plan, the reporter discussed it with the football captain. The story came out saying that next year in the gym classes 'all facilities will be co-ed.' You can imagine what a bombshell that was!"

In *We Cover the World,* one Associated Press correspondent recalls an interview years ago with the Shah of Iran. Since the time was to be strictly limited, he planned for limited questions. Unexpectedly he was invited to stay for an informal chat. "And there I was," he lamented, "unprepared!"

Learn to Prepare

The students gathered for the round-table discussion surveyed the leader thoughtfully. They represented many kinds of school papers from many sections, for they were delegates to the annual convention of the Columbia Scholastic Press Association in New York City.

"This question has been raised," the leader stated. "Where do most reporters seem to need the most help in getting a story?"

Smiles of common understanding flickered across the faces of the group.

"In getting the whole story," one said.

"A lot of students don't know how to cover a story," another added.

"Sometimes a reporter is asked to do a story he doesn't know anything about."

"A new reporter, someone who hasn't had any experience, takes 'No, nothing new here,' for answer when there's really a story if he knew the background."

"Some students don't know that you have to prepare for an assignment."

Answers Suggested

During that round-table discussion, the following points were suggested as helpful:

1. Covering the story requires planning and carry-through. On a small story this is simple, but on a big story or series of stories it can mean considerable effort.
2. Actually preparing for an assignment not only makes the story go better, but also gives the reporter a feeling of confidence and security.
3. Steps in preparing for a story include the following, the time put in on them determined by the importance of the story:

    a. Be sure you know exactly what the assignment is. Most staffs use an assignment card giving the subject of the story, the type of story wanted, sources suggested, special instructions, length, date due, editor making the assignment, and date the assignment was made. The editor keeps a duplicate of the card given the reporter. When the reporter turns his story in, he staples the card to it. Some staffs use a color for the editor's duplicate.

Key # 9—*Seek Background Material*

Reporter's assignment card design:

```
                REPORTER'S ASSIGNMENT—The High Times
        _____ Reporter's name
Subject _____
        _____ Length _____ Type of story
Sources _____
Special instructions _____
Date due _____ Editor _____
                        Date assigned _____
```

b. Be sure you know whether it is an advance story, a spot story, or a follow-up.

If a spot or follow-up, be sure you read the advance story and other publicity, not only in your paper but elsewhere. An advance story is an *expected* event. A spot story is the report of an event *as it occurs* or immediately afterward. Follow-up stories are written as long as there are new developments.

c. Find out whether this is to be a meeting story, a speech story, a program story, or what. If you are inexperienced, you should consult one of the journalism books available (including this one) to see what kind of write-up is expected.

Until you learn how to handle stories yourself, it is helpful to study stories others have written. You cannot be expected to write a good speech story if you do not know how a speech story should be written. Certain patterns are generally followed. It will help you to know what they are. After you have acquired skill in using the accepted patterns, then you can "dare to be different."

d. Study the background of your story. Inform yourself as fully possible on the subject. *This is the point at which most new reporters fail, according to this CSPA round-table group.* Advisers and editors with experience concur.

To gain background, you may need to consult the files of your paper or the editorial reference materials known as the morgue, or visit the library.

You will not, of course, use all this information as such in your story, but a number of the facts you discover will give depth and background to your story. You will have a longer story, a fuller story, and a more meaningful story.

For example: You are to cover a Hi-Y election of officers. After consulting the files, you find that this is the first midyear election. Why? In seeking the answer to this, you discover that the constitutional committee has been working. This is a change just now effective. Also, other changes are being suggested by the committee. You also find from the files that the new president is a brother of a former president and a cousin of a former president. You discover that this is the tenth year of the organization on your campus, that the membership this year is triple that of any other year, and that the club sweetheart tradition dates back eight years.

Had you not consulted the files, it is likely that the only information given you would be the list of new officers.

e. Find out whom you should interview as the best possible source or sources. Often more than one person must be interviewed.
f. Find out all you can about this person as related to this story so your interview will be as complete as possible.
g. Make an appointment for your interview or interviews.

h. Consider the total story you hope to get and carefully plan questions so that you can secure all the information you need.
i. Formulate a statement of exactly what you expect the story to cover.
j. Arm yourself with a notebook and pencil, polish up your enthusiasm for the assignment, and set off.

What Is a "Morgue"?

Is this preparing for an assignment just a schoolroom idea about a way to help students do a better story?

No. "The story behind the story" is explained in a publication put out by *Time,* entitled "Any Time, Every Time."

Key # 9—*Seek Background Material*

The following section appears under the heading "Every Story Has Its History":

> In New York the researchers go to work on their reports for the writers. Some of the material they will need is at their fingertips . . . in *Time's* own Bureau of Editorial Reference. There, 78 people compile and maintain the constantly changing collection of 45,000 books; 18,000 folders on United States and foreign business firms; files of some 900 magazines and technical journals; 225,000 biographical folders on individuals in the news; 100,000 subject folders containing current information on a list of subjects from acupuncture to zirconium.
>
> But most of the facts researchers are looking for are too current to have yet been published anywhere. For these they go to the people who know them best."

This "bureau of editorial reference" is usually called a "morgue." It is a specific place in a newspaper office where miscellaneous reference materials are filed.

In professional newspaper offices this "specific place" is a room or suite of rooms furnished with shelves, filing drawers, and storage space suitable for keeping reference materials easily accessible so reporters can find what they want as quickly as possible.

In most school newspaper offices the morgue is a filing cabinet or a drawer in a filing cabinet. Here filing folders are kept in alphabetical order by subject. Among them would be such as "Faculty—Current Year," "Principal," "Administrative Reports"—including such items as school board meetings, financial reports, committee reports, "Guidance," "Curriculum," "Annual Awards," "Clubs," "Student Council," "Special Programs," "Yearbook," "School Paper," "Homecoming," "Football," "Basketball."

Some schools where staffs have not yet discovered the tremendous advantage of having a larger "editorial reference bureau" keep a filing box—the kind used for legal papers—handy in the office. Here, too, the reference material is filed in folders with suitable headings. If this reference material is to be helpful, it must be easily accessible and easily handled.

Sadly, in many schools across the country, each September a brand-new adviser faces a brand-new staff across a shiny table top—lucky if they have even a typewriter to call their own.

The word to any adviser and staff in that situation is, "Take courage; start now." Begin collecting and filing any material that might serve as background help now or later.

A morgue is not a self-perpetuating institution. Someone should be appointed to be in charge of it to be sure that all material taken out is returned and that all returned material is properly filed again. Furthermore, every effort must be made by the entire staff to see that any material that can later be used for reference is added to the morgue.

A scrapbook as a supplement to the morgue is maintained in a number of schools. This is made up of clippings about the school and school activities from publications other than the school paper. If kept in chronological order and indexed, it is very useful. Each year's scrapbook is numbered as a volume and shelved. Over a period of time this becomes valuable reference help, especially if a master index is kept current so stories can be easily located.

OTHER REFERENCES

In addition to this editorial reference material, the office should include bound files of the paper. Every school should have at least two complete sets of bound files, one in the journalism office and one in the library. Because these files eventually deteriorate, especially if used very much, some schools are putting their files on microfilm. With projectors generally available, back issues thus become easily accessible, and yet actual files are preserved.

Another help in the journalism office is a card file containing the name of every student in school. Whether the school is large or small, this file is important. To be sure that every card has the student's name properly spelled, as the student wants it, have the students themselves fill out these cards, printing their names. Betty, for example, may spell her name Bettye, or Bettie, or Bette, or perhaps even Betti.

This card can carry additional information that you might find helpful—address, parents' name, telephone number, class, course of study, activities. You might even add hobbies, unusual interests. The additional information would give you material for stories on a number of subjects.

Every journalism office should have a standard dictionary, as complete as possible (Webster's unabridged dictionary is the most popular), and as many other reference books as the staff needs and can afford. Building up a journalism library is important. It should include a thesaurus, a book of synonyms, a handbook on grammatical usage, a book showing how to divide words, a state almanac, a standard desk book, a variety of textbooks in journalism, and as many books in special fields as can be acquired.

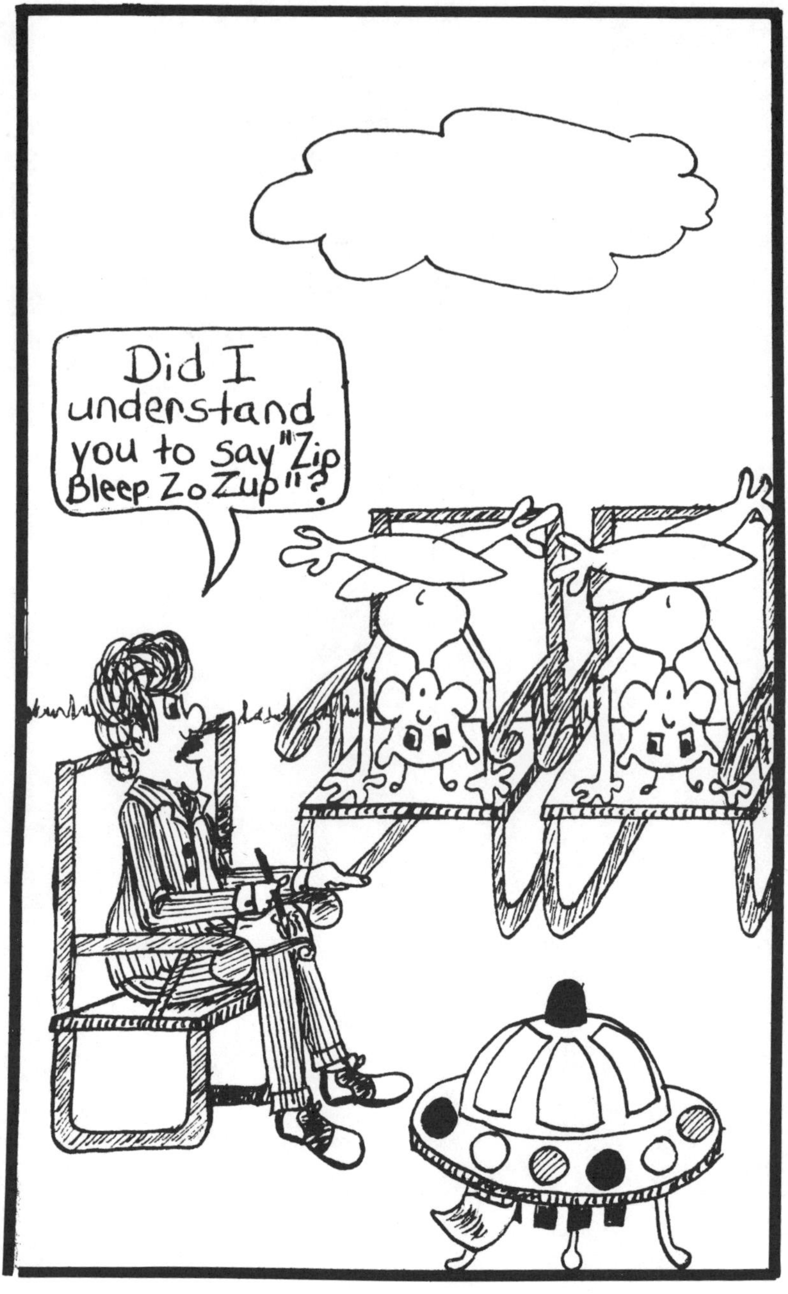
Did I understand you to say "Zip Bleep Zo Zup"?

Key # 10   *Achieve Skill in Interviewing*

... We speak of both the craft of news reporting and the art of news reporting. It is true that successful journalists have many plus qualities that are certainly more art than craft. But be encouraged. One of the basic needs of a successful journalist is skill in interviewing—and skill can be taught and learned.

You begin by wanting to develop this skill. Therefore, step 1—you decide to develop skill in interviewing; step 2—you find out what the basic procedures are; step 3—you ask successful journalists for suggestions; step 4—you observe those television interviews you consider effective to learn what you can from them; step 5—you practice; step 6—and practice; step 7—and practice.

You will find that successful interviewers make these suggestions: (1) Your enthusiasm for your story will encourage the interviewee to talk. This means being prepared with adequate background material and well-planned questions. (2) Develop an interest in people. Appreciate people. Thus the interviewee will feel that you consider him a person, not a subject. (3) Learn to keep the interviewee talking by asking plenty of meaningful questions—and then *listening* attentively to and following up his responses.

Asking Questions Is Basic

The art of asking the right questions and getting the right answers is essential for a news writer.

Fortunately it is an art that can be developed.

"There are books to read, suggestions to heed—but practice is what you need." This just about sums up the whole matter of interviewing.

Almost all stories are based on some form of interviewing—at least 90 percent, according to the estimate of Stewart Harral, of the University of Oklahoma, who considers the subject so important that he spent five years doing research on the secrets of successful interviewing.

Subjects Are Varied

Suitable subjects of interview stories include anyone who has done, said, or seen anything out of the ordinary.

1. They include the opinions of well-known persons who have done some thinking or study on subjects that would be of interest to readers, as a world-famous scientist on the importance of skill in communication.
2. They include the reporter's impressions of persons who are well known but who have not studied or thought about any particular subject, as television stars on tour.
3. They include how-to and we-did-it stories, by experts—or comedians—as how to take a pack trip and survive.

Finding Ideas

The most familiar cry among some journalism students is, "I can't think of anything to write about." (This is a familiar lament, too, in English classes when certain kinds of composition assignments are made.) Then they add hopefully, "If I had an idea, I could write a story."

These students seem to think that if an idea were offered to their minds, as a piece of information could be fed into some sort of thinking machine, a beautiful story would emerge as the fingertips were applied to the typewriter keys.

This is not so. Stories are based on facts, and facts come from a deliberate and businesslike effort to find them. Because people are tied in with facts and fact-finding, naturally the best way to start fact-finding is to locate the people who have the information you are seeking.

"From the start to the end of his career, the reporter is an asker of questions, a listener and recorder of the replies," says Carl Warren in *Modern News Reporting*. "Like Diogenes with his lamp searching for an honest man, the reporter searches ceaselessly for people in possession of opinions or facts which he desires. In his quest for news, the reporter successfully plays the role of prying detective, successful salesman, probing psychiatrist, wily diplomat, confidential friend, examining attorney and questioning quiz master."

SHORTCUT TO SUCCESS

There are not many shortcuts in the field of journalism. But if there is one at all, it is this: that you can help yourself to greater proficiency in all areas of journalism if you can develop skill and finesse in meeting people, gaining from them the information you need and at the same time understanding them as figures in the unfolding drama of history in the making.

To accomplish this, of course, requires that you understand the techniques of interviewing and that you apply them to your own situation and practice them as often as you can. This will build your confidence in yourself, help you overcome shyness about meeting people.

Most people you will interview as a school reporter are glad to cooperate in helping you get a story. They may not know much about how to direct the interview for you, but they are willing to answer questions. This gives you an advantage in trying out your wings.

PURPOSES VARY

Though you will employ basically the same procedures, you will have different purposes in mind from one story to another:

1. For some stories you will want to obtain information for a straight news story.
2. For others, you will want to discuss with the interviewee some subject in which he is interested or on which his opinion is important. The purpose here is to find out what he thinks about the subjects he has thought about. This is called an opinion interview. It is not based on mere random thoughts. The reporter seeks to find out what the interviewee thinks about some subject he has studied, or about which he has accumulated facts as a basis for his thinking.
3. For yet others, you will want to get him to give you information about something he is doing that will be interesting to your readers.

4. A fourth kind of interview story features the interview itself, as a visiting movie hero who might be colorful and interesting in himself but who would have little to say. This kind of story is based on the reporter's personal impressions.

The straight news story would be such as visiting the band director for details about the forthcoming concert, or the student body president about the district convention.

For an opinion story, you might visit the school nurse for a story about the use of stay-awake pills and tranquilizers among teenagers, or the municipal judge about ways of curbing vandalism locally, or the head of the employment agency about local opportunities for dropouts.

For the "interesting person" story, you might visit a student who had an interesting gun collection, or one who had just returned from an archeological expedition, or one whose brother was a racing driver, or one who taught skin diving and did some diving for "treasure" on the side.

ACTION MEANS STORY

People have been called "players upon the stage of life." Every person is a potential story, or stories. Stories are built on what people are *doing*. Therefore, if the "player" is really engaged in *action,* and you can get him to tell you about it, you have the beginnings of a story.

Prominent persons in the community might be suitable subjects for interview stories in your paper. In using these, relate them in some way to the school scene. For example, discuss with an optician the advantages and disadvantages of contact lenses. Or discuss with a banker the perils of get-rich-quick schemes.

Visiting celebrities are frequently refreshing subjects for interviews. Three approaches are possible: (1) What makes this person interesting? (2) What is he saying and doing? What impression does he leave? (3) What about his work, background, activity arouses attention?

FORMULA FOR SUCCESS

In interviewing, as in writing, the secret of success lies in the doing. The formula for success is $Y + O + U$.

Procedures, techniques, devices, methods, strategy—those are suggested and defined by master journalists. Whether you practice them, and how—that's what counts.

Key # 10—*Achieve Skill in Interviewing*

Learning to conduct a successful interview, as we said earlier, is a shortcut to success in news writing. It is not a shortcut in distance but in time. For if you work at this business of learning all you can and then devote your energies to practicing, you can travel at your own speed. The more you practice, the more you accomplish, the sooner you arrive at proficiency and skill.

"A" is for attitude. That is where you begin. The proper "mind set" actually determines your final success. An enthusiastic attitude influences every move you make, from planning your first step to the final word you write.

Enthusiasm, like the wind in the sail, carries you on. No one can teach you this. You have it, you develop it. The basic importance of an enthusiastic attitude is emphasized by Louise Moore, of the University of Oklahoma, in these words:

"You must have enthusiasm. Develop enthusiasm for your ideas, not like a pep squad but like a lamp, and develop enthusiasm for people. In meeting people, show that you are sincerely interested in what they are saying and doing."

There's a moral here: Don't let a dull eye defeat you. (*Your* dull eye, that is.)

SEEK TO KNOW PEOPLE

Since interviewing is based on meeting people, you can help yourself by learning all you can about the psychology of behavior. You do this simply by studying people—that is, by watching them to see what they do, how they do it, what makes them do it, what results they get, how they feel about the results.

The secret is simply to pay attention to people around you. No two people are alike, no two act alike. Yet by observing those around you, you can begin to understand that there are certain patterns in behavior, certain similarities that carry over from one situation to another.

Look at people closely, listen to them talk. Learn to concentrate on the individual. Pick out those qualities that make him different from others—in appearance, in action, in speech. Study him as a character in this play on the stage of life. Try to see how he plays his part. What contribution does he make to the dignity of man?

"If you can think, act and feel in tune with the other person, then you are sure to get results," says Stewart Harral in *Keys to Successful Interviewing*. "Try your hardest to become interested in each person—even a bore—as an individual. Then notice the difference in his reaction.

He will see your interest. He will feel it. And your assignment will be more resultful.

"Secondly, if you want the other person to like you instantly, let him feel that you are favorably impressed with him. Be a good listener and enjoy it.

"Be alive to others. Develop 'you-ability.' Get the other fellow's angle. If you want to sell yourself, develop genuine and sincere interest in others."

This enthusiasm for people concerns the characters who play the parts in the interview—*him* and *you.*

The enthusiasm must also carry over to the *action,* the *plot*—and you are the writer of that script.

PLAN AHEAD CAREFULLY

The word here is prepare in advance, thoughtfully and fully.

Decide exactly what you want to accomplish in the interview. Formulate this in words and write it so you force yourself to do this preliminary thinking.

For example: Suppose you plan to interview the superintendent about the new gymnasium. You want to know what plans are now definite, how the building will be financed, when it will be available, what the architects have suggested, where it will be located, what need it will fill.

For example: Suppose you plan to interview the school nurse on the subject of teenagers and tension. Is it true that teenagers are seriously suffering from tension? What are the principal causes? Symptoms of trouble? Preventives or "cures"? What does this mean nationwide? In this school?

With your purpose definitely in mind, *plan* questions that you will ask in order to direct the interview as you want it to go.

Consider the order and phrasing of your questions carefully. Being able to think of the right questions, phrasing them clearly and simply and making them short, is the easiest way to get direct and meaningful answers.

If a reporter has not prepared carefully, he is likely to ask questions that are involved or that cannot be answered directly or fully. Sometimes when a reporter fails to get enough information for a story, or if his information is not interesting or worthwhile, it is because he did not plan his questions with a story in mind—a complete story, that is—or his wording was poor.

Key # 10—*Achieve Skill in Interviewing*

Learn as much as you can about the personality and characteristics of the interviewee before you visit him. Is he shy? talkative? abrupt? friendly?

If your interviewee is prominent and the story is to be about him as a person, it may be very helpful to you to know about his background and activities. Learn, perhaps, about his family, his accomplishments, his hobbies, his outlook, his philosophy—all or any of these that may have a bearing on the story you plan to do.

A true story: Professor W. J. Lemke, of the University of Arkansas, illustrated the importance of preparing fully in advance by planning an interview at a student press day on campus. Charles Finger, noted author living nearby, was invited to be present for the occasion.

From the student delegates in attendance, a volunteer was selected and told that he had an hour before the interview. Rushing to the library, he consulted *Who's Who in America* and tried to glean some background material from other publications here.

Happily back, he began his questions:

Q.—How does it feel to be a successful author?
A.—Well, ummmmm . . . . ummmmm . . . . umm . . . . . .
Q.—Do you like to write?
A.—Yes.
And so on.

Highly discomfited, the reporter left the stage, but the point had been made for the delegates. Knowing Mr. Finger as he did, Professor Lemke had guessed that he would delight in showing the delegates that you never can tell about people—that an interviewee may not be cooperative.

"So it pays to prepare as well as possible—and always be mindful that this kind of thing could happen to you," Professor Lemke pointed out. "An interviewer must plan questions that will draw out the interviewee, no matter how reluctant he may naturally be. The reporter must manage to encourage the interviewee to talk if he gets the information he needs for his story."

The reporter should do research for any interview assignment, however trivial it may seem.

If the interviewee is a person of prominence, there are innumerable sources for information, including morgue clippings, magazine articles, *Who's Who* listings. This preparation should be organized in at least a few questions designed to draw from the subject comment worthy of publication.

However, beginning reporters on school papers frequently are assigned interviews with fellow students who are not prominent and therefore not included in such areas as the above.

Question: With no possibility for formal research, what does one do?

Answer: First, consider the interviewee in relation to the reason for his being newsworthy. Then try to fill in a background by visiting others who have had some part in this, or by reading about it if anything has been printed. Frequently, teachers, other students, school records prove to be helpful.

Once you have exhausted possible sources of background information, give special care to devising questions that will lead to worthwhile answers. Example of poor question: *Have you always been interested in science?* Better: *I've heard that your interest in science dates back to an experiment with cocoons when you were in grade school. What other experiments related to entomology have you carried on since then?* Poor: *Where do you plan to use the science scholarship you won?* Better: *Since your science scholarship for study in entomology is offered by the University of Texas, what plans for your college program have you made?*

Inform yourself about the subject to be covered in the interview. Never waste the interviewee's time by asking him for information that you could have found elsewhere. Your purpose in going to this particular interviewee is to obtain information that can be learned from him only or that can be substantiated best by him.

Make an appointment for the interview. Even to gain information for a short fact story, you will do better to let the interviewee know in advance what your story is and arrange to see him at his convenience. This will make it possible for the interviewee to allot you some of his time and will give him an opportunity perhaps to think about the subject and possibly afford you additional information.

This gives you confidence and also gives the interviewee the impression that you are businesslike and serious about the story. Time is a precious commodity these days. You do not want to waste his time, and you cannot afford to waste yours.

Consider your appearance and manners. Untidiness is not a pleasing quality. It is important for a news reporter to make a good impression. Some people think that untidiness in appearance and carelessness in manners are related to sloppy thinking and sloppy writing. Do not chew gum during an interview.

Key # 10—*Achieve Skill in Interviewing*

Even as a student journalist you are associated with a great profession. You owe it to your colleagues, both professional and scholastic, to do all you can to be worthy.

Be punctual. Never, never, never keep an interviewee waiting.

Do not enter a private office without knocking and being invited in. Some offices of school officials are considered private, so it is best to knock before entering. In public offices there is usually a reception room that you enter without knocking.

AT THE INTERVIEW

When the stage is thus set and the "play" is about to begin, bear this in mind: As a representative of the press, you are an important figure. This means that you not only have a responsibility but you have prestige. This should give you confidence and pride. This pride should carry over into your efforts and show in your work.

One city editor says to his new reporters: "You must learn to *walk* like a newspaperman."

Keep these points in mind:

1. Be friendly and courteous. Ask your questions in a businesslike way in a quiet voice.
2. Cultivate tact. Remember, more stories are won by kid gloves than by boxing gloves.
3. When the interviewee speaks, listen with interest. "You have to be a good listener," says Clark Porteous, veteran professional journalist. "Too many reporters talk too much. That's good, to a point. You have to know how to prime the conversation, get the interviewee started, ask something now and then, but it's best to give your subject time to express his views and not keep inflicting your own."

4. Be prepared to take notes in a small inconspicuous notebook. Learn to trust your memory, but take notes so you do not run the risk of a mistake. Figures, dates, names must be accurate. Be tactful and diplomatic about it, but make sure that you get this information right. In some stories you will want to quote the interviewee. Be sure that you make notes on these points so your quotes will be accurate.

   Think as you listen. If you question any point, check it at once. Cultivate an ability to listen to information critically so you can catch an error or inconsistency before it is too late.

   Some reporters advise against taking notes during an interview.

The kind of information to be included in the story would be a determining factor here. A scientist, for example, prepared to give you specific figures, data, statistics, would prefer to have you take notes in order to quote him exactly. An author, on the other hand, might enjoy talking more freely, expecting you to make notes only as necessary to insure the accuracy of facts included.

5. As you ask questions, be alert for new ideas that may grow out of some answer or comment. Cultivate agility in thinking, so you can skillfully pursue unforeseen developments.
6. Keep your reader in mind and try to think of questions that he might want answered as the conversation continues. Also, remember that sometimes what a person says is less important than how he says it. When this seems so, make a mental note to consider it later, perhaps for clarification, or evaluation. Occasionally such a situation is opportunity for delightful color in your story.
7. As you are getting the factual answers, train your eye and ear to be aware of the total scene so you can picture it for your reader if the interview lends itself to that kind of detail. An interview is really a little play, with setting, characters, action, and dialogue. Keeping this in mind as you write will help you add background.

If you listen attentively, you will find "quotable quotes" to give your writing character and personality. A person is characterized by the way he uses language as much as by the clothes he wears or the motions he makes. It pays to develop a memory for words, phrases, and structural patterns in speech and to listen for them.

8. Note the exact words used by the interviewee, because this insures accuracy. If there is any question in your mind, be sure that the interviewee is using the words as you understand them. Especially in instances where a word has more than one meaning, there may be misunderstanding or confusion. Also, be sure to make notes full enough that you have the answers in context. Frequently, a person's meaning is distorted if he is quoted out of context. It is important that the reader understand this context.
9. Make mental notes of additional stories that might be suggested by the interview.
10. Thank the interviewee for giving you the story. Let him know

that you are interested in the story and that you found him interesting. With a good reporter this is always sincere, no matter how difficult the situation might be.

Improving Techniques

Because interviewing is basic to thorough reporting, you as a student journalist will do well to consider a number of ways to improve your technique.

1. Find examples of what you consider good interviews conducted by professional reporters. Study these for content, form, and style. (Try pretending that you are that reporter when you conduct your next interview. Sometimes such a pretense helps you feel less self-conscious at first. It helps you focus all your attention on the interviewee.)
2. Develop an ear for questions as you hear them generally, and learn to choose and phrase questions skillfully.
3. "Think questions" as you move through the various experiences of the day. Ask yourself: How could I find out more about this subject, or situation, from this particular person?
4. Study the art of persuasion, and take a course in logic.
5. Develop your ability to write about people by watching them in action, hearing them talk, trying to see what makes them behave as they do.
6. Keep yourself informed as well as possible in general and in the areas of your special interests.
7. Practice writing, trying to "tune your ear" in order to capture turns of phrase, structural forms, devices, use of language—any means possible to give your writing color and depth.
8. Develop a set of guidelines for yourself. Although there are few rules as such in interviewing, you will soon discover that a core of "dos and don'ts" becomes obvious.
9. Never try to be "fancy," or "cute" in the effort to be creative and original in your interviewing. The secret lies in preparing well so you can ask significant questions that will bring forth essential information.
10. Cultivate a "sparkling enthusiasm" for life—awareness, aliveness. This is what gives your work vibrance, fresh color, significant new angles—the plus quality.

Was it S-M-I-T-H or S-M-Y-T-H or S-M-E-T-H? Oh, why did it have to be the principal?!?

Key #11 — Remember: "Accuracy Always"

. . . If a poll were taken, probably the chief criticism of newspapers would be related to accuracy. "They never get anything right," is a frequent complaint. Such censure is usually based on information with which the critic is familiar, as the spelling of a name or a word, or an incorrect grammatical usage.

Is it any wonder then that the reader questions the accuracy of other items? It is logical to assume that since these errors occur, there are others.

With all the possible margins for error, can a reporter expect to have a 100 percent accuracy rating? Answer: Yes. Yes, if he devotes himself to learning all the ways to try to insure accuracy. Yes, if he makes this a full-time concern. Accuracy, we might say, is a way of thinking, an attitude.

On this subject one student editor at a workshop said, "Every staff needs an adviser like our Sarge. Her theme song is 'If you don't care enough to get this story RIGHT, don't do it at all!'

"Get it right. Get it right all the way. Get it right all the time—that's our Sarge."

Briefly, this means "check." Check on every item, check on every aspect of your story, check on yourself. Remember Sarge.

ACCURACY COMES FIRST

Accuracy in news writing is basic. Better not try to give the news at all than to give it incorrectly—or than to give it so the reader is misled. However, although accuracy is usually mentioned first in any list of qualities that good reporters have, others are also important.

With care and determination you can develop accuracy in your procedures and your writing. The following guidelines will help you follow practices that will lead to effective news gathering and accurate news reporting:

1. Check all information thoroughly. Rely only on authoritative sources. In your stories be sure to state your source, or sources, of information. Whether your quote is direct or indirect, make certain that you give the exact meaning of the words the source used. (Caution: Many words have more than one meaning. Also, many persons use words carelessly. Suggestion: *Think* as you *listen.*)
2. Avoid hurried assumptions. Take time to listen carefully and thoughtfully to what your source is saying. Check to see that you have facts, not assumptions. That is, be sure that you are not assuming something that is not said—and at the same time, be sure that your source is giving you facts, not assumptions on *his* part.

    Lawsuits often are filed by persons who contend that they were misquoted or that their meaning was distorted. Do not guess or take chances.

    Caution: News sources are not necessarily accurate, nor do they necessarily give you the complete story. Remember to check and recheck statements of varying news sources against each other, and then remember to state the source of each item of information. And always, always, always remember that you are seeking the *complete story*—both sides of it—all sides of it.
3. Build up a background of general information. As this grows, you will find that you are able to check what you see and hear against what you already know to be correct.
4. Cultivate clear expression of your ideas. Know exactly what you mean to say. Then check to see that your words do say that, precisely.
5. Work hard at writing correctly. Watch your grammar, spelling, punctuation, construction, vocabulary. Study the "rules," for they are guidelines to help you and your readers get the same meanings from the same words.

Key # 11—*Remember: "Accuracy Always"*

The importance of consulting standard sources of reference for spelling, punctuation, and usage is stressed in many books for the professional journalist as well as for the beginner. Every person who wants to write so that he is fully and clearly understood is familiar with reference helps and uses them.

6. Remember that accuracy must be achieved by determined effort on your part all the time. Accuracy in small things every minute of the day will pay off.

In a time when other media can get information to the public even as the event occurs, it is imperative that newspapers supply this information in more complete and reliable fashion. As always with the printed word, the record is available not only for the statement of the information but for reference later.

School reporters, particularly, run into the problem of inaccuracies in information given the paper. Two examples are typical:

1. A club president hands in names of committeemen. They are misspelled, or the list is incomplete.
2. The Student Council reporter turns in information about the forthcoming student elections before he makes a final check with the election committee. Later he discovers that the date of the election has been changed, but he forgets to tell you. Unless you are alert, you appear in print—wrong.

Four B's for Accuracy

"There are four B's to help insure accuracy in news writing," one student editor tells his staff. Then he posts the following on the bulletin board:

1. Be sure to go to the correct news source.
2. Be thorough in research and formulation of questions to ask.
3. Be particular to take full notes—notes that you can read later.
4. Be alert to sources of error.

You may not be a brilliant writer, but you can be a successful reporter if you realize that these qualities are important. Practicing these Four B's conscientiously will help you learn to discipline yourself and develop self-confidence and a sense of competence and poise.

Other Qualities Needed

"A journalist has to be four men rolled into one," says Laurence Campbell, author of many helps for journalism students and a popular speaker at press meets. "He must be an applied psychologist, a resourceful researcher, a responsible analyst, and a facile writer." He works at being these "four men" if he hopes to be a competent reporter.

Not only must a good student journalist be intelligent and interested in improving his background and broadening his knowledge, Campbell adds. He must also be thoughtful and realize the importance of learning the craft of writing and of being a thorough craftsman.

Craft. Craftsman. Comforting words these are, for a craft can be learned. Skills and techniques can be mastered.

Specific Suggestion

If—after reading all these "helps"—you are less helped than overwhelmed, consider the following specific approach to your daily development of practices that are basic in effective news reporting.

This approach may be oversimplified, but it will provide a set of four ideas easy to remember that will serve as a checklist so that you can evaluate your efforts daily. As always, the secret of success will lie in the enthusiasm you demonstrate in following them—for yourself, by yourself. No one but you can create success for you.

1. Learn to judge news values.
2. Learn to sense human interest.
3. Learn to organize facts and ideas.
4. Study the language—as you read it, hear it, use it.

Specific questions to ask yourself in these areas:

1. *News values.* What will people want to know about today? What's new? What's going on? Who is engaged in something important? Interesting?
2. *Human interest.* What emotional overtones does this news have? Do I see anything that will interest people about people?
3. *Organization.* Am I working at organizing my material? Have I decided on an outline or sequence for the presentation of the facts with the specific purpose of gaining and holding reader interest? Do I observe various story patterns as I read so that I will know what story form is best for a particular story as I put it together?

4. *Use of language.* Do I make a studied effort to learn about the use of language? (Although English is a difficult language to learn, the rewards of reading the great masters are worth the effort of studying to understand.) Do I take the care necessary to produce a well-written piece of copy? (And there is great satisfaction in being able to make words do your will.)

Basic Characteristic

Obviously, there are many special qualities a journalist needs and many abilities he must develop if he is to succeed. But none of these will be meaningful or helpful unless they grow out of a curiosity about the world and its people.

Why learn at all about how to gather news and how to write it, if you are indifferent in the first place? Journalism is only for those who are interested in what's going on, who's making it go, and what difference it makes.

Curiosity may have killed the cat, but it keeps the news media alive and journalists on the go.

By Way of Illustration

The following editorial from the *Southwest Times Record* states that newspaper's feeling of responsibility for accurate reporting. The editorial appeared immediately after violence erupted at Fort Chaffee and hundreds of Cuban refugees swarmed through neighboring communities.

Let's Put Rumors to Rest

This newspaper will not spread unsubstantiated rumors that could lead to the death or injury of innocent people or a nasty incident that could be used against this nation by Fidel Castro's communist government for propaganda purposes.

We will print whatever happens involving the Cubans on or off Fort Chaffee, but the information must be verified by eye witnesses, victims or participants who will be quoted.

Hopefully, the Cubans now will be kept inside the military reservation until they are completely screened and processed for release to Cuban-American relatives or American citizen sponsors. Those found to be Castro agents, social misfits and outright criminals by American standards should be returned to Cuba. . . .

Thanks to Gov. Bill Clinton's mobilization of the Arkansas National Guard and reinforcements of state police, plus the governor personally conveying the seriousness of the situation to President Carter who sent in additional troops, we believe security has been effectively strengthened inside and outside the Cuban refugee compound for the mutual protection of residents of this area and the Cubans. The contributions of city and county law enforcement agencies to improved public safety also cannot be understated.

Now, perhaps the biggest remaining danger stems from frightening loose talk circulated through the rumor mill by civilians, military personnel and Cuban-American relatives of the people inside the refugee compound.

We have heard rumors of everything from rapes to bodies being tossed out windows, but have been unable to locate either an American rape victim or body, or anyone who personally has seen either at a hospital or funeral home. Such talk, however, naturally arouses public anger and fear. This can cause frightened people, who have armed themselves for protection of homes and property, to do frightening and tragic things, such as firing a gun through a closed door when a footstep falls on a front porch without really knowing who is outside.

We do not want such things to happen.

We have attempted to track down many of the rumors now in circulation, usually running smack into a dead end. Today, we are asking your help. When you hear a rumor, find out who it happened to, get the person's name, address and phone number. Do not repeat the rumor until you yourself are absolutely convinced it is true. Call us with names, dates, places, phone numbers and any other information you may have. We will attempt to follow through and get someone to either confirm or deny the story. If it can be confirmed, we will publish it.

We recognize that rational thinking and behavior are difficult because of recent events. But it also is essential.

Public confidence in spokesmen for the refugee task force has been shaken, especially when one government civilian calls what has been happening in and around Fort Chaffee "fun and games."

We see the situation as deadly serious and desperately dangerous. It was serious enough to involve the president of the United States. That is not "fun and games."

Please, be calm, demand facts and do not accept unfounded rumors on face value.

SECRET of SUCCESS
Apply seat of pants to seat of chair!
My deadline is not for 15 minutes. All I have to do is find someone to interview, interview them, organize my notes...

Key #12 Organize Your Story

... Putting the parts of a story together is something like riding a sled downhill. You load the sled, you shove off, and about all you can do after that is rest confident that you knew in the first place where you would be headed.

Putting the story together is more a matter of judgment than of rules. You have a "feeling" for the completed story, a "feeling" for how it should unwind.

If you have prepared well and have full notes, organizing the first draft is something like assembling a freight train. Once the locomotive units are in place (the lead), the cars are coupled on in the order of their destination. Just as the yard master knows what cars are to make up his train, so does the reporter know what facts his story is to include. He follows his lead with the next important piece of information, and then adds items in the order of importance or interest.

The plan for a story really begins when you get your story idea and progresses through the background preparation you make. Then when you actually cover the story, you begin to see the pieces of information fall into place logically.

This logical sequence gives your story coherence, and coherence makes for unity. Your reader finds it easy to follow and understand.

Story Takes Shape

Covering the story—that is, the actual seeking of the information—sets the stage for the next step.

Immediately after gathering the facts, the reporter is ready to put them into story form. Whether he is aware of it or not, he shapes the story in his mind. If he does not get the story shaped in his mind, then he has difficulty writing it.

This "story shape in his mind" is a guide to organization. Sorting, analyzing, weighing, arranging—he occupies himself with his facts until as a group they take on form. There is a play of the mind here, which is the factor that makes the writer's work distinctly his own.

Reporters seldom stop to think what steps they are taking, or to analyze their procedures, but there is a process. It is called "thinking journalism" by William Jay Stewart, an editor and free-lance reporter with wide and varied experience.

In speaking to a group of students at a press meet, he had this to say about shaping facts into a story:

> I believe that some people think journalism all the time, and others TRY to think journalism when they get back to the typewriter. A person who thinks journalism will be writing the story in his mind as he goes along.
>
> Each new fact changes the story a fraction, and as each fact is fed to the writer's mind, it is digested and, like a computer, the mind is constantly revising the story. You watch for crowd reactions, speaker's nervousness, the facts hidden on the third page of a printed handout. Everything seen, heard, or experienced is analyzed to see how it affects the event.
>
> Thinking journalism becomes a reaction, and then when you get back to the typewriter, there is no long searching for an angle, or a long session of trying to recall some minute fact that will plug a gaping hole in a story.
>
> If you are just going to an event to be a witness, you will have problems writing a complete story. Oh, you might do a good story—but it won't be complete. But if you are thinking all the time about a story, the story is three-quarters written when you sit down at the typewriter.

When a student understands this, he can gain experience by working at every story diligently and thus develop his ability. Writing is a craft that can be learned. Great reporters, however, are more than mere masters of the craft of writing. They have an added talent of being able to see more in a story than others see, and they have some immeasurable quality of expression—some intangible in their mind's eye—that is uniquely their own.

Basic Patterns

News stories fall into one of three basic patterns, determined by the nature of the event or situation to be covered.

They are (1) the fact story, (2) the action story, and (3) the quote story.

All three are similiar in containing the following:

1. A lead containing all the five W's, or those essential to the summary of the story.
2. The body written with facts in descending order of importance, so the end can be cut off if necessary because of space requirements.
3. And, if necessary, a tie-in between the lead and the body of the story to (a) fill in identifications too detailed for the lead, (b) bring in one or more secondary but significant facts, (c) attribute the lead statement to authority, and (d) explain one or more of the W's, usually the *why*.

Inverted Pyramid Form

The inverted pyramid form for news stories of these three types has long been popular and still is.

At present, however, there are surveys and studies to show that many news stories do not, nor necessarily need to, follow that form. The choice lies with the reporter.

If what is "new" or "different" serves his purpose and meets the need in print, or on the air, he should feel free to organize his story as he thinks effective. Many news stories are not written in the inverted pyramid pattern. Examples of variation can be seen in print and on the air, by writers ranging from beginners to experienced professionals.

Practical Reasons

The practical nature of the inverted pyramid as a basic pattern for news stories has long been demonstrated. There are four reasons for this:

1. Having the items arranged in order of descending importance makes it possible for the reader to get a quick summary and hurry on.
2. It satisfies his curiosity quickly about the essentials of the story.
3. It makes it easy for the make-up man to fit the story into the

space allotted, as he can cut off the closing paragraphs as necessary.
4. It makes headline writing easier, since the lead is the summary of the story and the headline is the summary of the lead.

"The failure to arrange information in the order of descending importance is one of the major faults in high school newspapers," says Max Haddick, reporting for the Texas Interscholastic League Press Conference after a survey of school papers across the nation.

The inverted pyramid arrangement is also called "spiraling." Either by definite grammatical reference or linkage of thought, each succeeding paragraph flows from the preceding one.

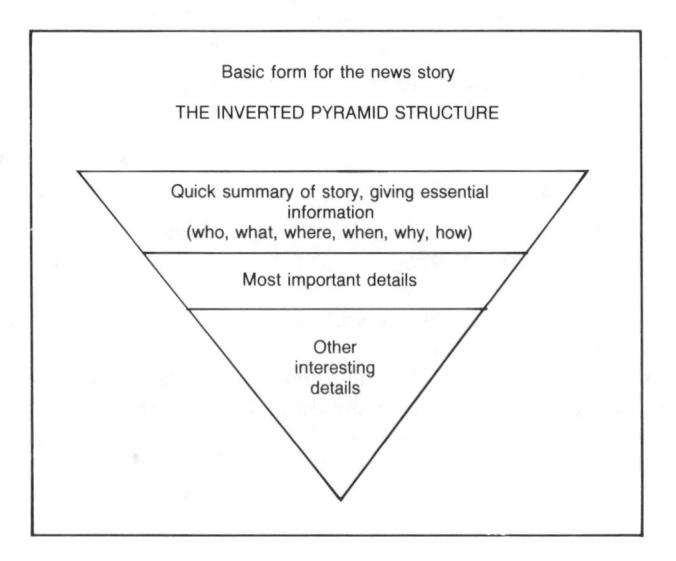

```
Basic form for the news story
THE INVERTED PYRAMID STRUCTURE

  Quick summary of story, giving essential
                information
     (who, what, where, when, why, how)

           Most important details

               Other
             interesting
               details
```

Human Interest Story

The human interest story is related to straight news stories in a number of ways, but it is never written according to the inverted pyramid plan.

In composing a human interest story, you have three choices of pattern to follow:

1. If your story fits into a narrative pattern, you tell it like a regular story, with a beginning, a middle, and an end.

Key # 12—*Organize Your Story*

```
┌─────────────────┐
│    Lead fact    │
├─────────────────┤
│ Secondary fact  │
  ├─────────────────┤
  │   Fact three    │
    ├─────────────────┤
    │   Fact four     │
    └─────────────────┘
```
FACT STORY—single feature

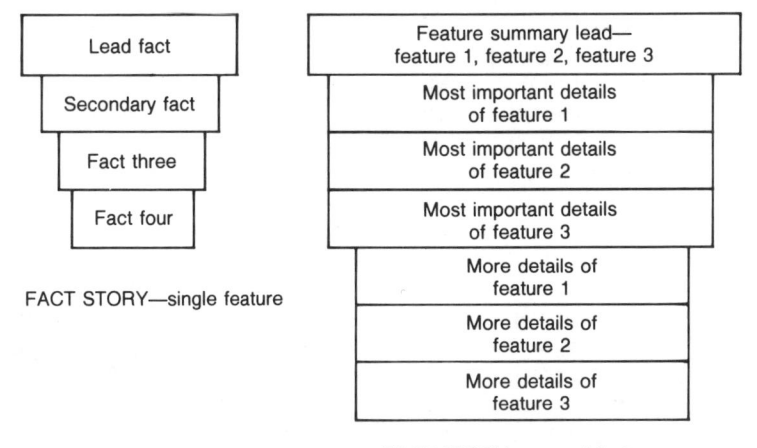

```
┌───────────────────────────────────┐
│      Feature summary lead—        │
│  feature 1, feature 2, feature 3  │
├───────────────────────────────────┤
│      Most important details       │
│           of feature 1            │
├───────────────────────────────────┤
│      Most important details       │
│           of feature 2            │
├───────────────────────────────────┤
│      Most important details       │
│           of feature 3            │
├───────────────────────────────────┤
│         More details of           │
│            feature 1              │
├───────────────────────────────────┤
│         More details of           │
│            feature 2              │
├───────────────────────────────────┤
│         More details of           │
│            feature 3              │
└───────────────────────────────────┘
```
FACT STORY—several features

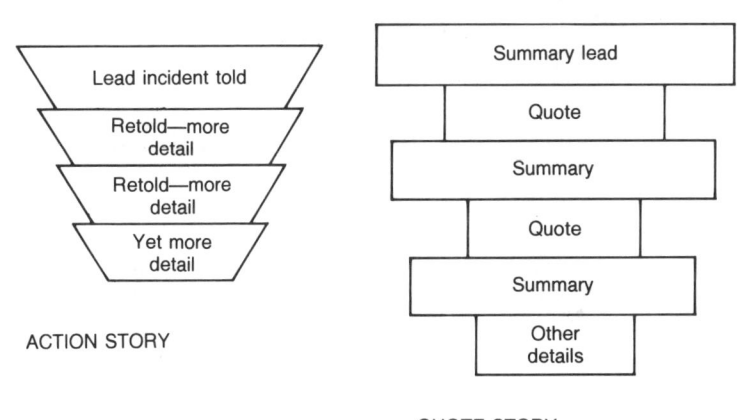

```
\     Lead incident told      /
 \                           /
  \   Retold—more detail   /
   \                      /
    \  Retold—more detail /
     \                   /
      \  Yet more detail /
```
ACTION STORY

```
┌───────────────────────┐
│     Summary lead      │
└───────────────────────┘
    ┌───────────────┐
    │     Quote     │
    └───────────────┘
┌───────────────────────┐
│       Summary         │
└───────────────────────┘
    ┌───────────────┐
    │     Quote     │
    └───────────────┘
┌───────────────────────┐
│       Summary         │
└───────────────────────┘
    ┌───────────────┐
    │    Other      │
    │   details     │
    └───────────────┘
```
QUOTE STORY

2. If your story lends itself to the surprise ending, you begin with a summary lead, continue with narrative, and end with the surprise or punch lines.
3. Occasionally a human interest story is highly dramatic. For this, you begin with an introduction in which you set the stage and bring in the characters, followed by the rising action, climax, falling action, and denouement. These stories are difficult for inexperienced writers.

Suggestions

1. The old complete summary lead, with all five W's and H crowded into one paragraph, is usually too long for today's reader.

    Pick out only the two or three most interesting facts for your opening paragraph. Select what you think would answer the first questions the reader would ask about the story.
2. In the light of studies made regarding easy reading, avoid weak words at the beginning of paragraphs. This applies especially to lead paragraphs.
3. If any sentence is more than 30 words long, take a second look at it. It may be wordy, poorly constructed, hard to read. The trend is toward shorter and more easily comprehended sentences in any writing intended for hurried readers.
4. Put only one main fact in each paragraph. Keep your paragraphs short, rarely more than two inches in length.

    The paragraphing in newspaper stories is not the same kind of paragraphing you study in expository writing in English classes. The development of a topic sentence in a well-constructed paragraph is a block of composition suitable for only certain kinds of prose writing.
5. In order to hold these separate-fact-paragraphs together, it is helpful to remember the following devices to gain continuity in writing:
    a. Repeat key words.
    b. Use synonyms or pronouns for key words.
    c. Refer to preceding fact or idea.
    d. Elaborate on preceding fact or idea.
    e. Use transitional words, as *formerly, also, in particular, additional, a further development, in connection with, since then.*

Leading Off "Right"

"A good story writes itself."

Though this optimistic statement might be debated, it is true that if you work carefully on your lead and get it "right," the remainder of the story will fall into place comparatively easily.

The reason for this is that if your lead is "right," it is proof that you have thought through the story and have arrived at the proper beginning. The reasoning that helped you arrive at this logical beginning will supply the parts to fall in place to tell the remainder of the story.

However, even after you complete a lead that satisfies you, there is still work to be done, and so the question: "After the lead, what?"

Key # 12—*Organize Your Story* 139

Finishing the story consists of arranging and then writing the remainder of the information at hand in logical and orderly sequence.

The first step at this point is to see if your story needs a lead-to-body link, that is, a few words, or perhaps even a paragraph or two, merging the opening paragraph with the main portion of the account.

The lead-to-body link usually serves one of these purposes:

1. To fill in identification too detailed for the lead.
2. To bring in one or more secondary but significant facts.
3. To attribute the lead statement to authority.
4. To explain one of the W's, usually the *why*.
5. To recapitulate what has gone before.

ORGANIZATION IS BASIC

Consider the arrangement of the additional facts you have to include now that the opening part is complete. The key here consists solely in judging the relative value of the facts. Since you arranged the facts for your story in order of descending importance in order to compose the lead, the parts of the body of the story should fall into place easily.

Some textbooks have heavily emphasized certain forms for beginners to follow. But the trend has always been toward readability of copy. Readability does not necessarily mean simplicity, as we usually think of it to mean starkness or barrenness. Readability is based on basic planning that is thought out with care. You do not achieve unity unless you "think unified."

There must be orderly progression of ideas. Transitions and connectives will follow naturally if you "think unified."

Make a paragraph of each fact, usually not exceeding 60 to 70 words. This block paragraphing, of course, is different from paragraphing in English class compositions.

The advantage of this kind of paragraphing in the news story is that a "loose" column looks more readable than a tight block of copy several inches long. Also, short paragraphs make it easier for the reader to grasp the full content, idea by idea.

The word *organize* appears in every discussion of news writing. Some define the word one way, and some another.

The important point is that the arrangement of your facts must be worked out so your story is a well-planned and effective whole. The parts must "hang together."

Somewhere along their way through school, many students acquire a hostility toward outlines and organization of ideas.

Let it be emphasized that by "outline" we mean an orderly, logical presentation of facts and ideas. This is a much broader and more flexible kind of outline than the formal outline taught in connection with the writing of research papers and other formal presentations.

This hostility is unfortunate for them if they had hoped to be writers, because a planned presentation of facts is much more efffective than a haphazard collection.

Many people say they write without an outline. If they actually do write well without an outline, they have acquired a quick way somewhere in their training to organize ideas in their minds.

Some writers really can do this. Others, however, like to think that they are some sort of geniuses who do not need to outline. Students who think they can write without organizing their ideas are just fooling themselves. They may think they do not need to outline, but the reader can tell. The end result is not that the reader takes issue and tries to prove this. He merely doesn't read the story—he doesn't really care. If the writer didn't try to interest him, then he isn't interested. It's that simple.

One of the world's great newspapers, the *Wall Street Journal,* advocates outlining news story material.

Sometimes the phrase *plot a yarn* is used. This means organize your facts before you start writing. Other professional journalists say it this way: "Have facts, and plan."

Some experienced writers agree with William H. Stringer of the *Christian Science Monitor,* who says he organizes a story "simply by passing out new and interesting points as the story continues." Then he adds: "One must make a continuing effort to keep his story appealing."

STARTER TROUBLE?

Occasionally even after planning, a writer has trouble getting started. As this is a common problem for all at one time or another, various suggestions have been offered. The following may be helpful for you:

1. To get started, try telling the story orally to someone, merely telling it naturally.
2. If you "freeze" at the typewriter, just start typing, any words at all that might be related to the subject, and keep typing as fast as you can for several minutes, not even hesitating.

Key # 12—*Organize Your Story*

This will force you to keep your fingers moving and your thoughts concentrated on no hesitating. This in turn will help you break the "freeze."
3. If you go a few minutes without any ideas at all, try doing something else, like eating an apple or glancing through some cartoons—something physical to interrupt the "nothingness."
4. Don't let your typewriter sit there and stare at you. Make it write something, even perhaps retype your notes as fast as possible.
5. If you cannot get a lead phrased to your liking, try to work out at least a "lead idea" and then go on to do the remainder of the story. Later you can return to the "lead idea" and work out a lead.

Having a "lead idea" at least helps you get the story together. Generally this effort on the body of the story will give you some ideas about what to do with the opening.

Be sure that in your story you identify all persons, all organizations, and the like. Never assume that the reader knows the background of the story or that he is familiar with the situation.

You put into each story as much complete information as you can, as if this were the only place where this information could be gathered. As you write, imagine that the reader to whom you write knows nothing at all about the situation or the people included.

Also, be sure that you state the authority for your information. This is important, since the reader wants to be sure that his information comes from what he considers an authoritative source.

COPY MUST "LOOK GOOD"

After you have finished your story, go back over it with this checklist:

1. Are the paragraphs kept to 60 to 70 words except where greater length is necessary?
2. Are the paragraphs of varying lengths to make the story look interesting in print?
3. Are the opening words in the paragraphs varied? Try including some quotations for variety.
4. Is each paragraph a complete single thought? If any one paragraph were replaced or removed, would the continuity of the story be affected?

"Try visualizing your story as made up of blocks," says William J. Good, of the University of Arkansas. "Put a one-paragraph

fact in each block. Then note how you can manipulate these blocks, even remove some if necessary."
5. View your story critically to see if it looks easy to read. Remember that newspaper readers are hurried readers. They are in the habit of merely glancing at a news sheet.

If their eye is not attracted at once, they will not come back. Furthermore, they do not expect to read more than the headline and possibly a few paragraphs. Therefore, if you want to keep the reader interested, you must keep his attention sentence by sentence.

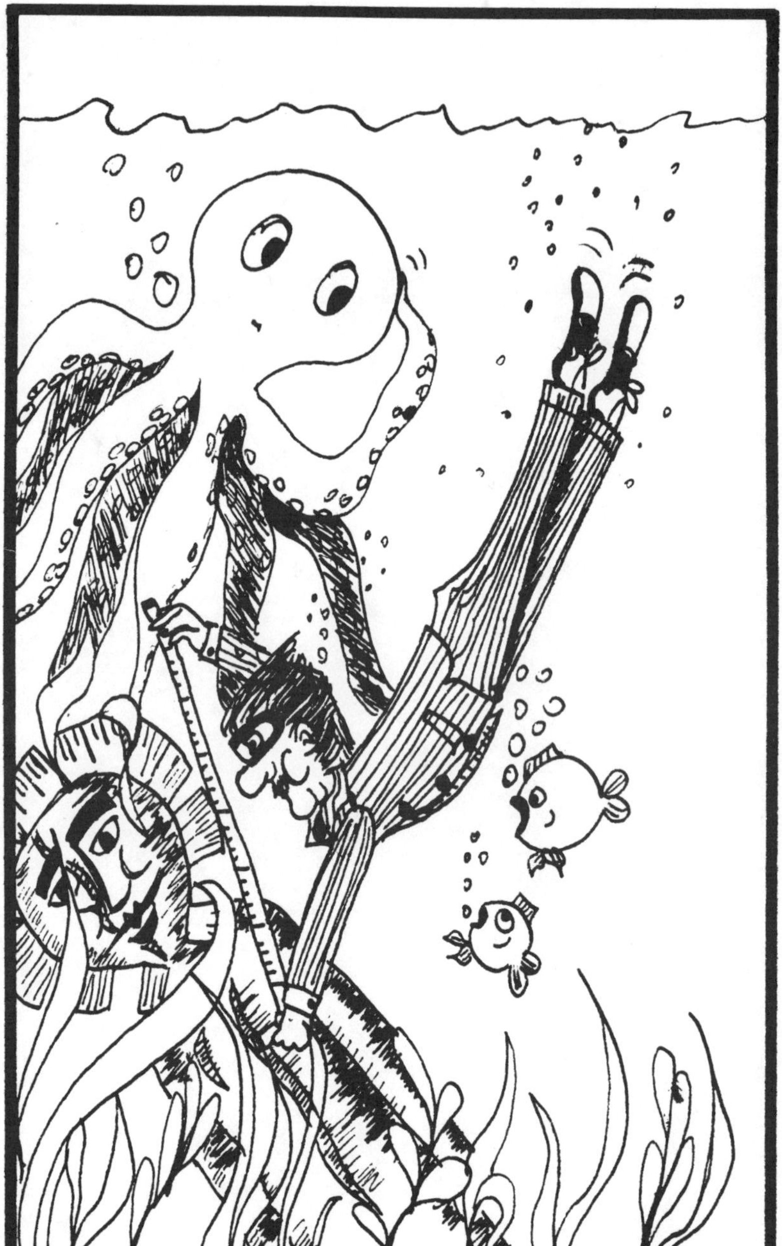

Key # 13 *Be Thorough—
Be Complete*

. . . To get there first with the facts is the key to effective news reporting—the facts, all the facts.

First reports are frequently bulletin-type summaries of the 5 W's. But immediately thereafter news stories are put together with as much of the information printed or broadcast as possible. The reporter, therefore, has the responsibility of gathering enough information to cover the event or situation thoroughly and completely. To repeat a popular simile: "Just as only one-tenth of an iceberg is above water, so a reporter's story is only a small showing of all the information he has gathered."

News reporters would do well to watch a sports reporter at work. Before a game, a good sports reporter already knows about the teams—players, standings, records. Because he follows every moment of play, he can report it in detail. What enthusiastic sports reporter would drop in sometime during a game, ask a few questions (of just anyone) and drift off?

The big question: Have I covered this so well that the reader will have no gaps in his information? Can he reconstruct from my words the total story?

Old saying: "See all, hear all, tell all."

Story May Need Revision

Although you think you have written a story that is thorough and complete, when you turn it in you are likely to discover that the editor or adviser thinks it could be improved.

This may mean that you have not included sufficient information, that you have unnecessary material for this particular story, or that you have put the story together so that it does not seem complete and satisfying.

You will benefit from working earnestly at revising your copy.

Aids in Revision

Revising a story means rewriting it in such a way that it is improved in one or more of the following ways: (1) coverage, (2) organization, (3) wording, and (4) that ever-elusive quality, style. Revision does NOT mean merely copying your first draft.

Revision may mean including additional or more specific illustrations or going forth in search of additional and more significant information. It may mean rewriting the lead, possibly from a new angle, or possibly even reshaping the entire story.

Where to Begin

The following checklist for revision is a short summary that many writers keep handy, for every writer who really cares about a well-done piece of copy is concerned about revision. It helps to have definite steps to follow.

1. Regarding coverage:
    . . . (a) Does the story answer all the questions the reader would ask—briefly the 5 W's—and such other questions as: What is this story all about? Who is involved or concerned? How important is it generally, and to me? Will it lead to something else? Is it related to or a consequence of something that has gone before? What difference does it make?
    . . . (b) Are there any interesting feature or sidebar possibilities?
    . . . (c) Is everything properly explained and supported with facts? Are sources quoted accurately?
    . . . (d) Is my coverage fully factual?

2. Regarding organization:
    . . . (a) Can the reader trace my line of thought from the lead to the conclusion?

Key # 13—Be Thorough—Be Complete 147

. . . (b) Is my lead adequate? That is, does the story follow naturally from this beginning? Have I phrased the lead so it is easy for the reader to grasp the summary of the story quickly? Is my lead in proportion to the story? (Sometimes enthusiastic writers turn out an ill-proportioned beginning in the effort to create an "attention-getter.")

. . . (c) Do the various parts of the story stand in proper relationship to one another and in proportion?

. . . (d) Are allusions, illustrations, examples, quotes, and the like well chosen?

3. Regarding wording:

. . . (a) Check all important words to be sure that you have the exact word in the right place to carry your information clearly and accurately.

. . . (b) Consider your verbs. Study each sentence with the purpose of finding the strongest verbs suitable for the phrasing of your idea. Verbs that show action are generally preferable to combinations of "being verbs" plus adjectives. Example: Note the difference between *He seemed to be interested* and *He listened with seeming interest.*

Also, sometimes in expressing your idea the active voice is preferable to the passive voice, or vice versa. If you do not fully understand the difference, study voice in a grammar textbook. Example: If your story is about a search for a sunken treasure ship being carried on by a salvage company, you will write *Divers radioed that they had sighted the wreckage about noon.* However, if your story is about the ship and its history, you probably would write, *The wreckage was sighted about noon by divers in the area.*

Also, verbs themselves have specific meanings. Note: Did he laugh or chortle? Did he putter or piddle? Did the team defeat their opponents or edge them out? Did he state this, or announce it, or declare it?

. . . (c) Check for misplaced modifiers, ambiguity, dangling constructions, trite expressions.

. . . (d) Note your transitions and connectives to be sure that that they are correctly chosen and that you do not repeat noticeably.

. . . (e) Scan the opening words of the paragraphs to be sure that you do not begin paragraphs too much alike.

. . . (f) Study your sentence structure. Avoid stringy sentences—that is, those with adjective clauses and other kinds of floating modifiers carelessly tacked on at the end. Learn to distinguish between loose and periodic sentences, and use them as you think they are suited to your purpose.

4. Regarding style:

... (a) Read your story aloud. Does it "sound right"? Cadence and rhythm are qualities that you will develop by cultivating a "listening ear."

... (b) Have you dramatized your story where possible?

... (c) Consider what you have learned about the devices of rhetoric to see if any apply here.

... (d) Check for parallelism, climax, figures of speech, and the like. Is the phrasing not only clear but colorful?

A Story for Study

The following account of the development of a story by a junior high school reporter is told by the adviser. It will give you an idea of what to expect.

The story as it first came in:

> *Slowly but steadily directories take shape as student council members check names, addresses, and telephone numbers of seventh-, eighth-, and ninth-grade students. Directories will be sold in home room classes by council representatives, also in SC room 121 and the school store. Price will be determined by the publishing cost, but should be about 35 cents.*
>
> *Topics to be displayed and discussed will be "Know Your School," "Know Yourself," and "Know Your Community." There will be different topics displayed each month. A committee of SC members are digging up information on these subjects.*
>
> *Last but not least, a mixer will be held in the gym tonight. It will honor the football team, cheerleaders, and band students. A jukebox with all the latest hits will supply the music. Those not wishing to dance may go swimming, play Ping-Pong, or delight themselves at the refreshment stand. There will also be a contest for the best decorated socks. A couple will be selected and awarded a prize.*

Adviser's Comments

> *The reporter who handed in this story had attended the student council meeting as part of her beat. Assuming that she knew all the facts, she wrote the story. She did have a good many facts, but she failed to include some important ones.*

Key # 13—Be Thorough—Be Complete

This kind of writing is fairly typical of most beginning junior and senior high school students.

Notice:
1. *She gave no authority for any of the statements.*
2. *She failed to give names of the committee members—and names make news.*
3. *She forgot to include the admission price of the sock hop.*
4. *She used trite phrases (slowly but steadily, last but not least, delight themselves, etc.).*
5. *She wrote the story in the order in which the items were discussed during the meeting, forgetful of timeliness and student interest.*
6. *She wrote the story in the present tense, though the paper was not to come out until later.*
7. *She seemed to be writing about three unrelated facts, making no effort to connect them.*

After I had glanced through the story, I asked her to read it aloud. Before she was halfway through, she said, "It isn't any good, is it? It's all jumbled."

I had to admit that it could be better, so we began to discuss the possibilities. I reminded her of the "several-feature story" outline we had discussed in class some time before.

Her eyes opened wide. "Why, this is a perfect example of that kind, isn't it?"

She recalled that a lead mentioning all three items should be written, making a unified story. Then she could develop each topic individually.

In branching out into the various topics, we had to decide which of the three should be mentioned first. When I asked which one was of most interest to the students, she immediately answered sock hop. I asked her which was most timely. Again the answer was sock hop. Then I told her to figure out the other two the same way.

Going back to her first paragraph, I wondered aloud how she knew the price of the directories. When she explained that the student council sponsor had mentioned it, all I did was raise my eyebrows, and she realized that that bit of information should have been included.

That gave her the idea that perhaps the student council president should also be mentioned, especially as he had played an important part in all three phases of the student council program.

She smiled a little wryly. "And I should have found out the names of the students on the committee."

Then I pointed to the second paragraph and asked, "Displayed where?"

"Why, you know, on the bulletin board."

"Of course, I know," I said. "And you know, and many of the students would also know, but what about those students who don't know?"

Then I asked which topic would appear first. In answering, she suggested that perhaps it should have more space given to it, especially as we could do a follow-up story on the others in a later issue.

And that did it. After our little discussion, she began to think. To get more facts, she interviewed the student council sponsor and president. Then she rewrote the story:

The rewritten version:

Preparing for tonight's sock hop, finishing the student directories, and giving the bulletin board a "new look" are the current projects of the student council.

Tonight's "mixer," the first of three sock hops planned by the student council, will honor the football players, cheerleaders, and band students. Music will be supplied by a jukebox with all the latest hits, reports Steve Lease, SC president.

"Those who do not want to dance may swim, play Ping-Pong, and, of course, visit the refreshment stand, which will be open from six until nine o'clock," Steve said. "Also, all students may enter the contest for the best-decorated socks. The winning couple will be given a prize."

Admission to the sock hop will be 25 cents stag or 35 cents drag.

The student directories, which will include all seventh-, eighth-, and ninth-grade students' names, addresses, and telephone numbers, have been compiled by student council members Lana Steadman, Glenda Allen, and Katie Harper.

Now at a local printshop, they should be ready for distribution within two weeks, says Richard Mulley, SC sponsor.

"As soon as we receive them, they will be sold by student council representatives in room 121, in the school store, and in home rooms. The price will be determined by the publishing cost but should be about 35 cents," Mr. Mulloy stated.

Acting on a suggestion given at the last student council meeting, the topic to be displayed on the SC bulletin board next month will be "Know your School."

The committee to gather information for this subject includes Rudda Mansell, Glenda Allen, Linda Laney, Sharon Stevens, Linda Watson, and Richard Mask.

Other bulletin board displays still in the planning stage include "Know Yourself" and "Know Your Community." Committees to carry out these topics will be appointed at a later date.

STEPS TO FOLLOW

If you are an inexperienced student journalist, bewildered by so much that you have to think about, you will probably feel much more secure if you have a definite set of steps to follow as you write your first story.

This section is intended as a guide so that your first assignment will be successful.

1. Sit down with your notes as soon as possible after you visit your

Key # 13—*Be Thorough—Be Complete*

news source. Imagine that you are going to tell the story to one of your friends out of town.

2. Carefully think through your notes and write a summary of the total story as if you were sending a telegram of 35 words and were determined to say as much as possible for your money. Label this "telegram" the *story summary*.
3. Number your items of information in what you would consider the descending order of importance if you were paying for additional words in the "telegram."
4. Mark any items that seem especially interesting.
5. Consider those carefully and decide which item, or items, to feature as most likely to gain the reader's attention.

6. Write six or seven ideas for beginnings, each as different from the others as possible and yet based on what you selected as the item, or items, to feature. Choose the one you like best and label this the *lead idea*.
7. Using this lead idea as a starting point, add the remaining ideas in your notes as you think they fall in place. The least important must be last. Consider this carefully so that if the story has to be cut, only the least important ideas are lost.
8. Now go back through the story and see how much background and detail you can add so that the reader can visualize the action. Give him something to look at. Most news stories are stories of action, which, like a play, have a setting. A few words here and there to describe that setting will appeal to your reader.
9. Go back to the lead idea and work on that until it "sounds right." If you cannot get it to sound right, try using another approach—or two. Of course, this is all more easily suggested than carried out.
10. The secret is to keep on trying. You will not succeed in writing a lead if you quit writing. As you write, you will eventually give yourself an idea.

11. Now write a headline for the story. If you *can* write an adequate headline, your story is probably worked out properly. If you cannot phrase an adequate headline, then very likely something is wrong with your organization.

    In trying to see where the shortcoming is, ask yourself these questions:
    a. Is the lead not really a lead but a fact only? Leads are ideas, not just items of information.

b. Is the lead too cluttered? That is, does it include too many items of information not properly related? A lead is like a bouquet. It is made up of parts, but they form a whole that has a beauty of its own, a meaning of its own.

Remember, a lead is the first part of a news story and is called that because it *leads off.* The term would not be applied properly to just any group of words or sentences occupying the first part of a piece of copy. The lead is the appropriate beginning carefully worked out to spearhead the recounting of your news.

c. Did I make a poor choice in selecting the lead idea? Many times student writers overlook their lead ideas and bury the most important part of the story deep in the body, often even using it at the end.

12. When you see where your difficulty is, revise accordingly. Do not be afraid to rewrite, and do not try to patch and piece out if major changes seem necessary.
13. Now go through the story and cut out all unnecessary words, check all sentences for errors in grammar, spelling, and punctuation.
14. If the story is too short, do not pad it with extra words. Go find more interesting facts. Never, never, never pad a story.
15. Verify all facts, check spelling of all names.

Example to Study

The analysis of a prize-winning story may serve as a guide for those seeking to learn to recognize a well-written news story. The article is from *The John Marshall Rocket* of the John Marshall High School in Rochester, Minnesota. The comment was prepared by C. J. Leabo, in a National Scholastic Press Association critique.

The story:

*Will Citizens Approve
School Bond Issue?*

In four years Rochester will have a new high school . . . if the citizens support the school bond issue in a city election Tuesday.

Dr. James Moon, Superintendent of Schools, explained the new high school, its advantages and disadvantages, during a recent interview.

A school bond issue of $7.7 million has been presented to Rochester citizens. $4,850,000 of that will be needed for the construction of the new high school, and the remainder will be used for new elementary schools.

Key # 13—Be Thorough—Be Complete

If the bond issue is passed, planning for the school will begin immediately. Dr. Moon, Dr. Ralph Wright, JM's principal, Mr. Jennings Johnson, JM's assistant principal, and Mr. R. J. Rehwaldt, JM's assistant principal of student affairs, will be doing preliminary planning for about ten months, according to Dr. Moon.

After one or two months of bidding by contractors, and the final contract awarded, the high school will take about twenty months to build, according to Dr. Moon.

Dr. Moon said, "If everything goes as smoothly as it can, the building will be ready within four years. The school will have to be economical, pleasing to the eye and just right for Rochester."

The high school will be located in the northeast corner of the old airport in southeastern Rochester and its students will be determined simply by dividing the town in half so that an equal number of students will go to each school.

This year at JM there are approximately 2,100 students. JM is five years old. Originally JM was planned for a capacity of 2,000, Dr. Moon explained. "This was just before IBM came here . . . we added an addition to JM even before it was completed."

Rochester is growing faster than the average city in this country, he pointed out. Next year there will be 160 more students at JM than this year.

When asked about more additions for JM instead of a new high school for the increasing enrollment, Dr. Moon explained:

"We can put on classrooms, but the real problem is the size of the library, art rooms, cafeteria and shops.

"If we were just going to use classrooms, it would be all right, but in the long run it would be uneconomical because the building would be unbalanced."

The most important assignment in building a new school is to have a comparable educational system at both of the high schools.

Moneywise, the planning committee will rearrange things more efficiently and cut down on the number of feet in the new high school.

For example, instead of separate entrances for the gym, auditorium, and cafeteria, such as at JM, there will be one main hall leading to each part of the school.

There will be no stadium at the new high school, but there will be a swimming pool and an auditorium to hold 900–1,000 students.

Both JM and the new high school will each have their own sports teams.

"When schools are split, there is a problem of who gets the trophies, school colors, etc. We will look to the Student Council for help on this matter," he commented.

"Of course, the new high school may create a competitive spirit between the two schools. I hope this competition will be carried out in a gentlemanly way," Dr. Moon said. "This is why it is important that the students have the right attitudes."

Even if the school bond issue is passed, Dr. Moon explained, there is a possibility of a variation of a double shift at JM beginning next fall.

If double shifts are used, both student and teacher morale is expected to drop. *One of the major problems with this system is having students run the streets while the other shift is in school.*

If Tuesday's bond issue does not pass, another will probably be tried at a later date.

"However," Dr. Moon said, "it's all or nothing now."

The comment:

> This is a story of a type too seldom recognized and covered in high school papers, in an approach too seldom used.
>
> First of all, it deals with an inherently interesting subject—*the possibility of a new high school for the community where only one now exists. This is a subject that affects students, faculty, and parents alike.*
>
> Actually, the news peg *is a bond election four days away. Many schools might report briefly the coming election and pass it off with a few paragraphs stating the bare facts.*
>
> Instead, The Rocket *delved into the story and lifted it from a dull and dry recitation of time, place, and event into a meaningful, well-rounded story.*
>
> The reporter went to a basic *source, Superintendent James Moon, to get his extra information. He searched for the meaning of the story, what the election means in terms of the future for Rochester education.*
>
> The reporter backgrounded *his story well. He played the present (see the ninth paragraph) against the future. He gave the reasons why the school is proposed. And he gave facts: What it will be like, when it will be built, how it will be built, how it will function vis-à-vis the present school.*
>
> These are the ingredients of a story that goes beyond the surface facts.
>
> But they must be organized skillfully and presented in a readable and interesting fashion.
>
> The lead *is superb—pungent, crisp, to the point. It summarizes the entire story in 22 words. And it interests the reader, leading him into the body of the story.*
>
> The reporter lets his authoritative source do the talking; note the good use of *direct quotes.*
>
> The story is written in short, direct paragraphs, proceeds logically to an end, *and leaves no reasonable questions unanswered.*

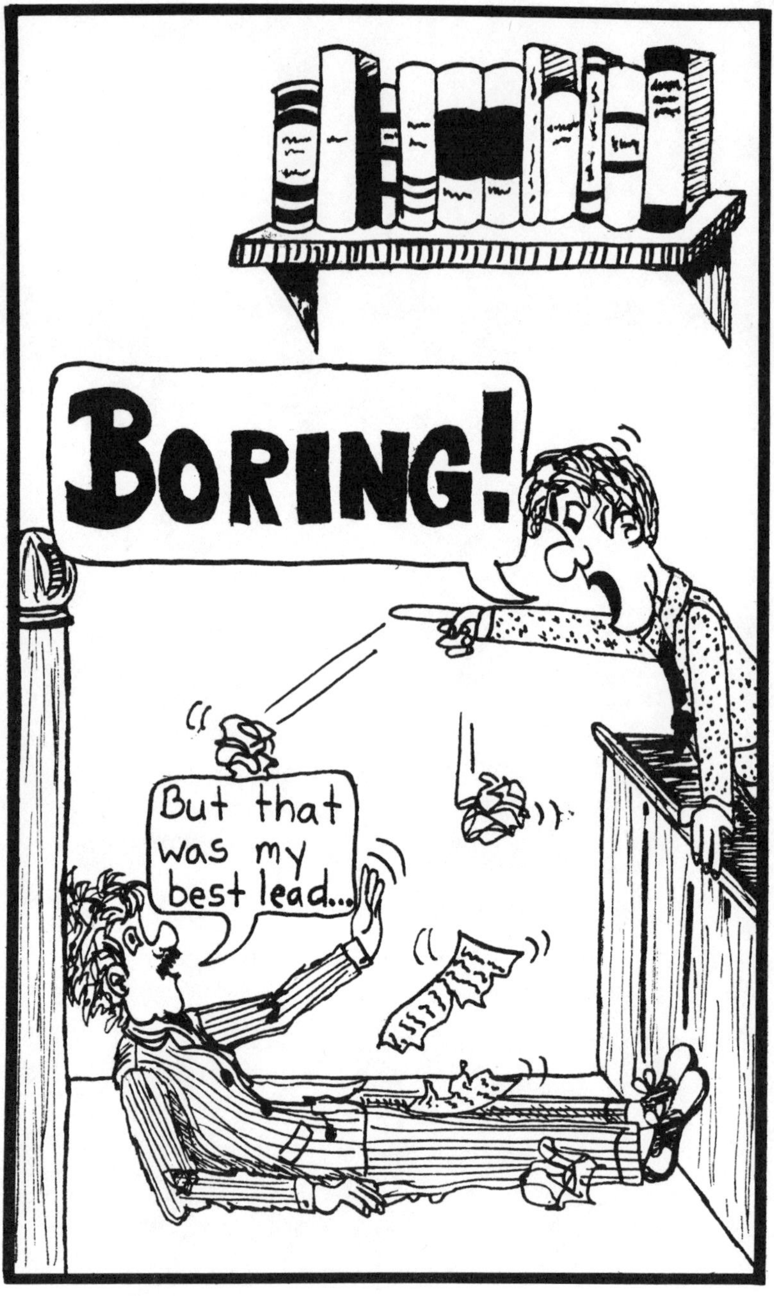
BORING!
But that was my best lead...

Key #14 Consider the Lead

. . . A quick way to help yourself succeed in writing an effective news story is to develop skill in composing leads. If you lead off well, you usually attract the reader's interest.

To achieve this "leading off well," ask yourself: What is likely to interest the reader the most? What is colorful? Important? Funny? Different? Weird? Dramatic? Spectacular? Then think: If I should have my story cut to one paragraph (and there are many occasions when this occurs), exactly what facts would I want included?

Once you have this basic answer, you have what we call the "lead idea." Write this information in a carefully worded sentence, simply stated but as complete as you can make it in about fifty words. Studying this single statement, draw upon all your skills to rephrase it as effectively as possible, with the purpose of attracting the reader's attention. Then add a dash of hidden talent for flair.

Suggestion: If you have "starter trouble," begin by typing first the words "Dear reader, do I have news! Listen to this!" Then give first the information you consider most important.

Writing a news story would be simple if you started by typing your notes in any order you pleased—and that's just the way too many stories look in too many school papers.

The Gist of the News

"President Reagan was shot in the chest this afternoon by a youthful gunman who tried to assassinate him in a blaze of 22-caliber pistol fire."

Thus began a news story written March 30, 1981, giving the gist of the news in the first few words. It was written more than a hundred years after another newsman had reported, "The President was shot in a theatre tonight and perhaps mortally wounded."

Both statements are clear answers to the question every news writer asks himself, "Where do I begin this story?"

In the years that have elapsed since the death of Abraham Lincoln, the simple statement of the main point of the news has become more than a matter of necessity controlled by the fortunes of war and the frailties of newly installed telegraph service. It is recognized as the natural way to tell the news.

This kind of simple statement giving the heart of the story, followed then by details, has become a pattern for prose writing as well established as the short story or the essay.

The *lead*, we call it—this opening statement for a news story. It is very simply and obviously named, for it serves a very simple and obvious purpose: to lead the reader into the story. Or, from the point of view of the writer, you might say: the writer leads off with this statement.

But although this is simple in purpose and in phrasing, it is vital to the story.

Even the best news writers labor over their leads. They work painstakingly to get the story off just right, because they know very well that if you lose your reader in the first sentence, he will not read the second—and hopefully, if he reads the first sentence, you have him for at least the second.

If you can keep him for the second, he may read the third—and so on. Most readers do not read more than a few paragraphs of a given number of stories. Knowing this, a writer who wants readers must make every effort to lead the reader into his story instead of making it easy for him to drift away.

The Five-W Formula

Because the gist of the news contains the answers to all the questions the readers would want answered at first, news writers have successfully made use of what is called the *Five-W Formula—Who? What? Where?*

Key # 14—Consider the Lead

When? Why? And because sometimes the *Why?* does not adequately satisfy the reader's questions, a *How?* is added.

How do you combine these?

Since the *who* and the *what* are generally more important than *when* and *where*, the subject-verb order is not only direct and effective but satisfying to the reader.

Briefly, the lead is defined as "the essence of the news," *regardless of the depth it covers in the story*. It should bring the essentials of the story to a quick focus.

The following examples from school papers illustrate what we mean by this:

> *A major cut in bus transportation, affecting about 300 AHS students, has resulted from a March decision of the Board of Education to reduce school district costs.*

> *Honors in several fields have come to individual WHS students in the past few weeks.*

> *FSHS science classes will sponsor an open house on the evening of March 17 for the general public.*

> *Clayton High School made national headlines this week when two seniors on a Nature Study Club outing discovered what may be a Viking runestone.*

> *Table the proposed club charter regulation—that's the decision of the Student Council after a poll Monday showed 34 home rooms for and 32 against it.*

> *This week has been set aside as National Newspaper Week, an event designed to acquaint the American public with the role of the free press in safeguarding the ideals of democracy.*

> *Cristy Foley was named Editor of the Year at the 51st annual AHSPA convention on the Ouachita University campus April 22–23.*

Lead Helps Reader

You as a writer must design your leads to serve two functions: (1) to win the reader's attention, and (2) to tell the reader the news as quickly as possible.

Thus, effective leads are not only informative but short and attractively phrased.

The current trend in leads is to use every device to say as much as possible as well as possible in as few words as possible.

This means that you use simple streamlined sentences with little if any internal punctuation. Following a number of studies and research in speed reading and comprehension, shorter sentences are being stressed. Many careful writers are trying to keep their leads to 25 words or less, giving the most significant points.

Note this, however: These shorter leads used for attention-getters are effective not by startling the reader but by thoughtful summarizing.

Generally in discussing news writing, we stress the importance of the lead as the beginning of the story. We emphasize the fact that an effective lead is an essential of a well-written story.

Lead Helps Writer

However, the lead is also of prime importance to you as the writer. Why?

Because if you work on your lead and succeed in thinking through your information until you can arrive at a suitable lead idea, you have managed to organize your story in your own mind.

Furthermore, if you then take care to work on the phrasing of your idea in an effort to present it as attractively as possible, you have increased your skill as a craftsman.

In associating with professional writers, you will find that no matter how great his experience, the master reporter never stops working on leads.

As in learning to swim or play the flute, for example, you learn to write leads *only* by practicing.

Once you have drilled sufficiently to compose summary leads with ease, you are well on the way toward skill and speed in writing long and difficult news stories.

"Most old-timers even have trouble with leads," says Louise Moore, of the University of Oklahoma. "Actually, a story may have several leads, all good choices. The reporter just uses his judgment about the 'master lead' he finally comes up with.

"Don't think you have to have feature leads on every story. Some stories carry themselves if written simply and directly."

Headline Is Test

How can you tell whether you have a good summary lead?

Ask yourself this question as a test: Can a crisp headline be written easily on this story?

If your answer is no, obviously you have not succeeded in your lead.

Key # 14—*Consider the Lead*

The relationship between a well-written summary lead and a concise headline is generally recognized.

Although she does not necessarily recommend the practice to others, the successful editor of the *Lepanto News Record* has this to say: "I write the head before the story, as a rule."

Secret of Success

Can you learn to write a good lead? Yes.

The steps in writing a lead are simple. The secret of success lies in the writer's approach to his work.

1. Study the facts you have gathered for the story.
2. List the five W's and H and match the facts with them.
3. Number these in order of importance. Arrange them so as to give the proper emphasis to those that are most important.
4. Write a sentence including these in the order listed.
5. Usually the *who* or *what* is most important in a straight news lead. However, often one of the other W's or H is unusually interesting. If so, play up that one. This is called emphasizing the feature.

    To find this, say, "What is the point of interest or point of significance in this story?"

    Playing up the feature is important because often the entire tone of the story is determined by it. When no outstanding fact is apparent, the reporter must use his judgment.
6. Once you have phrased this summary, emphasizing the feature, your next problem is to work at expressing this in forceful English.

The opening sentence does not necessarily contain all the five W's and H. A popular practice is to play up the most important W's in a fairly short sentence (ranging up to about 25 words) and run it as one paragraph. The remaining W's are then given in the next paragraph. Some writers use two sentences but put them in the same paragraph.

Examples showing how various W's are featured:

Who:

> Doug Sanford, sophomore, placed first in piano at a contest sponsored by the South Plains Music Teachers Association at Texas Tech Museum last Friday and Saturday.

Four JM juniors, winners of gold seals in the sixth annual Rochester Science Fair last weekend, will participate in the 11th annual SE Minnesota Science Fair in Winona April 10–11.

Senior Colvin Idol came home with a first-place trophy, a plaque for the school, a medal, a certificate, and $15 after speaking in the district finals of the oratorical contest at the American Legion March 2.

Who—when the *identification* of the person is more important than his name:

One of today's outstanding coaches, Lou Holtz, will give RSHS students the how and why of physical fitness when he is featured in an assembly program here December 10.

What:

The Christmas card post office, sponsored again this year by the student congress, opened for business Wednesday and will carry on its activities all next week.

Ceremonies for the dedication of SAA's new buildings and the consecration of the chapel will be performed Sunday, March 8, at 11 a.m. by the Most Rev. Clarence E. Elwell, Auxiliary Bishop of Cleveland and School Superintendent.

When:

Friday, October 11, marks the absolute deadline for Purple and Gold sales. No orders for yearbooks will be taken after that date.

Sunday, in recognition of Mother's Day, FHA members and their mothers will attend a Mother-Daughter tea sponsored by the LHS chapter of FHA.

Where:

Behind the new library doors, swinging open today for the first time this year, lie 125 new books of entertainment and knowledge for use by FTHS students.

Why:

To recognize and encourage literary talent at Central, the Quill and Scroll chapter is sponsoring its third annual creative writing contest.

Key # 14—Consider the Lead

As a result of the recent school bond defeat and continued lack of expansion in Ottawa High School, three school rating officials visited here December 5 to review present building facilities.

How:

Without muffing a single question, Grosse Pointe was victorious for the second year in a row on the Detroit News show "Quiz 'Em on the Air" last Saturday.

In a rousing display of public opposition, approximately 300 Fort Smith residents turned out for the monthly meeting of the Board of Education, March 27. The Board room, normally sparsely filled at such a meeting, was packed, with citizens overflowing into the hall.

The cause of the large turnout was the Board plan to condemn 37 residences near Darby Junior High School to make room for a new elementary school.

Use of two sentences for opening idea:

For those students who wish to improve their study habits early in the semester, here is the answer:
Miss Dorothy Beatty, junior counselor, is conducting a "How to Study" class, to be held from 3:45 to 4:30 every Tuesday for six weeks.

WHS students are among the first students ever to take the new Test of Academic Progress, published by Houghton Mifflin Publishing Company of Boston.
The test was administered to juniors Monday and Tuesday as part of a nationwide program to tabulate . . .

CONSIDER YOUR WORDS

Many student journalists are able to find the feature for the lead and thus are on the way to writing an effective lead, but then they desert their story and do nothing about trying to express it in forceful English.

We say they have a good "lead idea" but that they failed to write a lead. The point is that the actual wording is important.

For example, this is a "lead idea": *An evening of hilarious entertainment is in store for everyone who attends the donkey basketball game tomorrow night in Farmer gym when the faculty plays the varsity.*

The finished lead, after care is given the wording: *One of the wackiest evenings of ball-bumbling, basket-blitzing, and burro-baiting ever seen* is on tap for tomorrow night as the fabulous faculty all-stars tackle Haywood's victorious hoop squad in a donkey basketball game at 7:30 p.m. in the Farmer gym.

In composing your lead, remember that a lead should not be out of proportion to the story.

That is, do not put a long lead on a short story, or a short lead on a long story. A well-written story shows a sense of proportion.

(Remember, by *lead* we mean the gist of the story, not necessarily the first sentence only.)

Many leads require a statement of authority.
The following are illustrative examples:

> Plans for a new elementary school near Darby Junior High School are being considered in spite of widespread opposition.
> In an open letter in the local paper, Dr. C. B. Garrison, superintendent of schools, stated yesterday that the Board has unanimously passed a resolution designating this building site and instructing attorneys to secure the land for construction.

> A local SWTR reporter has gained national recognition for a story that she entered in a feature-writing contest last spring.
> Becky Meeks, who won third place in the annual Writing Awards Contest, will be featured on the Today Show, Friday, according to Writer's Review, the magazine which sponsored the competition.

> With the concurrence of the principal, Major John M. Torode, PMS announces the following promotions of Cadet Personnel in the Cadet Corps:

If a lead is a summary of two items or more, be sure that the same order is followed in the headline as in the lead.

For example: If the *lead* says that the student council will stage a carnival and a Christmas play, then the *headline* should read: Student Council Plans Carnival, Christmas Play—not Student Council Plans Christmas Play, Carnival.

CONSIDER GRAMMAR

In the effort to give their leads variety, student journalists often make use of faulty construction, grammatically speaking. Check carefully to see that you do not make these errors:

1. Use of a reversed verb phrase followed by the subject. Example: *Winning scholastic honors this year are three seniors.* Better: *Three seniors have been named for scholastic honors this year.* Or: *Returning to the faculty this year are all eight English teachers.* Better: *All eight English teachers are returning to the faculty this year.*

2. Use of *according to* in the sense of stated or said. Example: *The board report will be filed later, according to Principal John Mason.* Better: *"The board report will be filed later," said Principal John Mason.* Or: *Tests are being given all this month, according to the schedule posted by the guidance office.* Better: *Tests are being given all this month, according to an announcement by the guidance office.*

Initial words in leads are the reader's introduction to the story and as such should be considered very carefully. Avoid beginning a lead with the words *a, an,* and *the* unless absolutely necessary. If you do not watch these words, you may discover to your chagrin that all your stories begin with the same word.

Sometimes, of course, these words are necessary to the meaning. Example: *The Jonesboro Hurricane travels . . .* or: *The Central High band will stage . . .*

Other openings to avoid are such phrases as *there are* and *there is.* These are not only weak in themselves, but they occupy space that should be given to attention-catchers.

Great care in phrasing the opening of the lead will serve two purposes: (1) your stories will be improved, and (2) you will gain skill in apt and adequate expression.

As a beginning writer seriously undertaking to produce effective leads, you will soon discover that if your story is newsworthy, often your best choice of lead is to summarize briefly the five W's, being sure that you have them in the order of importance.

You will discover that generally the simple statement is effective, with the usual subject-verb order. That is the trend in today's writing, for it is easiest for the reader to follow.

If you can communicate your idea simply, the reader can follow your thought quickly and understand you clearly.

Skill in this kind of expression is basic. Later, when you have mastered it, you can acquire polish.

But polish without basic strength is meaningless.

Gaining Variety

Obviously, however, leads should show some variety. Furthermore, sometimes elements are present that would lend interest to the lead if they were played up.

One way to avoid sameness is to see that you vary the grammatical structure of your opening sentence. The following are commonly and effectively used to vary the subject-predicate pattern:

Prepositional phrase:

In recognition of National Newspaper Week, when newspapers across the country are in the limelight, the Bulldog staff takes time out to do a bit of checking up on what Selina's own special newspaper has accomplished since moving into the new building, in addition to publishing regular school news each week.

Participial phrase:

Selected on the basis of their acedemic ability and the type of work they have done in science and mathematics, 13 KHS seniors are participating in a special research class.

Introductory adverbial clause:

As this year comes to a close and the seniors are planning their parties, the juniors and sophomores are making plans of another kind. Nomination and election of class officers . . .

Infinitive:

To point up the importance of a free press in today's world, Holy Angels Academy initiated its first School Newspaper Week, October 13–19.

To give more emphasis to fine arts and to stimulate greater student interest in the related arts fields, Fine Arts Week will be observed at CHS beginning today. Special programs planned will include two concerts and an art exhibit.

Gerund:

Exchanging calling cards, addressing graduation announcements, distributing caps and gowns—each is a reminder to Arthur Hill's 796 seniors of the nearness of commencement.

Variety in leads can be achieved by considering another kind of classification of opening sentences. Leads thus identified include the following:

Key # 14—Consider the Lead

Simple statement:

May 8 will be a busy day.
Teachers will be in Ann Arbor for the Schoolmasters Conference. (Note: For students there will be no school that day.)

The two-semester system at state universities and colleges is on its last legs. "What this means for high school students will be explained by guidance counselors at special class meetings," said Dr. H. R. Williams, chief counselor.

Striking statement:

Last Friday night was a bad night all the way around for Westside High School.

Eat your way through school and get credit doing it. That is what the girls in second-year foods classes are doing.

I had 10 minutes with Santa Claus yesterday.

Question:

Are students under too much pressure?
This is the "conversation topic" to be discussed at the Parent-Teacher Association meeting Monday night.

Quotation:

"If we're not going to be the biggest football team in the city, then we're going to be the strongest," claims Head Football Coach Carl Falivene.

"A penny and a prayer isn't a very impressive offering, but multiplied by 500 Marywooders and five days a week, a wonderful product results," remarks Virginia Lee, CSMS president.

Narrative:

The audience arrived, the gong crashed, the orchestra played, and the freshman class presentation of a Chinese fairy tale, "The Stolen Prince," began.

Novelty:

Question: Button, button, who's got the button?
Answer: Everyone. Everyone, that is, who wants to "keep up with the Joneses" in this modern space age.

Guns—January 20—a general assembly—sixth hour—fit the pieces together and they come up a lyceum on firearms.

Verbs, prepositions, conjunctions . . . travel, gardening, photography . . . These are two different worlds, and Mrs. Alyse Westbrook will soon be leaving the first to devote all her time to the second.

Like the little train going up the hill, band and orchestra members set off for Lansing last Saturday saying, "We think we can, we think we can, we think we can . . ."
And they did . . .
. . . take straight firsts in the finals . . . for the sixth year in a row.
Bands and orchestras from every part of the state gathered for the Michigan Music Festival to see who would be the best in the state.

Suzie Anderson? Jeri Fredricks? Donaleen Kramer? Kay McLeod? Tyra Parson? Penny Roberts? Which one of these girls will be chosen to reign over the Homecoming Festival this year?

These divisions are also broken down to help the writer see possibilities for gaining variety in other ways. They include these:

Contrast:

Scientists might call it a theory, politicians a breakthrough. But modern linguists have termed the new concept of language instruction a revolution.

San Francisco public school students will take a holiday from school, teachers and studies October 11. Teachers, on the other hand, will be visiting local business establishments on their annual Business-Education Day trip.

Cartridge (summary of important news in as few words as possible):

Tom S. is dead.
After six years of being Tom S. Lubbock High School (more commonly known to the general public simply as Tom S.) LHS had its original name restored at the last meeting of the school board, January 16.

Punch (brief attention-getting statement, often epigrammatic):

It is now official: the Uarkettes have been booked for six concerts in major European cities in August.

The four-quarter system is not the answer.
This is the vigorous reaction of parents replying to a questionnaire which accompanied a recent letter from the Board of Education.

Picture:

"The flowers that bloom in the spring, tra-la—!" with multicolored shifts, baby-blue sheaths, backless shoes and straw purses with flowers on top!
This floral scene was the Girls League Annual Cotton Day Assembly, April 2.

Clutching maps and program cards, confused parents will be dashing around Moorville this Thursday night, hustling to classes and asking directions of their equally confused peers.

Here on the gentle hill overlooking the point where the Arkansas and Poteau rivers flow together, the bright January sun reflects sharply off the frigid waters. On this same hill, 148 years ago this month, the first "Fort Smith" was established.

Allusion:

"He that troubleth his own house shall inherit the wind."
This phrase comes from Proverbs and contains the title, if not also the theme, for this year's term play, "Inherit the Wind."

CREATIVE IMAGINATION

Up to this point we have discussed the five W's and H. Occasionally a sixth W is listed: Wow—which, as might be expected, is an effort to point out that there is often an element of unusual interest. This usually grows out of the special interest of the information. The *wow* is thus a feature of the most striking facts.

Suppose we add another letter to the W's and the H. This additional letter would be U—standing for YOU—for every successful lead writer does his work with a touch of creative imagination.

Frequently this turns out to be a light touch. In school papers this is very important because so much of the news is either routine or similar in nature, possibly even "old" news retold.

The following leads taken from school papers indicate how this light touch is achieved. When the writer thus shows that he finds the story interesting, the reader is likely to be drawn into it.

A word of caution: Avoid attempts at cuteness at the expense of accuracy. Consider this lead: *The school's best baker, seamstress, dishwasher and dietitian will be determined on Tuesday when senior girls compete for the Homemaker of Tomorrow award.*

This not only gives the wrong impression, it is actually untrue, for the winner of the contest is not expected to be a baker, seamstress, dishwasher, and dietitian.

Leads with a light touch:

Santa and his helpers will take a rest from toymaking when the Girls Glee Club takes over the task at Santa's workshop today at 3:30 in the student lounge.

Excitement, tears, cheers and the successes of the Muir championship football team and pep squad will be brought back to life Tuesday night at the school's first pep banquet.

An unpaid mortgage, a moustached villain and the all-American hero set the stage and plot for the first melodrama of Ottowa High School, to be presented May 1 and 2 in a large tent south of the school.

Fun, food and frolic are in store for froshies attending the senior-freshman Christmas party sponsored by the senior class in the Manual cafeteria after school December 19.

The weatherman may still be debating whether spring has really sprung, but in the girls intramural program the outlook is positive.
With spring and summer in focus, all activities have changed. For girls interested in . . .

Armed with briefcases and file boxes of statistics, SMN's debate squad talked their way to three trophies last week.

"Push that pawn, grab that rook; we're going to win by hook or crook."
But the fight song of the Cross Keys chess team was hardly prophetic.
The St. Pius X chess team defeated Cross Keys in a four board match Friday, January 24. Having won over Briarcliff two weeks earlier, the St. Pius team is still undefeated.

Shakespeare came a-visiting in Fort Smith and Van Buren last weekend to help the sister cities celebrate his 416th birthday with scenes from his Macbeth, The Taming of the Shrew, Romeo and Juliet and A Midsummer Night's Dream.

Some laugh, some lead, some dance, others work; some have talent, others looks, some learn it all from books.
These are the various qualities of the 24 seniors who were chosen yesterday as MSHS Senior Personalities of the year.

It looks as if Muirites may be shoveling dirt in the new quad by March 1 as Project Q gets under way, headed by a steering committee of seniors Dennis Sweet, Don Pike and Bert England under Adviser Dominic Acossano.

Key # 14—*Consider the Lead*

A landscape architect is drawing plans for the quad, and Don and Bert have submitted blueprints to the school board for final approval before construction begins.

April Fools' Day gets a new twist this year as 145 eighth graders come to FTHS for indoctrination.
The soon-to-be freshmen will gather in the girls gym for briefing before a tour of the campus and lunch in the cafeteria.

Sloshing through the breezeway may become a thing of the past if the Board of Education approves the enclosure plans now being formed for remodeling for the NHS campus.
This would be welcome news to students who must resort to coats, scarves, boots and umbrellas for trips between the annex and the main building.

Snowflakes falling, candles glittering and music ringing will help create a Yuletide atmosphere for festivities Monday night, December 23, at the Municipal Auditorium, from 8 to 12.
Sponsored by the Student Council, the "Christmas Frolic" is something new added to the school calendar.

Nicholls High produces scholars.
It produces musicians.
It produces athletes, debaters, homemakers, journalists, dramatists, bookkeepers and stenographers.
It also produces . . . RUBBISH. Pounds and pounds of it—tons of it.

Professional Examples

The following leads are clipped from stories by professional reporters:

Things are quiet today at the Fort Chaffee Cuban refugee complex—quiet but tense.
Officials of the Chaffee Security Task Force are continuing their investigation following the weekend riots.

What is electronic, can "see" despite rain, snow, fog or dark of night, and if aimed your way can cost you a small fortune? Traffic radar, of course.

A blinding storm that dumped up to three feet of snow in parts of Ohio, Pennsylvania and New York fizzled to flurries Sunday, but forecasters said it may be the calm before another onslaught.
A heavy snow warning was issued . . .

Was it Groucho who first said, "You can call me anything, but don't call me late for dinner"?

Whether he did or not, he would find today that dinner itself is being called late in numerous households.

A couple of decades ago, railroads could set their watches by the 6 o'clock dinnertime in middle-class American homes. But with the variety of family lifestyles during the 1970s and the assistance of ever-improving appliances, dinner and the hour at which it is served have done their own thing along with everything else.

A snowfall that sent motorists in western Arkansas skidding into ditches and closed some Oklahoma roads Thursday night could be only a preview of Friday, according to the National Weather Service.

Both Oklahoma and Arkansas were under travelers advisories for Friday, Fort Smith schools were closed, and snow was stacking up at the municipal airport.

Arkansas voters kept the sales tax on food and drugs, told the legislature it could create an intermediate appeals court, decided to vote on a new constitution at the 1980 general election, swept David Pryor into the United States Senate, and made Bill Clinton the country's youngest governor at 32.

These were the results on the five statewide questions and races that appeared on Tuesday's general election ballot.

They are the handsomest men in the world, and their livelihoods depend on their remaining so. They are jetted to posh resorts and exotic locations to be photographed wearing the latest creations from Paris, Rome and New York.

They must look their absolute best—and better than their competitors—or they will be replaced. They are male fashion models for whom potential earnings are high—but so is the possibility of months without work.

They're doing it again—and this time it will be bigger and better than ever.

Members of the Junior League have been picking up, sorting out, and squirreling away merchandise since last April for their king-sized sale, which will be held Saturday in the Industry Building at the fair grounds—their third annual "Bargain Barn" where there will be something for everyone.

Auburn's James Brooks ran for 218 yards and three touchdowns and Charlie Trotman passed for two other scores Saturday to power the Tigers to a 45–32 season-opening victory over Kansas state yesterday.

Brooks, a sophomore in the starting lineup only because of an injury to regular Joe Cribbs, gained . . .

A severe Atlantic storm Tuesday slammed into 330 yachts off the Irish coast, turning an international yacht race into a struggle for survival.

Key # 14—*Consider the Lead* 173

At least 10 yachtsmen drowned, 12 were missing, and 58 craft were sunk, wrecked or abandoned.

With the last measure of strength that his pride and ego could summon, Muhammad Ali revived his flagging skills long enough Friday night to become the first heavyweight boxer ever to win the world's championship for the third time.

Stretch-running Pleasant Colony moved one step closer to the Triple Crown Saturday and breezed by Bold Ego with a scorching finish to register an impressive victory in the 106th running of the $270,800 Preakness Stakes at Pimlico.

In a virtual replay of the Kentucky Derby, jockey Jorge Velasquez again chose to keep the colt well off the early pace set by Bold Ego and then made his move at the turn from home.

High-flying Bobby Unser captured the pole position for the 65th Indianapolis 500 with a sizzly four-lap qualifying run of 200.546mph Saturday at the Indianapolis Motor Speedway.

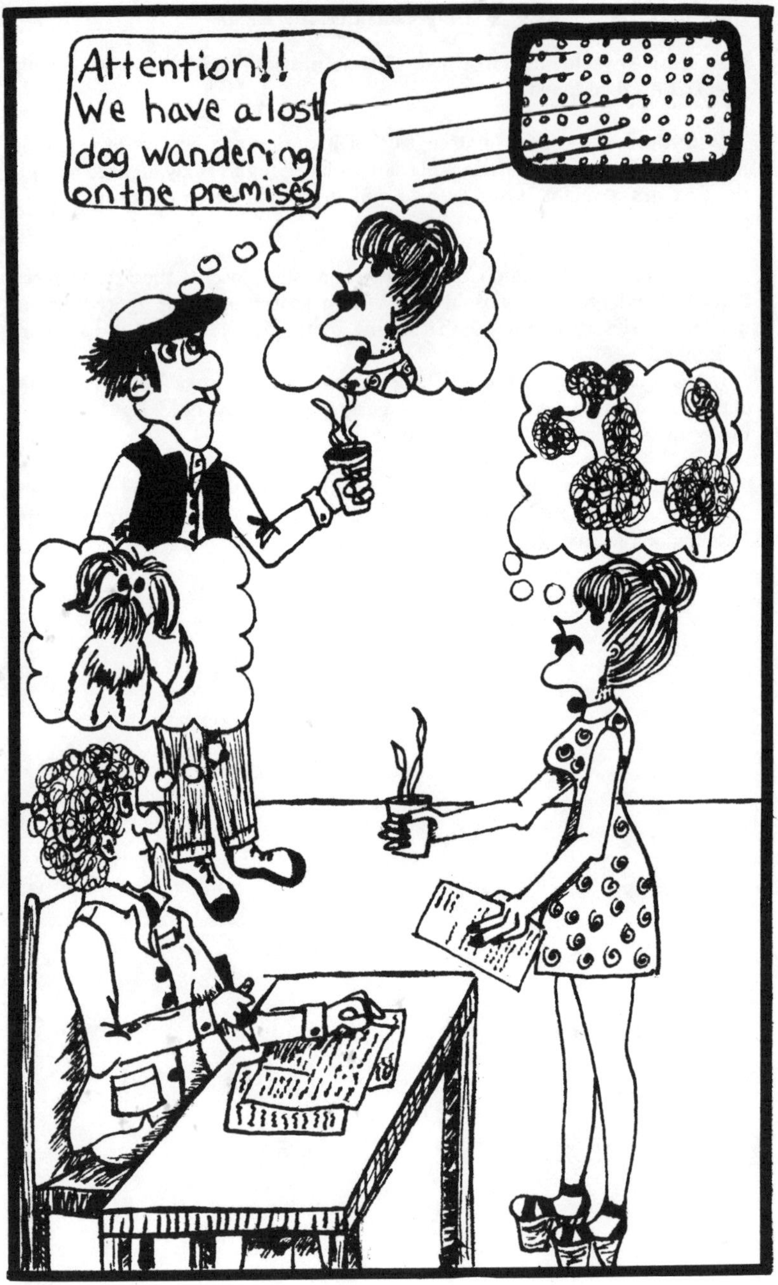
Attention!! We have a lost dog wandering on the premises

Key #15   *Be Specific*

. . . Vagueness can be very effective in a foggy seascape or a picture of a desert sandstorm, but in news reporting, vagueness is a no-no with top priority. The watchword is BE SPECIFIC.

Specific—in knowing exactly what you want to communicate to your reader. *Specific*—in knowing exactly how to phrase your sentences so that you do communicate exactly what you had in mind. *Specific*—so the reader knows exactly what's what. *Specific*—so he can see, hear, smell, taste, feel.

A veteran copy editor was addressing a group of high school editors: "You kids need to learn how to express yourselves precisely. How to get the idea across. How to help the reader see the picture. Sock it to 'em precisely like it is. Steaming hot, smoking hot, sizzling hot—which way do you want your steak? One word makes a difference in meaning, doesn't it?"

Learn *to think* in specifics. Compare: *(1) A colorful crowd filled the stadium. (2) A cheering crowd jammed the stadium with the red and white of the Bears and the purple of the Pirates.* Note the difference: *(1) Putting the fish on the stringer, Joe turned to rebait the hook. (2) Slipping the bass on the stringer, Joe grinned as he reached into the minnow bucket for more bait. "That's three!" he chortled.*

A Matter of Attitude

Being specific is much like being accurate—a matter of attitude, a sense of completeness. It is a concern for seeing that the reader knows exactly what the total story is. It is precise coverage reported in precise language.

To put it differently: Being specific is:

(A) Knowing exactly what you want to report,

(B) knowing exactly how to phrase your sentences for communicating adequately,

(C) so the reader knows exactly what's what, and

(D) so the reader can have a full understanding and appreciation of the event or situation by being able to see, hear, etc. in reconstructing the story in his mind.

More About A, B, C, D

. . . (A) By the time you, as a beginning reporter, have become acquainted with the basic principles of news reporting, you have become aware that knowing exactly what you want to say is dependent on two activities: (1) covering the story thoroughly, with full and adequate notes for reference, and (2) organizing your thoughts so you can tell the entire story and so the reader can follow your account easily.

This is fundamental, for unless you have in mind exactly what you want to say, the other phases of being specific in your reporting are meaningless.

. . . (B) A genuine interest in language that leads to a study of the use of language is basic for writers with a concern for adequate communication. The English language is a versatile language. There is always a right word for the right place.

. . . (C) So the reader knows what's what—that's our purpose in news reporting.

. . . (D) He has the pleasure of the reading. He recreates the scene, the occasion, the action for himself.

The writer cannot allow himself to fall into language patterns followed by the general public. For example, to listen to ad lib answers to questions in television interviews reveals that the English language is loosely used. Following a national tournament, athletes on the winning team were responding to the usual questions of, "What factors contributed to your team spirit and winning game plan?" Answers given by the two star players included the sentence, "You know what I mean" seven times.

Key # 15—Be Specific

Not only is this true of impromptu interviews on television but also of carelessly written copy in the printed media.

Three Suggestions

Specific procedures to help you be specific:

Note details as you cover a story. Think of your story as a script for a movie, with an awareness of props, background, items that would help the movie-maker reproduce the situation as you saw it.

Listen for words. Discipline yourself to consult a dictionary or thesaurus to develop your vocabulary and extend your understanding of the shades of meaning in words.

It is helpful to note derivation when you are trying to ascertain the difference between words that are seemingly synonyms. For example, *senile* and *anile*. Both refer to the characteristics of old age. *Senile*, however, is derived from the Latin word meaning *an old man,* whereas *anile* is derived from the Latin word meaning *an old woman.*

Another example: The word *prostrate* is generally used and generally understood to mean that a body is lying flat, as trees prostrate after a heavy wind, or victims prostrate after an earthquake. In specific use, however, if one wants to indicate exactly how a person is lying prostrate—as perhaps an investigator would want to report after a murder—he would choose either the word *prone,* meaning lying face downward, or *supine,* meaning lying face upward.

(Incidentally, fortunate is the young reporter whose education has already included a study of Latin. There is no better way to learn correct usage than to study Latin and other languages that are part of the background of the modern English language. The study of any foreign language is a help to a writer, for he learns not only meanings but nuances, subtleties, rhythm of utterance. It is never too late to begin a study of language, and there is much to be gained by a continuing study of languages, either specialized in one language or two, or general, with no more than a passing acquaintance with several.)

Use direct quotes, or quote indirectly. In both instances, be sure to quote accurately, fully enough to convey the exact meaning intended by the speaker or writer, and using the same words so the meaning is the same.

Although the English language contains many synonyms and near-synonyms, there are very few pairs of words that have exactly the same meaning. In fact, one of the advantages of the language is its numerous synonyms or near-synonyms so that a writer need not repeat the same word tiresomely.

In using the exact words of the speaker, however, it is permissible to correct grammatical errors if the correction causes no change in meaning. For example, the word "ain't."

A reporter covering a story on the drowning of a small child was interviewing the grandmother, who had been keeping the child that day. In telling about it, she said, "I ain't sure when he left the house."

The reporter used that sentence verbatim in his copy. The copy reader corrected the grammatical error before the story went to the composing room, saying that the use of the word "ain't" tended to characterize the speaker unfavorably and did not affect the meaning of her statement.

The reporter did an excellent story on the event, an award-winning story as it turned out, including much detail that gave the reader a full understanding of the situation—the distraught grandmother's frantic efforts to summon help, the surge of rescue squads coming in to search for the child, the desperate waiting for news, the final discovery of evidence that the child had fallen into the water, the huge bonfires built on the river's edge as night fell so the search could continue . . .

It is true that frequently use of direct quotes is an excellent way to characterize persons. Colloquialisms, foreign phrases, colorful or interesting combinations of words, barroom language, sports jargon, pedantic phrasing—the list is long, the possibilities for the writer are innumerable.

It is important that the reporter not embarrass his interviewee or other subject when he is covering any kind of news story. The eagerness to find colorful phrasing should always be tempered by a sense of fairness and a sincere consideration for the feelings of people.

BE CONSISTENT, CORRECT

Be *consistent* in the use of details. In a story about an automobile accident in which seven vehicles were involved, either the reporter or the copy reader or the proofreader was at fault (or perhaps all three), for the story appeared in print with the ages of only four drivers—one 17, two 18, and one 16.

Interestingly, this occurred during an extended debate in the legislature regarding teenage drivers and the issuance of driver's licenses. If the reporter thought it significant that the four drivers were teenagers, he could have commented on this editorially, but editorializing has

Key # 15—*Be Specific*

no place in straight news reporting. Also, the discrepancy in giving the age of the drivers involved was not fair reporting.

Be careful to see that the specific details you are incorporating in your copy are *correctly phrased.*

For example, in the giving of specific time, the word "about" means "approximately." Thus it is correct to report, *The fire is thought to have started about 9:30 p.m.* However, the exact time can be used thus: *The fire was reported at 9:32 p.m.*

Also: In reporting on the reentry and landing of the Columbia at Edwards Air Force Base, the television newscaster said, "The craft has landed after 54 and a half hours in flight." NASA officials reported: "The craft is down after two days, six hours, 26 minutes, and 52 seconds."

An Example

A review of coverage of the reentry and landing of the Columbia shows how professional journalists report a news event:

One more remarkable step [regarding the flipping of the craft just prior to reentry] *in a remarkable event*—This statement taken out of context would seem to be an editorial comment. However, in this story the reporter supported the statement with a block of evidence quoted from NASA headquarters, facts regarding the design, the manipulation, the performance of the craft manned by astronauts Young and Crippen.

The astronauts saw fifteen sunrises and fifteen sunsets each day—A colorful way to explain the orbiting of the craft.

Space is black, one astronaut remarked, *not black like black velvet, but shiny black, like patent leather. We don't know why, but it's that way.*—Direct quote of colorful detail, giving the reader something to see.

The Columbia reentered the earth's atmosphere at 400,000 feet, after 36 orbits, 12 miles northeast of Guam, at a speed of more than 18,500 miles per hour.—Specific detail.

You couldn't have hoped for better weather conditions or a better day for the first landing of an untested shuttle spacecraft.—Direct quote of a NASA official. *This dry lake bed forms an ideal landing strip. In the shape of a kidney bean, it affords a runway five and two-tenths miles long, twice the length of the usual landing strip.*—Colorful detail, figure of speech.

The Columbia is coming down like a falling brick—Television newscaster's use of a figure of speech in following the reentry and descent of the Columbia. And then, *She is flying like a glider right down Interstate Highway 5 at 22,000 feet, 325 miles per hour.*—Specific detail.

John Young is the first American to fly five times in space, and the first in a space shuttle craft.—Specific detail.
There are 30,000 of these black and white tiles on the craft—black on the bottom to radiate heat, and white on top to reflect heat.—Specific detail.

At 200 feet they're to put the landing gear down. Everything is looking good, right on the money. She's in—the landing gear is down! The crew is down—on the ground. Welcome home, Columbia—beautiful, beautiful!— NASA official quoted for specific information and climactic effect.

Watch for Pitfalls

In the effort to produce "picturesque expression," the writer must consider his words carefully. For example: In a newspaper story about Mount St. Helens after the first major eruption, the writer was reporting that the President would be touring the region immediately after designating it a major disaster area.

The story read: *Meteorologists predicted that clouds obscuring the 8,377 foot peak—1,300 feet was chopped off in the blast—would make it unlikely that the mountain would be visible for viewing.*
"Chopped off" is a form of a transitive verb that means "to cut by striking with a sharp instrument, hence to cut into pieces, to cleave." This definition implies an exterior force applied. However, in the case of the volcano, the disappearance of the mountaintop was caused by the internal force of the explosive action of erupting lava and steam.

Another illustration: Frequently the connotation of a specific word makes a difference to readers.
Covering a football game between two schools that had long maintained a fierce rivalry, a young reporter on the local paper wrote: *The Collinsville Pirates overwhelmed the Selina Bulldogs 32–16 last night before a record crowd in Pirate Stadium, bringing the 30-year series to a 14–14 tie.*
The next day the Selina coach called the editor of the paper. "Tell that kid reporter of yours," he shouted into the telephone, "that we may be outscored, but we're NEVER overwhelmed!!!"

ENCYCLOPEDIA
NEWSWRITING
LEADS
DICTIONARY
Of course I have a dictionary.

Key # 16 — *Learn to Use the Language*

... "The use of correct language is basic to effective news reporting"—the words of an Associated Press editor who coaches inexperienced reporters.

"This does not mean a slavish following of rules—it means (1) precision of diction and grammar, (2) orderliness of structure, and (3) simplicity of phrase. It means no wordiness, no clumsiness, no vagueness."

With so many words thrust upon us by the media every day, it is no wonder that much of what we read and hear is poorly written. Indeed, some of it is gross violation of what is generally accepted as standard English. However, let us never assume that since we are in journalism "just anything goes."

Words, it has been said, are the writer's tools of the trade. If so, it's time to fit out your toolbox. Suggestions: a desk dictionary and access to an unabridged dictionary, a manual of correct usage (perhaps one or more grammar texts that carry especially helpful illustrative material), a thesaurus.

Learn to revise your copy, painstakingly if necessary at first. Ask yourself: Is this the best word? Is this usage accepted as correct? Does this passage have impact?

Communication Basics

In news writing, where the reason for writing is communication, *correctness* and *clearness* are essential. *Color* is an added quality that comes from enthusiasm for your subject and an appreciation of words.

Why *correctness?* Because people have learned to read by certain rules.

A question mark, for example, means something to a reader. If you want to ask a question but fail to put the question mark, the reader does not get your meaning.

The same holds true for grammatical construction. Incorrect grammatical construction can mislead the reader so he will fail to understand what you are trying to communicate—or even worse, he may misunderstand. That is, he not only will not see your meaning, he may actually get a wrong meaning.

For example, a simple word like *only* determines the meaning of a group of words merely by its position.

1. Only Joe called the police. (No one else called.)
2. Joe only called the police. (He called but did nothing else.)
3. Joe called only the police. (He called no one but the police.)
4. Joe called the police only. (He called no one but the police.)

Why *clearness?* Because if you have a story worth telling, you want the reader to read it, and he will not read if he is confused.

Note this example. The meaning in this sentence is determined by the word accented: (1) *I* never said John stole money. (2) I *never* said John stole money. (3) I never *said* John stole money. (4) I never said *John* stole money. (5) I never said John *stole* money. (6) I never said John stole *money.*

Know EXACTLY what you want to say, and then say it EXACTLY.

Why *color?* Because you want to give pleasure in reading as well as information. You want the reader to say, "Gee, that's a good story."

When you write a story that you offer to a reader, you are showing him how that event looks to you. What you show him through your "glasses" is what he will see, and that view is what gives him understanding. You have two chances to interest him. One is *what* you show him, the other is *how you show* it to him.

Summary Checklist

Much has been written on effective expression, but briefly these are important points to remember:

Key # 16—*Learn to Use the Language*

1. Never forget that clear writing begins with forceful, ordered thinking.
2. Keep sentences fairly short and compact. A general average of 15 to 25 words is suggested. Use very short sentences occasionally for variety. When longer sentences are necessary, be sure that the meaning is clear and the sentence easy to read.

    However, shortness is not necessarily a synonym for readability. *Ease in reading depends not on sentence length but on thought.*
3. Avoid stringy sentences made up of subordinate clauses carelessly sandwiched in or tacked on.
4. Check all compound sentences to see that they are correct compounds rather than two separate ideas merely joined by "and."

    For example: *The newsletter is a new venture for Eastside High and it will be sent to all schools in the state participating in the debating conference.* This is not a correct compound sentence, *for a correct compound shows balance or contrast of ideas.*

    The sentence is merely two ideas and should be worded something like this: *A new venture for Eastside High, the newsletter will be sent to all schools participating in the debating conference.* Or: *The newsletter is a new venture for Eastside High. It will be sent to all schools participating in the debating program.*
5. Consider your wording carefully. The following examples of poor, awkward, and confusing passages were taken from various school papers:

    Students are reminded that the prom is formal, but a coat and tie will be sufficient wear for the boys.

    The prom budget this year is $1,025, although not all of the money may be used, according to Richard Harris, junior class president.

    Cards are carried by all seniors identifying them as such. In this way they can exercise their privileges as they might be prevented from doing otherwise.

    "Twelfth Night," the Glee Club Christmas concert, and the combined Band and Glee Club Winter concert will be presented to the high school on January 6 and late in January respectively.

    Of all the events entered by the Mohawk girls, they took none less than one second and four of the first places were new state records.

6. Check your story for connectives to see if it reads smoothly.
   The following connectives show how paragraphs can be linked together:

   Another development in the . . .
   At the same time, word came from the capital that . . .
   Earlier in the day, Central High won . . .
   Coincident with the arrival . . .
   Piecing the clues together, he learned . . .
   On the heels of this disclosure came a report that . . .
   As a climax to the celebration, the . . .
   As an aftermath, the various . . .
   Citing these various items, he explained that . . .

   However, at best the writer's connectives are little more than literary tools. Essentially, preparation of a readable story is a problem of organization and arrangement.
7. Choose the adequate word. Generally this is the common word, the simple word—as "give" instead of "contribute" and "end" instead of "terminate." The length of a word, however, is not necessarily the measure of its value. For example, there is no substitute for "extracurricular" or "automation."

   "The most accomplished journalist has a naturally simple way of writing which offers little difficulty to those with only average word knowledge and does not, on the other hand, offend the better educated by over-simplicity," says Laurence Campbell, of Florida State University.
8. Do not waste words. Avoid padding. Avoid unnecessary repetition of words and phrases.

   These sentences, taken from school papers, are typical:

   Projects were judged on the quality of work done on them. What the writer means is: *Projects were judged on quality.*

   Two new courses will be added to the regular curriculum at Herman and Lowell next year. Building Construction Technology will be offered at HHS and Electronics Technology is to be taught at LHS.

   Better: *Two new courses will be added to the regular curriculum at Herman and Lowell next year, Building Construction Technology at HHS and Electronics Technology at LHS.*

   Or: *Two new courses will be added to the regular curriculum at Herman and Lowell next year. Building Construction Technology is to be offered at HHS and Electronics Technology at LHS.*

The Tennis Club held a discussion on membership rules. Better: *The Tennis Club discussed membership rules.*

The secretary said the records were completely destroyed. Better: *The secretary said the records were destroyed.*

There is no vacancy at present. Better: *There is no vacancy.*

The tournament will open on Saturday. Better: *The tournament will open Saturday.*

The testing will continue for a period of three weeks. Better: *Testing will continue three weeks.*

Robert Jones will be the speaker for the meeting to be held on Thursday. Better: *Robert Jones will be the speaker for the meeting Thursday.*

Mary Smith, who is president of the Pep Squad, will lead the cheering. Better: *Mary Smith, president of the Pep Squad, will lead the cheering.*

9. Avoid wordy phrases, such as "a sufficient number of" when you mean "enough" or "in the event that" when you mean "if" or "in the immediate vicinity of" when you mean "near."
   Consider your sentences in the effort to cut out unnecessary words.
   Because space in print costs money, we often hear the admonition "Be brief." This, of course, does not mean to omit fact, but rather to avoid wordiness.
   Today's top writers who are paid by the word do *not* earn dollars for *just any word.* Their dollars are earned for *the right word in the right place.*
10. Avoid triteness. These phrases have been used so often that they are worn out: *last but not least, scanty attire, dull thud, glassy stare, dead silence, radiant bride, a wonder to behold, in the wake of.* Think of picturesque phrasing, colorful word combinations, fresh figures of speech that are your own. English is a magnificent language, rich and versatile.

11. Avoid "fancy writing and purple passages," as well as technical phraseology that is meaningless to the reader. If the facts are hard to understand, it is your task as a reporter to simplify and explain so the reader knows not only what the facts are but what the facts mean to him. "The real trick is to 'write plain,'" says Louise Moore, of the University of Oklahoma. "Usually you can write your story as you would tell it."
12. Keep your reader in mind. Editors have long followed this rule: *Never overestimate a reader's information, and never underestimate a reader's intelligence.*
13. Remember that "Clearness plus color equals copy that clicks."

    This often repeated idea is one that you might tape to your typewriter where you can see it as a daily reminder.
14. Search for the most suitable words in every sentence. Avoid all blanket and general words. Every word has an exact meaning. Very few words have synonyms.

    Many writers use the words "reveal" or "disclose" when they merely mean that an announcement was made. "Reveal" and "disclose" are not correct unless the matter has previously been kept secret intentionally.

    The word "charge" is also used carelessly. "Charge" implies accusation.

    "Claim is erroneously used in the sense of "assert." Thus: He claims to be the owner of the car and asserts that he has proof of title.

    "Explain" is not a synonym for "said"; neither is "declared."

    The workers won a wage boost means one thing. *The workers were given a wage boost* means something else.

    The rule is BE PRECISE. To be precise, you must know exactly what meaning you want to express. Then you must check your wording and construction to be sure that the sentence conveys that meaning.

    Care in choosing the exact word for the exact meaning is illustrated in this story:

    David Brinkley, NBC news commentator, in the telecast of a Republican convention, mentioned one of the NBC reporters on the convention floor.

    "He's with the Michigan delegates," Brinkley said.

    Then he shook his head with a slight smile. "No, I better clarify that. I mean he is on the floor where the Michigan delegation is seated."
15. Use verbs and nouns for strength and color, rather than relying on adjectives and adverbs. Merely to tell the reader *about* some-

thing is not enough. Show him in pictures. Dramatize the action for him. Beware of abstractions and generalities. Note these sentences by professional writers:

Hurricane Hilda howled her way across the Florida Peninsula yesterday and died last night in the pine-covered hills of Georgia.

Moscow today just about owns Cuba—lock, stock, barrel and beard.

Last night New York glowed with embellished brilliance, smelled of freshly cut spruce and rang with cash registers and the bells of sidewalk Santas.

Smoldering discontent among French-Canadians has recently burst into flames of violence and political action which could change the map of North America.

16. Personalize your stories. Seek aspects that will bring a response from the reader.

This does not mean to editorialize. Editorializing has no place in a news story, for your obligation as a reporter is to state the facts only and state them accurately and objectively. You must see that your opinions never creep into your words.

In a news story, if you try to convey your impressions of occasions and people, you must substantiate them with proof. That is, you must cite facts that will support what you are saying. "Impressionistic reporting" must be thorough reporting—facts, not your feelings.

Punctuation, a Friend

Punctuation can be your friend and assistant.

Punctuation marks have meaning. In clear writing, the punctuation is an aid. Too many commas in one sentence, for whatever reason, tend to be confusing and to slow the reader.

No poor sentence can be rescued by adding punctuation.

Some students punctuate their copy as a cook might add spice to apple pie—sprinkle to taste. Others have heard that a comma means a pause. Therefore, they seem to think, every time you pause, you use a comma.

If you want to succeed in writing clearly, you need to make friends with the punctuation rules. You do this not so you can pass a test on punctuation but so you know what each mark can do to help you express your thoughts clearly and help the reader understand exactly.

Avoid semicolons in newspapers stories unless needed. Generally, the semicolon is used in a series with internal punctuation. Example: *New officers of the Don Quijote Club include Susan Harris, president; Lila Carter, vice-president; Marsha Hayden, secretary; and Ruston Pharis, treasurer.*

The effort to make punctuation meaningful is illustrated in the following examples in which the use of the dash is borrowed from contemporary professional writers:

> ... *Central's spring sports teams—tennis, track and golf—are entered in competition this weekend in Amarillo.*

> ... *Three new teachers—Mrs. Sharon Berdeaux, Miss Nancy Glaspy and Mr. Roy Hancock—joined the Benton High School faculty at mid-term.*

> ... *New student council officers—Keeton Zachary, president; Jimmy Poe, vice-president; Sandy O'Neal, secretary; Lynn Langston, treasurer; and Gin Turner, head cheerleader—will take their oath of office as is the tradition at PBHS.*

Ways with Words

As a student journalist learning to write, you will find many interesting uses of language in what you read and what you hear on radio and see on television newscasts. Developing a "listening ear" will help you in your writing.

Frequently words can be used to distort meanings or to serve a special purpose.

For example: The day Commander Alan B. Shepard made the first trip in a rocket, an item concerning his flight was read on a Russian newscast at noon that day.

Sandwiched between other items of little consequence, it read:

> *The United States tried to send a man into space this morning in a very small rocket which stayed up only 15 minutes and then fell into the sea, but the pilot was in good condition.*

Although there is no actual misstatement of fact, the piece is so worded that the reader who did not know the truth would get an erroneous impression.

To Summarize

A final word of "advice for success" is given by Louise Moore, of the University of Oklahoma.

"Care enough about the little stories to write them well," she says, "and then you can write the long ones well. If you are careless in the little ones, you will be careless in the long ones."

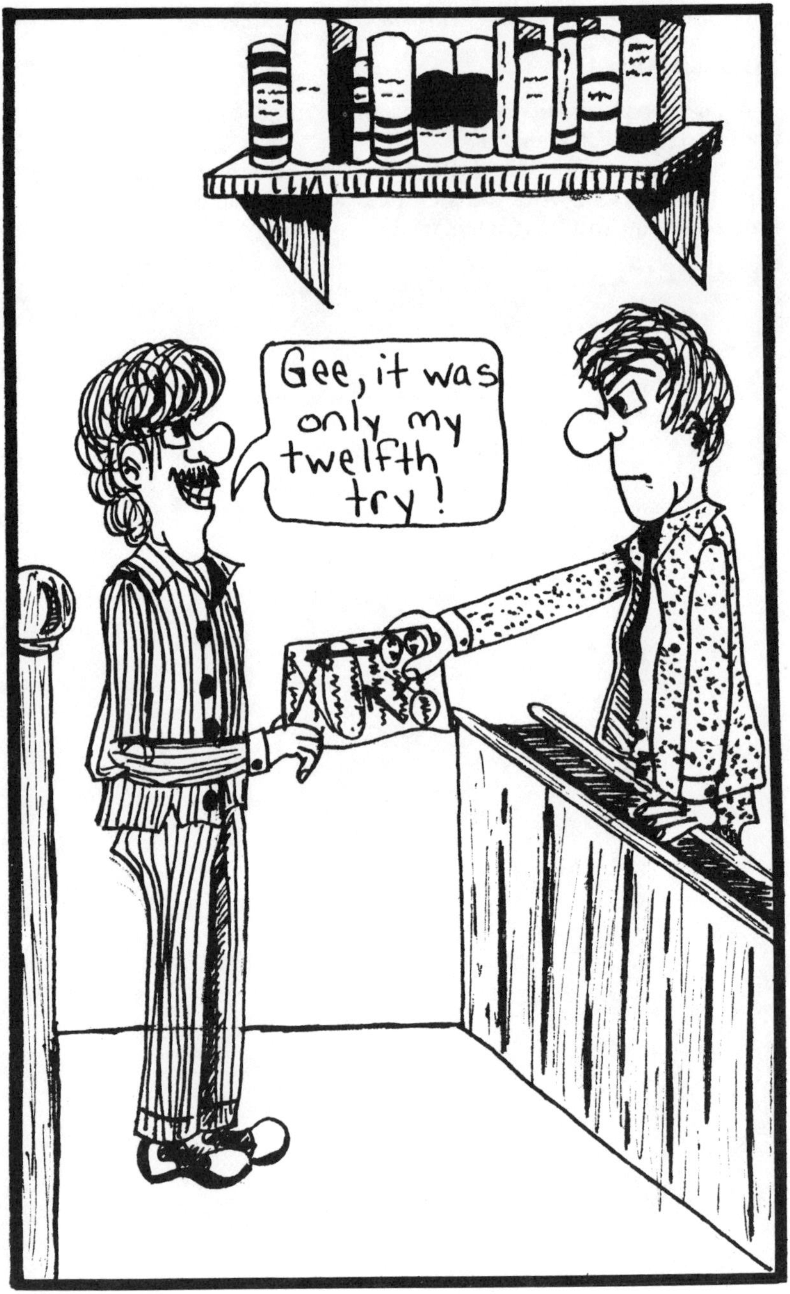
Gee, it was only my twelfth try!

Key # **17** *Cultivate an Effective Writing Style*

... *Correct* writing is "the proper use of the proper word in the proper place." *Effective* writing adds a plus quality, some smoothness and flair that make it easy to follow with clarity and pleasure.

This *plus quality* has something to do with really wanting to write. The reporter who is enthusiastic about his story already has a fluency and liveliness of thought that will make his ideas flow from sentence to sentence coherently and colorfully.

One professional journalist puts it this way: "If you want to write, you want to be read. Okay? Then think of the reader. After you've written your story, study it carefully. (1) Do the sentences flow easily from one to another? Is the thought easy to follow? (2) Does it have some sort of pleasing quality? Like maybe the use of an unexpected word that seems just right? A pleasing rhythm of thought? Apt figures of speech? Quotes that add color and flavor to the story?"

Helpful hint #1 for those who decide "the plus is for us": Keep books by your favorite authors and read aloud for a few minutes every day to develop a feeling for words and an ear for sound.

Helpful hint #2: Learn what the word "revise" means and then discipline yourself to revise your copy—every story you write. Check for clarity, coherence, unity, color, impact.

Basics First

In addition to learning how to express himself clearly and coherently, every ambitious writer wants to develop an effective way with words, a special quality we call *style*.

Again, this is a word that is hard to define but, like the wind in the trees, obviously there or not there.

An example: Using language might be compared to selecting clothes. Many persons choose correct apparel for a rainy day—raincoat, umbrella, perhaps boots. But only a few of those one sees on any one rainy day show any sense of "style." This "style" lies in a combination of choices that leads to some pleasing or special effect.

Communication Problems

It is generally agreed that communication is one of the greatest problems that citizens face today. In the United States, with the sudden "immigration explosion" of the 1970's and the "freedom flotilla," current difficulties arising in connection with the alien population (both legal and illegal) prove the importance of communication.

This is a problem of immediate concern to those interested in the use of language.

In this situation the newspaper is extremely important. News writers should know how to use the language to best advantage. They should know how to express ideas accurately and achieve readability at the same time.

TO BE REPEATED often: Readability begins with clear thinking, but writers must have skill in choosing words and in combining them in such a way that the reader understands the meaning.

Writers and Nonwriters

It seems to be generally agreed that some people can "write" and generally assumed that most others cannot. Now to define "write" is not simple. Probably one who can "write," if questioned about how to write, would say something such as "I've always liked to write," or "I love words."

Again the secret seems to be in wanting to—wanting to say something you think worth saying, and wanting to put the words together so that the something is well said.

About the Language

There is much to be said in praise of the English language. It is exceedingly flexible. That is, there are usually several ways, structurally

Key # 17—Cultivate an Effective Writing Style 195

speaking, of expressing an idea. Also, the language lends itself to expressing complex thoughts.

Although English is a combination, now several hundred years old, of two languages, with extensive borrowing from others, a fairly stable grammar has developed. Thus, it is possible to learn to use standard forms so we can understand one another.

HISTORICAL NOTE

English is a branch of Low German, the speech of the lowlands of northern Germany. About 450 A.D. various Low German tribes—principally Angles, Saxons, and Jutes—invaded the area we now call England, pushing back the Celts, who had been living there. The invaders in time came to be known as the English.

Their language was a combination of dialects known as Anglo-Saxon. It is the basis of American English.

In 1066 the Norman Conquest caused changes in the language used by the Anglo-Saxons. Speaking French, the Normans required the use of French in all governmental areas. Thus, French came into wide use.

At the same time, along with French, another language was introduced. This was Latin, used in connection with law, medicine, and science, and in education and the church.

This use of French and Latin lasted for more than two hundred years. All the time, however, Anglo-Saxon ("English") was still the popular language, spoken by most of the people in their daily lives.

Chaucer's decision to write in "English" marks the beginning of literary English as we know it. The use of French and Latin gradually faded. However, with "English" as only the popular language for so long, most of the vocabulary was made up of words associated with daily living. Also, many of the old grammatical forms were lost in careless and uneducated use.

This brought many problems, one of which was the extensive borrowing of words in all areas where French and Latin had been used. This addition of a huge "foreign" vocabulary means that we often have choices among words and thus can express ourselves clearly. Generally, the use of the old "English" words leads to simplicity, and simplicity is a characteristic of effective writing.

MASTERS TO STUDY

Understandably, English spelling and grammar are difficult to learn.

Difficult but possible. And no literary language is more beautifully used than is English in the hands of master writers.

Masters in the use of written English have left us a vast treasury of wealth in the body of English and American literature. This means that the student of language, the writer, has invaluable opportunity to study the techniques of the masters. Nothing can limit him but his own efforts.

To Summarize

The language of the careless is usually imprecise, redundant, awkward, and limited in the degree of complexity it can express. Those writers who have preserved correct forms and distinctions that have developed in the use of language have found them aids to clarity, precision, and beauty.

Where Do I Begin?

The beginner can immediately follow these suggestions:

1. Choose your favorite authors and read aloud to develop an ear for sound and a feeling for words.
2. Find for yourself (by asking teachers, visiting the library or book shops) one or more books written to help students develop an effective writing style. Choose *only* those books that are meaningful *to you.*
3. Make a practice of paying attention to what you read. If you think the material is well written, study it carefully to see why you think so.
4. Study your own writing, trying to avoid pitfalls and practicing correct and effective procedures.
5. Learn what the term "revise" means, and discipline yourself to revise conscientiously and painstakingly *all the time.* Always keep in mind the question, "Is there a more effective way to write this?"
6. Work consistently at increasing your vocabulary so you will have the precise word you need. The manner in which we express our thoughts is next in importance to the thoughts themselves.
7. Remember: *The mastery of English as a tool can be learned but cannot be taught.* That is to say, we must acquire it through *self-cultivation.*

Areas to Consider

As you study books on developing an effective writing style, you will find discussions of the following:

Diction. Diction refers to the *kinds of words* a writer uses. The lingo of sports columnists, the slang of the teenager, the sonorous phraseology of the Supreme Court, the elliptical language of informal conversation, the abstruse terminology of the philosopher, the technical vocabulary of the research scientist—all are kinds of diction and all have validity.

What kinds of words do you choose? Answer: Appropriate words. Failure to choose properly results in clumsiness, ineffectiveness, and lack of clarity.

Suggestions:

1. Use words that exactly express your meaning. Avoid words that are vague or misleading or "just sound good." Make certain that you know what a word means before you use it. Because many words have more than one meaning, check to see that there is no possible confusion as you write.
2. Avoid triteness. Strive for originality in expression rather than use of time-worn phrases that have lost much of their force. For example, *red as a rose, sadder but wiser, last but not least.*
3. Avoid wordiness. Write economically. Do not use several words if fewer will suffice. For example: *The meeting is scheduled to be held next Wednesday afternoon at 3 p.m.* Better: *The meeting is scheduled for Wednesday at 3 p.m.* or *The meeting is scheduled for 3 p.m. Wednesday.*

Awkwardness. This is the name given to clumsy construction and unpleasing phraseology, both of which should be avoided even though they may be grammatically correct. Three examples:

1. Clumsy repetition of sound: *The policeman's car's headlights suddenly went out.* Better: *The headlights failed on the policeman's car.*
2. Repetition and lack of subordination: *He did not appear at the meeting but he intended to, to the best of my knowledge.* Better: *Although I did not see him there, I think he had expected to attend the meeting.* Or: *Although he had expected to attend the meeting, he did not appear.*
3. Careless mixture of constructions: *Everything that is important—*

sometimes it is funding or maybe personnel, or at another time planning—these are discussed by board members. Better: *Everything that is important—funding, personnel, planning—is discussed by board members.*

Stiffness. A writer's style should be easy and natural, free from unnecessary formality. For example: *One should study one's lessons for one's own sake, and not for the sake of one's teacher.* Better: *One should study his lessons for his own sake, not for his teacher's.*

"Fine writing." The expression of ideas in fancy, highflown, affected, and exaggerated manner should always be avoided. For example: *Never have I been blest with the delight of viewing such an aspect of beauty as that sunset.* Better: *I have never seen a more beautiful sunset.*

Monotony. A monotonous style is caused by using a succession of sentences of similar construction, generally all of them the subject-verb pattern. Example: *The mayor had risen to speak to the crowd. Suddenly a gust of wind blew across the park. His notes fluttered to the ground, and everyone laughed.* Better: *As the mayor rose to speak to the crowd in the park, a gust of wind blew his notes to the grass. Everyone laughed.*

Lack of concreteness. This means use of generalizations and vague terms rather than specific, definite, precise words. Example: *This is an excellent book.* Better: *This is a dramatic adventure about Alaska.* Example: *He said he didn't like that at all.* Better: *He said, "I detest this kind of cake."*

SPECIAL DEVICES OF STYLE

The effectiveness of a writer's style is greatly increased if he makes occasional and varied use of many special devices, some of them *structural,* some of them *imaginative.*

These devices, of course, are not equally adapted to all kinds of writing. It should always be understood that the writer must exercise care and discretion in following them. That is, even though a writer understands all the various devices that he could name, he will employ only those that serve his immediate purpose.

In news writing, simplicity is basic—no ornamentation as such.
Suggestions:
As a guideline to help themselves improve their style in news writing,

Key # 17—*Cultivate an Effective Writing Style* 199

the *Grizzly* staff of Northside High School (Fort Smith, Arkansas) worked out the following. Since they originally presented it at a summer workshop it has "been around." Here it is again, with current modifications:

How to Succeed in Writing in 13 Easy Steps

1. Know *exactly* what you are going to write about.
2. Be sure you have facts, concrete information.
3. Be specific—use exact words for exact meaning.
4. Think in technicolor. Give the reader something colorful to see in his mind. Use picture-making phrases.
5. Appeal to his other senses, too. Give him something to hear, smell, taste, feel.
6. Dramatize the action. Use strong active verb constructions. Avoid weak passives. Example: *There were forty people yelling all at once.* Better: *Forty people yelled all at once.* Or: *Forty people were yelling all at once.* (Note the shade of difference in meaning between *yelled* and *were yelling.*)
7. Avoid stringy, run-on sentences. Example: *The election ended in a very close vote, but it was according to the constitution so the results were certified, leaving about half the student body disappointed in the outcome.* Better: *Since the election ended in a very close vote, about half the student body was disappointed. However, the constitutional requirements having been met, the count was certified.*
8. Carry an imaginary camera. That is, think in terms of pictures. In a way a news story is something like a play—it has a setting, characters, and action. If you examine these imaginary pictures in your mind, you will be able to write your story more completely because you will be filling in meaningful detail.
9. Avoid the "chop-chop" habit—that is, trying so hard to be "readable" that you fall into a succession of short simple sentences. In addition to the choppy sound, this kind of writing causes repetition of antecedents and pronouns and thus creates more words than meaning.
10. Avoid the "too-too" temptation—that is, control the "fine writing." Unfortunately, there are those who think that improving your writing means using more fancy phrases.
11. Develop an awareness for relationship of ideas. Subordinate clauses and participial modifiers are two of several structural patterns that help readers follow the flow of a story.

By reading the daily papers, one would think that many news writers do not understand the importance of showing readers such relationship of ideas. For example: *The Cuban refugees were to arrive at Fort Chaffee last Friday but were diverted to Little Rock. Unexpected rain necessitated the change in plans.* Better: *The Cuban refugees who were to arrive at Fort Chaffee last Friday were diverted to Little Rock because of unexpected rain.*

12. Develop a sense of rhythm and cadence—not the regular rhythm of poetry but a pleasing flow of language that gives a writer's work personality. To achieve this sense of rhythm, read aloud well-written prose, study the masters.
13. Watch for variety and contrast in passages of prose—variety, for example, in length of sentence, structure of sentence, combinations of words in such areas as parallelism and balance.

And REMEMBER that every story is different from other stories. Each deserves special consideration on its own merits. If there's a story worth telling, the enthusiastic writer can find the way to write it well.

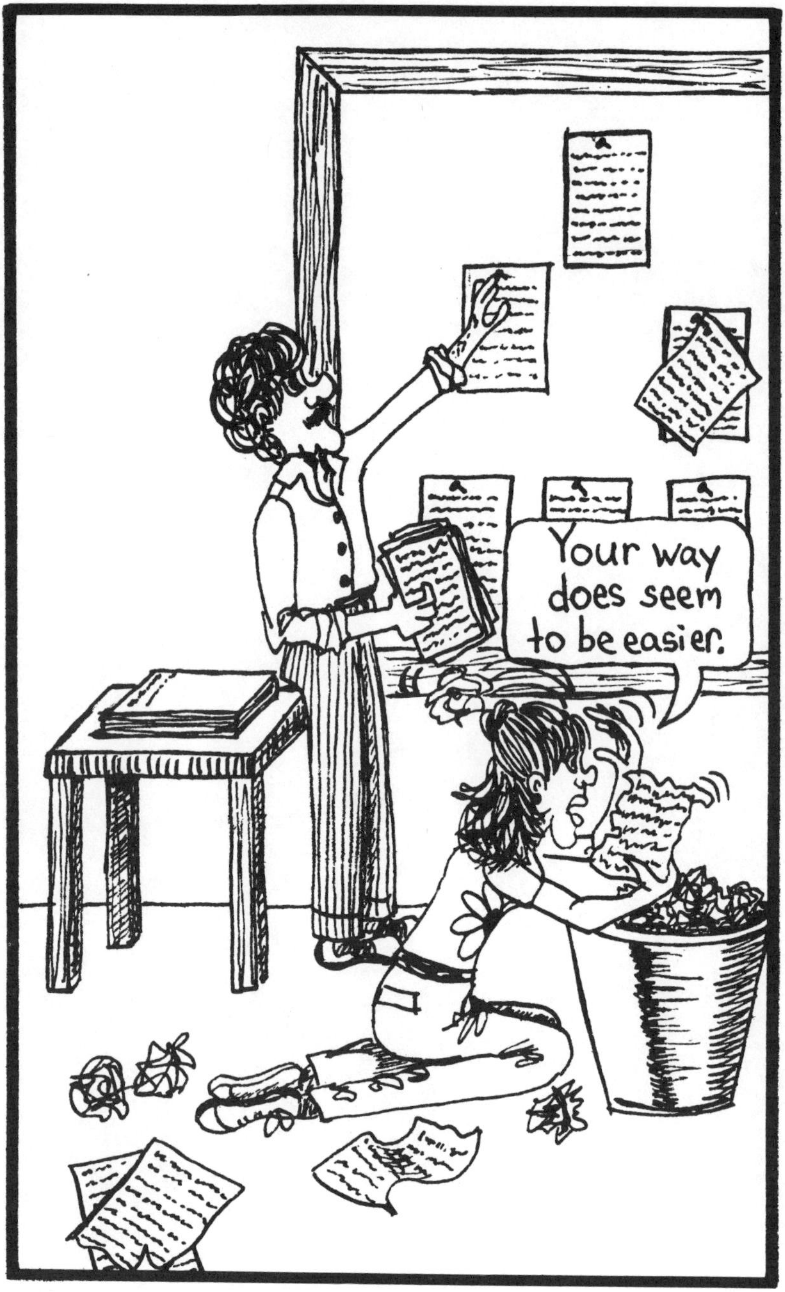
Your way does seem to be easier.

Key #18 Employ Effective Work Habits

. . . Do you lose things easily? Do your pencils turn up missing and your notes turn up in strange places? Does your story sometimes end with page two because you lost page three? Do you scribble so hastily that you can't read your notes? Do you lose important papers people ask you to return?

If your answer to even one of these questions is "yes," then you are probably messy, careless, and disorganized. It's time for you to develop effective work habits. That means to conduct your affairs in a businesslike way.

First, observe what others do. If they don't seem to be having your difficulties, consider following their practices. Probably they are neat and orderly, everything "under control."

Suggestions: (1) Develop a plan for filing or keeping up with important papers and materials and take time to follow it carefully, all the time. (2) Write neatly, legibly, no strikeovers. (3) Eliminate trash carefully but consistently, so you keep what is important and discard scrap. (4) Learn to keep up with your things. (Sage advice: "Put it UP instead of down.") (5) Keep your working space cleared. Never, never, never go off and leave anything important on your desk—it can easily be lost.

About "Housekeeping"

Some do's and don'ts:

1. Keep up with *your own things*. Never toss off the important job of filing your notes or putting away your material by calling to a friend, "Will you take care of this? I gotta run!"
2. Keep (in a safe place) your original notes so you can refer to them until the story is in print. Also, keep them if you see any possibilities for feature or sidebar stories.
3. Discard what is unimportant. If you make a copy of your story, dispose of your original draft. However, if you *revise* a story, keep both the original and the revision until all is in print. Frequently the original story will have something you need for reference. Also, frequently the first draft has more "fire" than a revision does.
4. Think "organized." Act "organized." Self-discipline is needed.
5. Begin work on your story early enough that you are not a victim of haste or desperation.

Work Space Needed

It is helpful to have adequate work space, but most student journalists have to cope with limited facilities and crowded conditions. This is a problem that individuals have to meet for themselves in the best way they can.

Two basic needs have to be worked out: (1) you must have a place for keeping what is important, and (2) you must have a place for keeping your materials—paper, pens, pencils, note cards and notebook, etc.

These will be of little help to you unless you can devise a way to have everything convenient and orderly. If you are among the fortunate who have a desk with drawer space and a filing section, your problem is one of arranging that space to best advantage. If you have limited space, the problem is more difficult.

Many journalism students, too many, have no private space at all. For them, their notebook is their "desk." Sadly, whatever limitations have to be met, the needs remain the same.

In many cases, however, one can provide himself with some means of containing (neatly) his supplies and the notes and other material he needs to keep. Some students, for example, find a shallow box (such as that used for packaging typing paper) to be helpful—*if* they can find a safe place to store it. This can serve as a miniature desk that affords both convenience and security.

About Taking Notes

One of the most important procedures for a beginning journalist is learning how to take—and use—notes for the stories he covers.

In a three-year survey conducted among incoming college freshmen recently, practically all students answered "yes" to the question, "Do you know how to take notes on material you read and lectures you hear?" Yet later, when tests were run in classroom situations involving both research and lectures, many students discovered that they could not produce adequate or useful notes.

Whether you use formal shorthand or a kind of personal shorthand, you will have to rely on your notes when you sit down with typewriter or pencil ready to begin your story. Even those who use recorders have to rely on notes at some point or other.

Learning to take notes is like learning to swim. The teacher gives you instructions, but you succeed only by earnestly following the instructions in repeated and meaningful practice. This is a skill that the journalism student can and must acquire.

1. You must be able to take notes very rapidly. Some professional journalists use a tape recorder now and then, but most of us don't need this kind of help yet.
2. You must know that a "note" is not a sentence written word for word, except for quotations to be repeated. A note is an abbreviation made up of some sort of shorthand system that makes it possible to crowd a great deal of meaning into a few words. Some journalists learn shorthand, some do not—but all note-takers must use some sort of "quickie" writing.
3. Notes must be *readable.* That means legible. That means understandable. That means usable.
4. The note-taker must *think* as he takes notes in order to follow the pattern of thought of the speaker or of the action in progress. Notes that indicate no relationship in thought or action are sometimes worthless.
5. In taking notes on a speech or on other prepared materials, the note-taker should do his best to see what the speaker's outline is as the speech progresses. If the notes can follow this outline guessed at, the speech can be more easily reported, especially in meaning and summary statements.

Individual System

Most reporters take running notes in covering a story. Each person works out some system of his own to show relationships of ideas, importance, special quotes, and the like. Some reporters use folded sheets of paper, others use notebooks.

Advantages of the notebook for the student are these: (1) he is less likely to lose the notebook than loose sheets of paper; (2) he can go back to his notes later if necessary; and (3) he can jot down ideas for related stories and have them where he can find them later.

In taking notes for background preparation, if much reading is involved, most people use 3" x 5" note cards. If such cards are given subject headings, they can then be indexed and filed. The source of information and page number should be included on each card.

Too many notes are better than too few. Remember, however, not to miss part of the speaker's next remarks when making a note.

Think as you make notes. Try to anticipate when an apt remark or pertinent point is coming so you can catch it and get it down.

OTHER CONSIDERATIONS

Beyond the basics of housekeeping and general work habits, there are other more subtle aspects of effective production. They have to do with attitudes rather than with habits or skills.

One such aspect is one's responsibilities to others. As a member of a staff on a school paper, your work is necessarily related to others. Similarly, a professional journalist has definite responsibilities as a member of a group who must work together to produce a newspaper on a daily or weekly schedule.

What are your responsibilities as a staff member?

1. *You are expected to meet your assignments.* A newspaper cannot run without copy. No copy means a blank space. Newspapers cannot run blank space. If for any reason you cannot get your story in, you are honor bound to notify your adviser or editor or someone who can meet the assignment or get another story. If the story assigned you is not turned in, coverage for that issue is incomplete.

2. *You are expected to meet your deadlines.* Failure to meet deadlines makes trouble and costs money. If an emergency arises so that you cannot get your story in on time, notify the adviser or editor at once. Failure to meet deadlines or rushing at deadline time results in errors and inaccuracies. Printing inaccuracies and errors is not only a foolish waste of money, but also a loss of prestige for the paper. Furthermore, occasionally errors result in misinformation that can be troublesome or disadvantageous for readers— as perhaps a wrong date for applying for a student loan or the wrong place for boarding the band's chartered bus.

3. *You are expected to do your best on every assignment.* This is not a halfway business. There is no place on the school paper for indifference.
4. *If someone gives you a story* thinking it is going to be in the paper and then the story is not run, you should tell him that the story will not appear as planned.

More about Deadlines

Most school paper staffs are organized so that they work on a staggered time schedule. This means that there is no single great push. This in turn means that day to day stories can be turned in, checked, and revised as necessary, with time enough for the writer to do a good job.

The time problem on school papers is not really lack of time. It is too much time.

Many student journalists seem to define "deadline" as "last frantic dash to get a story in."

Perhaps they do not realize it, but they associate this desperate rush with newspapering. A news story, they seem to think, is one that just barely makes it by press time.

A student who is assigned a story a week before the paper goes to press is in no rush in the sense that a professional on a daily is in a rush. But the student who has that much time to get a story in is usually the one who is late. With too much time, he waits too long.

The way to beat this desperation-dash is to get the story written as soon as possible after it is assigned. This insures the longest time available to revise it, gives you time to check for possible errors and verify facts, affords the copyreader and headline writer time to do a good job, provides opportunity for possible sidebar features and photographs, and gives you a feeling of orderliness and satisfaction.

If you let your notes lie unnoticed a day or two, you'll find the story much harder to write than if you composed it as soon as possible after covering it, while the experience was still fresh in your mind.

Your editor considers that a poor story turned in on time is better than a great story too late.

And Something Else

It may seem insignificant to beginners, but personal relations and public relations are important in journalism. As a reporter you are in a business where you are dependent on people, for without people you would have no news story, and without people you would have no readership.

Professional journalists are well aware of this when they give such advice as "Develop your contacts," or "Keep the lines open," or "Protect your sources."

Illustration: A reporter on a Southern daily produces a column that has a very high rating in readership surveys because it is made up of innumerable items gleaned from a varied and wide range of sources. His success in developing his contacts is proved by the fact that he has a long list of people on whom he can rely for information. One of his techniques is that his telephone line is always open to anyone calling in with a little news, be it that a parakeet is flying around the neighborhood or that a scandal is brewing in City Hall. (Big bonus: Tips from those contacts have afforded him story ideas that he covers for the free-lance market.)

To Summarize

Developing effective work habits and attitudes may be difficult for you, but it can be done. It must be done if you are to function well as a reporter.

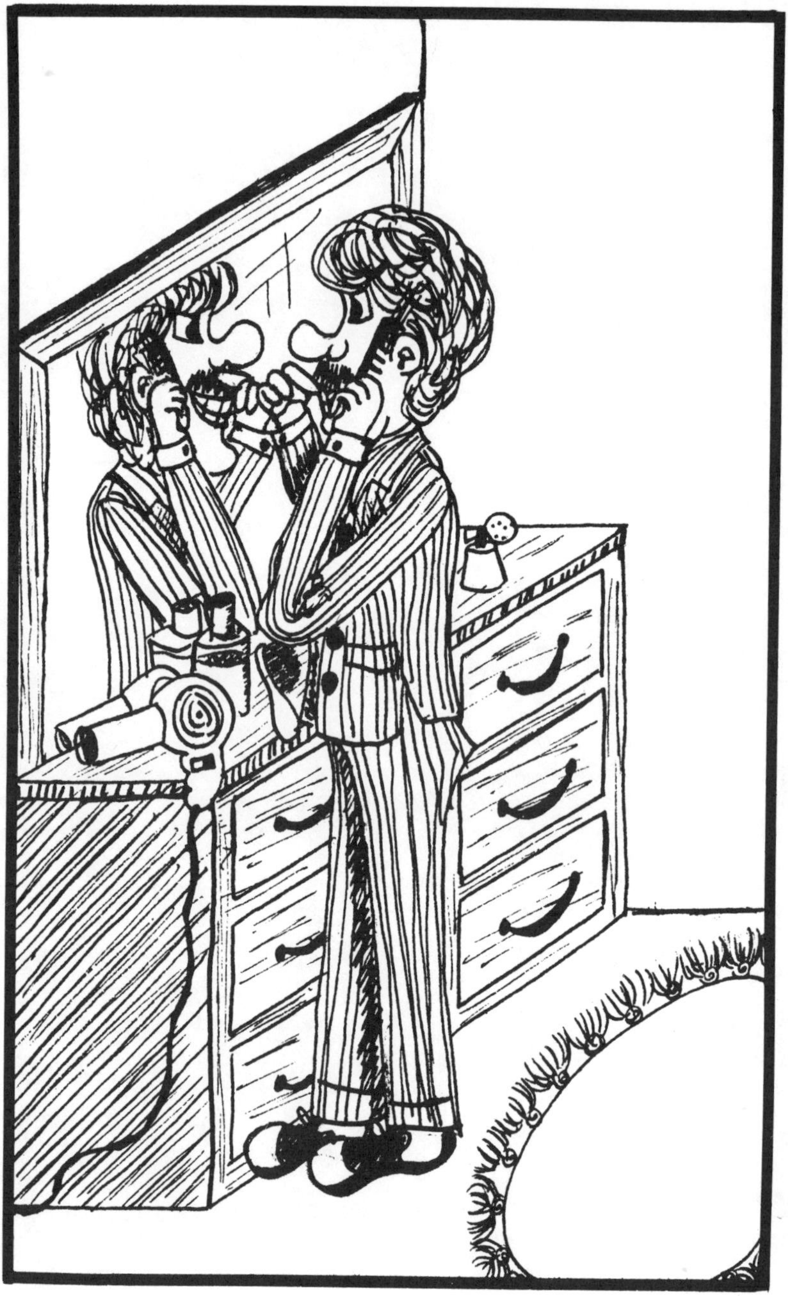

Key # 19   *Develop Confidence*

. . . Confidence, simply defined, is a state of mind characterized by reliance upon oneself.

As a student journalist it is important that you learn to perform well. Since a journalist is very much in public view, you must feel that you look presentable at all times, feel that your manners will never embarrass you, and feel that you know how to conduct yourself in any situation.

But the most important factor in your feeling confident at all times is your knowledge that you are well prepared, that you have done your research, that you are ready to go out and cover the story. You know how to think questions and get answers.

Remember the old ditty: "Be sharp, look sharp, act sharp."

Training on the school paper is training for one of the most important of all professions, for the journalist is the guardian of the First Amendment. This gives him both responsibility and stature. As the school paper is important to the school community, so is the student journalist important to the student body. Some writers record and reflect the story of society while others help shape the course of history. As a student journalist you are an important person. You must "walk tall."

A Matter of Feeling

Confidence is a matter of feeling. Confidence means that you feel comfortable: (1) feel that you make a good impression in your personal appearance, (2) feel that you know how to conduct yourself in any given situation, (3) feel that you are able to communicate effectively, (4) feel that you appear to be at ease, poised, that you have a sense of competency, and (5) feel that others seem to think that if you speak, you have something worth their attention.

Personal Appearance

Two factors must be considered if you desire to make a good impression in your personal appearance: (1) being well groomed, neat, clean, and (2) wearing apparel that is in good taste and appropriate for the occasion.

Whatever your personal likes, it is wise to remember that the public has a "public taste," an average taste that the public considers, just as a person has a personal taste. Fair or not, right or wrong, reasonable or unreasonable, this fact of "public taste" has to be considered.

An illustration: When a well-known, capable, and highly respected young public official lost his bid for reelection, his aides stated publicly that one reason for his defeat was the personal appearance of many of his staff.

General Conduct

If you feel that your appearance is acceptable, you are in a position to devote your full attention to your manners and your conduct of your affairs.

This begins with making sure that you are fully prepared, that you have done all possible research, that you have planned your approach, framed whatever questions seem helpful, considered a story guideline.

To be thus prepared means that you can anticipate changes in a situation or meet unplanned situations or unforeseen developments and face problems effectively. Obviously this requires either actual or vicarious experience: either you have had this experience before or you have read about it.

(Remember: When reading material that you expect to be beneficial, consider the source, the authoritativeness of the information. How sad to follow advice or example that foils your need.)

If your story involves interviewing individuals, make an effort to schedule an appointment. This is easy for interview-type stories, but frequently a reporter is faced with an impromptu situation. Experience helps here—experience and reading and heeding what seasoned reporters do.

Having made an appointment, *be punctual.* You are always at a disadvantage if you are late. Also, it is not fair for you to ask someone for his time and then waste it. Usually, too, if you are late, you expect the interviewee to give you the full amount of time you need, possibly running over into other appointments he had made. This is not wise.

Be courteous. Most persons you will interview for the school paper will be disposed to help you and will be glad to answer your questions or give information if they know what you want. Therefore, all you can learn about good manners and courtesy will be to your advantage.

Grizzled editors and salty old reporters occasionally advise others to "treat 'em rough, if necessary" to ferret out information that is hard to get or obtain answers to questions the interviewee does not want to answer. This is not wise for beginners.

Be honest and fair. Occasionally in their need to cover a story or in an attempt to track down information not easily available, professional reporters feel it is within their journalistic right and the public interest to resort to subterfuge, if not actual stealing or breaking and entering. This, too, is not for beginners.

Be businesslike. Since you know what the story is and have already prepared your questions and approach, you can proceed according to plan.

Take notes, but also make every effort to *cultivate your memory.* (If you want to improve yourself here, get a book on mnemonics. Study the art of improving the memory.) Even for those using a recorder, notes and memory are basic for accuracy, thoroughness, and easy reference.

Effective Communication

Anyone who desires to speak correctly, to think logically, and to be effective in communication can learn to do so. Communication is a subject taught in schools, covered in books, discussed by authorities, presented in special courses—and demonstrated everywhere all the time.

One charts his course for himself and proceeds at his own speed. He is his own critic and judge, and it is he who suffers the consequences or enjoys the rewards of his efforts.

Specific Suggestions

1. Read widely: newspapers to keep you informed about general news and a range of editorial opinions, and magazines, choosing a range of coverage to broaden your general background.
2. Prepare yourself particularly well in a few areas so you can discuss a subject with some understanding and knowledge, feeling that what you say will be significant rather than vague and meaningless.
3. Study the psychology of human behavior. This will broaden your understanding and enable you to deal with people in varying circumstances.

In this matter of developing confidence, one's opinion of himself is important. If you do not feel that you make a good impression when in a group or with an individual, do not despair, for there are specific ways to help yourself. No one can do it for you; this is another area in which, although others may teach, you must do the learning for yourself.

As you move from assignment to assignment, maturing a little with each one, you will gradually become better acquainted with yourself and your potential. Whereas in the beginning you may have had trembling knees and butterflies, you will discover that being prepared gives you confidence, confidence that perhaps you had never thought could be yours.

Public Shows Respect

You discover something else. You discover that other students and faculty members have a certain respect for good journalists.

There are few areas of school activity in which a student can join such illustrious adult company as by working on the school paper. One reason for this is that professional journalists now are taking a great deal of interest in school papers and student journalists. In fact, for some years now professional press associations, as well as individuals, have been supporting student journalists who have been involved in court cases over such matters as student rights, the First Amendment as applying to school papers, censorship by the school administration, and protection of sources of information.

If your local editor is typical of editors across the country, he is putting money into scholarships, affording training in some degree for ambitious students, and giving time and effort in appearing on programs, supplying you material, and offering you encouragement and support.

Reporting—and thus the reporter—is increasingly important to society. Even the smallest communities often have a local newssheet or are represented by a column or a page in a paper in a neighboring community.

Whatever the situation, the student journalist may have an opportunity to learn the craft through a one-to-one association with an older person who is interested in both the profession and the young journalist. The broadcast media, too, offer many at-home opportunities for the beginner.

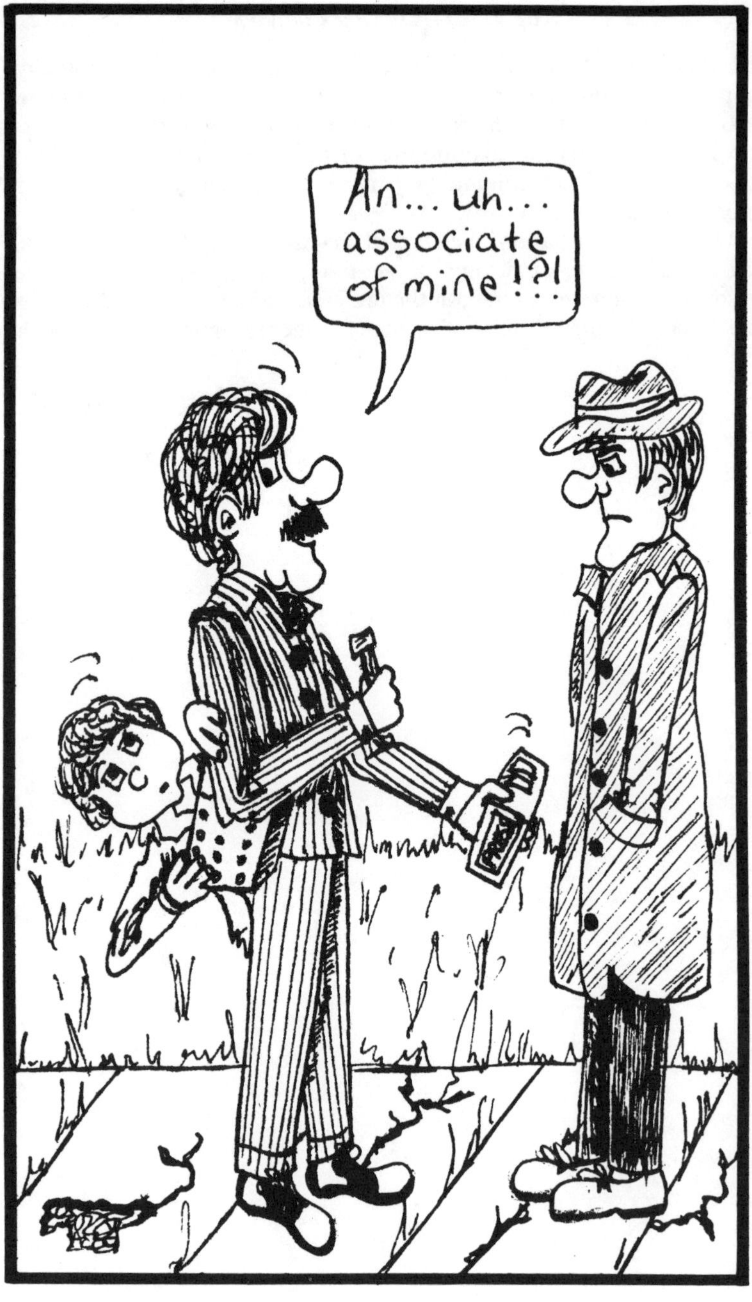
An... uh... associate of mine!?!

Key #20 *Learn by Seeing What Others Do*

... One interesting way to learn about news reporting is to be where professional journalists are at work.

Students often have experiences like these:

A. "Being news photographer when I learned that the President was flying in to our small airport, I managed to be cleared for the parking lot and arrived early to see what the Big Boys did. When one of the cameramen set up his equipment on top of his car, I climbed up on mine. When he clicked, I clicked in nervous excitement. His pictures were better than mine, but I learned a lot."

B. "Last fall when the Irish Foreign Minister was in town, the local editor invited school editors to the press conference. I had a chance to see professionals in action. They were sharp!"

C. "When Miss America was here for the city centennial, I managed to get a seat on the press bus. Luckily I sat beside a TV news editor. He gave me lots of suggestions, like watching for unexpected things, like maybe even getting an unexpected word with her."

D. "As a newly appointed editor, I spent a day in the newsroom of the local daily to see editors and reporters at work. I learned a lot from watching everyone doing his job."

Suggestion: Seek opportunities to watch professionals at work.

Professional Advice

"Read, read, read—write, write write."

This advice offered by an executive of United Press International many years ago is still sound. Although a book of rules and a set of guidelines is a help in knowing what to do, there is much to learn from the work of others.

The following story is told by a student at the University of Oklahoma enrolled in a professional writing class. The instructor was Foster-Harris, editor-reporter-author-professor, whose classes have included many of the well-known journalists and authors of contemporary acclaim.

"Well, I went to the first class session with the usual notebook and all set to learn how to be a great reporter after hearing a great lecture by a great teacher.

"You know what he did? He came in, sat down, cleared his throat and growled, 'The first assignment is to clip a feature story from any newspaper published today. Then you write a story just like it—exactly like it—only different. Class dismissed.'

"It took me more than sixteen hours to complete that assignment. I look back on it as one of the greatest lessons I ever learned.

"Maybe it was the challenge, or the outrage I felt at first—but I don't think so. I think that's a master stroke by a master teacher—delivered with that wonderful growl. And, you know, I'll never read another good feature that I don't hear him in my imagination—and I'll clip it and keep it and study it. That was the point—'just like that—only different.' "

Clipping File

Many writers consider their clipping file one of their most valuable possessions. There's always much to be learned from others.

Helpful Hint #1. Begin a file of clippings for yourself now.

Helpful Hint #2. Decide how to file them so they will be easily accessible and usable. Then keep your file in proper order.

Helpful Hint #3. Scan the daily papers and magazines available. DO IT TODAY, for today's newspaper will be in tomorrow's trash.

Helpful Hint #4. As you read them, make notes if you have any ideas for your own writing. And keep those notes.

Key # 20—Learn by Seeing What Others Do

Helpful Hint #5. Refer to this file often, for the reading of well-done stories will help improve your feeling for language and perhaps will serve as a source of ideas.

The following selections are offered as examples:

CAPE CANAVERAL, FLA.—Space shuttle Columbia shot straight for the heavens on a tower of white-hot flame Sunday and sailed a perfect course around earth: a spectular beginning to an American era of making space a workplace for mankind.
Everything worked.
"The vehicle is performing just like a champ," astronaut John Young said 9½ hours after lift-off. "It was as smooth as it possibly could go . . . better than anyone expected on the first flight."
Flight One of the winged space freighter got off on time, soared smoothly into orbit, and . . .

CAPE CANAVERAL, FLA.—After two flawless days in orbit, the shuttle Columbia and her crew prepared Monday for the searing, dangerous test of a spaceship's ability to survive a winged reentry and land like an airliner.
There remained questions concerning the integrity of heat-shielding tiles on Columbia's underbelly, adding extra tension to mission end. But a flight controller said simply, "We see no problems. Everything is going good.". . .

EDWARDS AIR FORCE BASE, CAL.—Space shuttle Columbia triumphantly passed her first trial by spaceflight Tuesday, sailing hypersonic through the heat of reentry to a perfect landing on a sunbaked desert runway.
The moment of triumph—12:20 p.m.—belonged to astronauts John Young and Robert Crippen, who inaugurated a revolutionary space transportation system with a mission lasting two days, 6½ hours.
Columbia, two years delayed, a $10 billion question mark, a white and black ship with the American flag on its left side, landed precisely as scheduled.
"You can't believe what a flying machine this is!" Young exulted. "It's really something special." . . .

EDWARDS AIR FORCE BASE, CAL.—The space shuttle Columbia, its maiden voyage described as "a 100 percent successful flight" after landing, has earned its wings as the flagship of a new American era in space, a mission official said Tuesday.
"I look at this reusable space vehicle as being the start of a whole new era in the space business," said Donald Slayton, the shuttle flight manager from Johnson Space Center in Houston.
The Columbia—the biggest craft ever put into orbit and the first one with wings—is a cross between a spaceship and an airplane designed as a space-going freighter that will make 100 or more round trips beyond the earth.
The National Aeronautics and Space Administration says the $10 billion

Space Transportation System could turn the heavens into a scientific laboratory, a weightless workshop.

Even as the Columbia was circling the globe, the shuttle Challenger, still just a partial fuselage with wings, was taking shape inside a Rockwell International hangar near Palmdale, 20 miles south of here.

Construction of the Discovery and the Atlantis shuttles should begin in the next year or so, forming the world's first real fleet of spaceships. . . .

NEW YORK—His whiskers betraying not a trace of gray, Mickey Mouse, a timeless hero, returned Saturday to the scene of his debut 50 years ago.

In celebration of Mickey's birthday, about 2,000 men, women and children jammed mid-Manhattan's Broadway Theater, where exactly a half century ago America's favorite rodent appeared in "Steamboat Willie," the first sound cartoon.

In the lobby, Mickey was greeted by smiling children perched on their parents' shoulders—some screaming "Mickey, Mickey" and some sporting mouse ears that bobbed over the crowd . . .

VANCOUVER, Wash.—A new mushroom cloud of volcanic ash and pebbles settled on cities across the Pacific Northwest on Friday as Mount St. Helens erupted for almost six hours in its third major explosion in a month.

The unpredictable volcano sent a plume of steam, ash and marble-size pumice 10 miles high late Thursday night, giving some cities their worst dusting yet.

Geologists expressed surprise at the force of the blast, which dropped pebbles of pumice up to an inch in diameter on Cougar, 10 miles southwest of the mountain.

"It was a major eruption," Pete Rowley, a U.S. Geological Survey geologist, said Friday. "It is silent for now, but it could do the same thing it did last night again." . . .

NEW YORK—Trim is the word that you heard.

Trim is the effect you'll be after for fall clothes, and the adornment that you'll want, and, if you're lucky, the shape your body will be in.

It's a trimmed season, Eleanor Lambert said, in assessment of the collections displayed in her American Designer Showings here.

The trim line is announced through shape: Broadened shoulders, smaller waist, definite hips and skirts that graze the knee.

The clothes themselves are trimmed, too: It's passementerie, beading, sequins, feathers, baubles and bugle beans. There are appliques and quilting, trapunto and contrasting colors. There are belts and muffs, hats and gloves.

And if you haven't got your body in shape by now, you'd better get after it now for real, because one of the season's big stories is the return of knits. And that means everything you wear is going to spill the beans on your every sin of overindulgence.

Everything, from coats to evening wear, is slimmed down and gussied up . . .

Key # 20—Learn by Seeing What Others Do

MIAMI, Fla.—The fearsome winds of a storm called David dwindled to a stiff breeze driving heavy rains Wednesday in the rolling hills of the Piedmont region of the Carolinas.

But in the islands of the Caribbean they were still counting their dead, buildings lay in shambles on Florida shores and scenic Savannah, Ga., was cluttered with thousands of felled oak trees.

The storm was one of the worst in the Atlantic this century. It slaughtered at least 900 persons in a sweep through Dominica, Puerto Rico and the Dominican Republic and left millions of dollars in damage when it sideswiped Florida.

At nightfall Tuesday, it smashed ashore again with full hurricane force near Savannah and spent its fury over gentle farmland and timber country.

At 6 p.m. EDT Wednesday, the storm was centered near latitude 36.0 north, longitude 79.5 west, near Greensboro, N.C. It was moving north . . .

NEW YORK—He told you about men on the moon, about the murder of a president, about the violent birth of civil rights. He told you about rice paddy warfare, campus bloodshed and landslide elections.

Now he is telling you goodbye.

Walter Cronkite. "Uncle Walter" and "the most trusted man in America" to a generation that scarcely remembers when he was not there to wrap up the day with, "And that's the way it is," signs off the CBS "Evening News" Friday March 6 after 19 years behind the anchor desk . . .

LIVERMORE, Calif.—Amid shattered windows, upended furniture and broken chemical bottles, workers returned to the Lawrence Livermore Laboratory on Friday to try to stanch radioactive water seeping from a tank cracked by a powerful earthquake.

Thousands of workers reported to the 640-acre nuclear weapons laboratory complex to begin the cleanup after Thursday morning's quake, which registered 5.5 on the Richter scale. . .

WASHINGTON—Skylab's 1,855-day career as an orbiting laboratory and then as a space derelict comes to a shattering end today between 6:50 a.m. and 3:14 p.m. (CDT). The most likely time was predicted as 11:02 a.m. (CDT).

Optimistic space scientists forecast that India, China, Europe and Russia need no longer fear being struck by Skylab debris.

On the other hand, the National Aeronautics and Space Administration acknowledged, the 77.5-ton spacecraft probably will fall during an orbit that carries it over the United States, South America, Africa and Australia.

Richard G. Smith, Skylab's director, said at Washington that the current prediction calls for the satellite to fall to earth along a 4,000 mile "footprint" in the South Atlantic or Indian Ocean.

However, as he has emphasized for a week, the prediction is only an estimate that could vary widely.

Smith said the latest data indicate it is highly likely that Skylab's final *plunge will occur within three orbits before and three orbits after the 11:02 a.m. equator crossing. . .*

WASHINGTON—With the fall and demise of Skylab imminent, the real mission of Skylab has been all but forgotten.

Nine men spent a total of 171 days in Skylab, proving that man can function effectively in space for long periods of time.

Among the scientific achievements of Skylab were the study of the sun, the improvement of crystals and alloys by producing them in the weightlessness of space and the surveying of earth's sources of energy, food and water. Skylab was launched in May 1973.

WASHINGTON—The time is now set at 11:10 a.m. (CDT) Wednesday. The place, Ascension Island in the South Atlantic with debris from Skylab falling along a 4,000-mile path starting in the southern Indian Ocean and ending in the northern Pacific just south of Alaska.

In announcing this forecast Monday, Skylab program officials said they hoped it proved to be accurate, as the track would allow most of the 500 or so large pieces to fall harmlessly into the water.

Only two large bodies of land—Australia and New Guinea—lie in the path as currently predicted, and since both are sparsely populated it is probable that Skylab's ground controllers would settle for this track—or one on either side of it—in favor of others that might pass over and thus endanger more people.

"The set of orbits with the least population under it," is the way Richard G. Smith, the Skylab project director, described the latest prediction.

Smith told a news conference here that at a "confidence level of 95 per cent," the re-entry time could be as early as 1:10 a.m. (CDT) Wednesday, and as late at 9:10 p.m. (CDT) that day, but most likely at 11:10 a.m. (CDT).

The 77.5-ton satellite, which has already traveled more than 87 million miles through space since it was launched six years ago, has accelerated its descent to 10 miles a day from one mile a day two weeks ago and now is at an altitude of 118 miles.

Smith said that four and a half hours before re-entry, ground controllers at Houston would command Skylab to tumble end-over-end to improve the accuracy of the predicted impact point. Ground controllers are best able to predict the ballistics of an end-over-end re-entry and thus are better able to determine how long it will take and can better calculate the fall of debris.

If the vicinity of Ascension Island is the point of re-entry in the atmosphere at an altitude of about 60 miles, it will take about 20 minutes for the first piece to land on the earth's surface, with pieces continuing to fall for the next 40 minutes.

Ground controllers could also order maneuvers to prolong Skylab's lifetime several orbits so that its debris would fall along a different track. Unless the current prediction is completely wrong this is not likely to happen.

The forecasts are made by feeding into the mammoth computers of the Johnson Space Flight Center at Houston the tracking data acquired by radars of the North American Air Defense Command.

Key # 20—Learn by Seeing What Others Do

FORT SMITH, Ark.—It's like something out of a science fiction movie.

Skylab swung in lazy ovals around the planet for years, receiving little attention from the public and only an occasional check from its guardians at NASA.

It sped over Arkansas twice a day, crossing over Little Rock, and then Fort Smith, two minutes later near Tulsa and then on a three-minute trip past Oklahoma City.

It moved fast for years, and as it now drops closer to its planet it moves faster.

And the faster it moves, the lower it drops.

But unlike late-night science fiction double features, people haven't poured into the streets in fits of screaming frenzy.

In fact, local folks are taking it all in stride.

Two Fort Smith radio stations are offering contests, with prizes, to Skylab-watchers.

A local donut shop advertises itself as a "Skylab shelter."

Area television stations will stay up all night and, if necessary, sound a warning.

About 500 pieces weighing a total of between 20 and 25 tons will survive the space station's fiery reentry into the Earth's atmosphere and fall to the surface.

They will range in weight from a pound to 2½ tons, including a 5,100-pound titanium protective shroud and a 3,900-pound lead safe.

Most chunks will be under 10 pounds, but NASA predicts that 10 pieces weighing more than 1,000 pounds each will make it.

The small pieces will be traveling about 30 mph and the larger ones about 250 mph.

A donut shop may not even be able to withstand the fall of a safe from a hundred miles up, traveling at that speed.

Though it's still mathematically unlikely that the flaming wreckage of the stately craft will fall ungracefully atop some unsuspecting pedestrian, the state Office of Emergency Services is prepared for it in any event.

"With the plans we have devised, we feel we could handle Skylab," said Richard Lucy, information director for the Conway-based civil defense agency.

The agency, in cooperation with local lawmen and the Federal Preparedness Agency, will follow standard disaster procedures should bits of Skylab pock across Arkansas.

The only unusual action by OES officials was the mailing of a lined piece of paper, with spaces for reports from citizens who claim to have seen Skylab on its descent or found a bit of metal which may have come from the craft.

Lucy said his agency would have about two hours notice of the imminent crash if Skylab were headed toward Arkansas. He noted the craft's path would be about 150 miles wide and 4,000 feet long, with particles and chunks scattered along a "footprint."

"People should not all run out and jump in their cars when they hear something. They should stay inside, away from windows, preferably in the basement or center part of the house.

"We have plans that have worked in the past for other disasters," Lucy said. "We have disaster plans for every county in the state.

"There's no real way to prepare for this. It's going to come down whether we like it or not."

WASHINGTON—The $2.5 billion Skylab space station fell to a fiery death Wednesday in the midnight skies over the Indian Ocean and a sparsely populated area of Australia.

Red-hot fragments of the 77.5-ton laboratory streaked down along a 3,700-mile-long swath of the ocean and Australian outback.

No injuries, damage or actual impacts were immediately reported. But ground observers and one airline pilot said they saw glowing chunks of the space debris hurtling through the sky shortly after 11:30 a.m. (CDT).

From 20 to 50 falling fragments of the disintegrating space station, the largest man-made object ever to fall out of orbit, were seen at Kalgoorlie, a remote gold-mining town at the edge of Australia's vast interior desert.

Other sightings were reported in the coastal city of Perth and at Albany and Esperance, all in extreme southwestern Australia. None of the pieces was recovered immediately.

An Australian woman who said she witnessed the debris falling described the scene as "a shower of sparkling lights." She said it appeared the pieces were heading toward the uninhabited Simpson Desert.

The spectacular nighttime display ended days of suspense for a world waiting to see where Skylab would hit and added yet one more surprise to the unpredictable 874-million-mile journey of America's errant space station.

Both the National Aeronautics and Space Administration and the North American Air Defense Command had been expecting the pieces of Skylab to plunge quietly into the Indian Ocean and fall short of Australia," Richard G. Smith, manager of NASA's task force on the Skylab re-entry, said at Washington.

"We were surprised when we heard of the sightings there."

NORAD, which tracked the orbiting station on a worldwide network of radar stations, announced at 11:42 a.m. (CDT)—just before the reports of visual sightings began coming in—that it thought the rain of metal had been taking place at least 1,000 miles off the Australian coast.

NASA had consistently maintained that its final prediction of the impact zone might be off by as much as half the distance around the world.

Ground crews lost all contact with Skylab as it sped over the tracking station at Ascension Island in the South Atlantic and began breaking up in the atmosphere.

NASA officials expressed surprise then that the silo-shaped space station still appeared to be in one piece as it tumbled end-over-end past Ascension at an altitude of 66 miles.

By then, they had expected that the friction of the upper atmosphere would have torn off the laboratory's windmill-like solar collectors and the outside telescope mount.

"We do not expect any further signals from Skylab," an official at Houston's

Key # 20—Learn by Seeing What Others Do

Johnson Space Center reported as contact with the space station faded out at 11:10 a.m. (CDT). "Skylab is on its final descent."

That was NASA's sentimental farewell.

The formal goodby to Skylab came much earlier, in the wee hours of Wednesday morning when authorities relinquished their last control over the falling laboratory.

At 2:45 a.m. (CDT), ground controllers in Houston fired the thrusters on the outside of the station and sent it tumbling toward its final re-entry.

The timing of that last move was the last crucial factor in determining where the tons of molten space debris would hit.

NASA actually initiated the tumbling maneuver earlier than it had expected to because it appeared from tracking data at midnight that Skylab's final plunge might end somewhere over the northern United States or southern Canada.

By tumbling the spacecraft earlier and increasing the space station's forward momentum, NASA hoped to keep it aloft for approximately 30 minutes longer, a time sufficient to carry Skylab out over the Atlantic.

It worked, but not quite the way that NASA had anticipated.

The midnight predictions from NORAD's command center inside Cheyenne Mountain in Colorado turned out to have been based on incomplete tracking information.

NASA concluded later that Skylab probably would have splashed down harmlessly into the Atlantic—as it had been expected to do for a day—without the early use of the tumbling maneuver.

As a result, the additional 30 minutes of life that NASA gave to its dying space station carried it an additional 8,000 miles downrange—past the tip of Africa and out over the Indian Ocean.

It was that move—the last act of human control in Skylab's 34,981 orbits of the earth—that provided Australia with its unexpected and unprecedented space-age fireworks.

Skylab was launched May 14, 1973.

SAN FRANCISCO—A shy Australian teen-ager on Friday collected the $10,000 bounty offered by the San Francisco Examiner to the first person who turned in pieces of the wayward Skylab space station.

The money went to Stan Thornton, a 17-year-old trucker's helper, after a federal laboratory determined the handful of black nuggets he scooped up in his backyard was indeed Skylab debris.

Thornton turned the $10,000 check nervously in his shaking hand and stared with frightened blue eyes at the gaggle of reporters in the Examiner offices who pressed him for comment on his fortune.

"I'm glad it landed in my backyard," managed the youth from the tiny town of Esperance in sparsely populated western Australia.

Scientists from the National Aeronautics and Space Administration laboratories in Huntsville, Ala., spent nearly a week testing the charcoal-like bits found near Thornton's home.

On Friday they told the Examiner that they had determined the pieces were probably souvenirs of Skylab.

"Although there is no scientific proof that the materials came from Skylab, neither is there scientific proof that they did not come from Skylab," the experts concluded, according to Examiner columnist Jeff Jarvis.

And for Jarvis and his paper's promotion department, that verdict was "good enough for us."

They declared Thornton the winner of the $10,000 prize since he was the first person with Skylab fragments to reach the Examiner office within 72 hours after the craft crashed on July 11.

Just as NASA could not predict exactly where or when the doomed Skylab would plummet to the earth, the space agency had a tough time making a precise analysis of the fragments found by Thornton.

"The examination of some of the pieces did strongly suggest that the remnants could have come from elements of the Skylab that were made from wood. Both hard and softwoods were used in Skylab as thermal insulators and cushioning materials," said NASA's W. R. Lucas.

"Other debris from entry 0021 (NASA's tag for Thornton's nuggets) give indications that they are pyrolized electrical insulating material."

Jarvis, who chronicled the contest for the afternoon paper, translated: "Pyrolized means burned."

Thornton said he'd most likely use his windfall for a "caravan (trailer) or for a down payment on a house" near his parents' home. His parents and girlfriend were en route to San Francisco.

While waiting for his find to be analyzed, Thornton had been seeing the city from cable cars—when he wasn't being besieged by autograph hounds. The visitor from the Australian backlands was clearly overwhelmed.

"I'd heard of San Francisco, but it's a little big bigger than I thought," Thornton said.

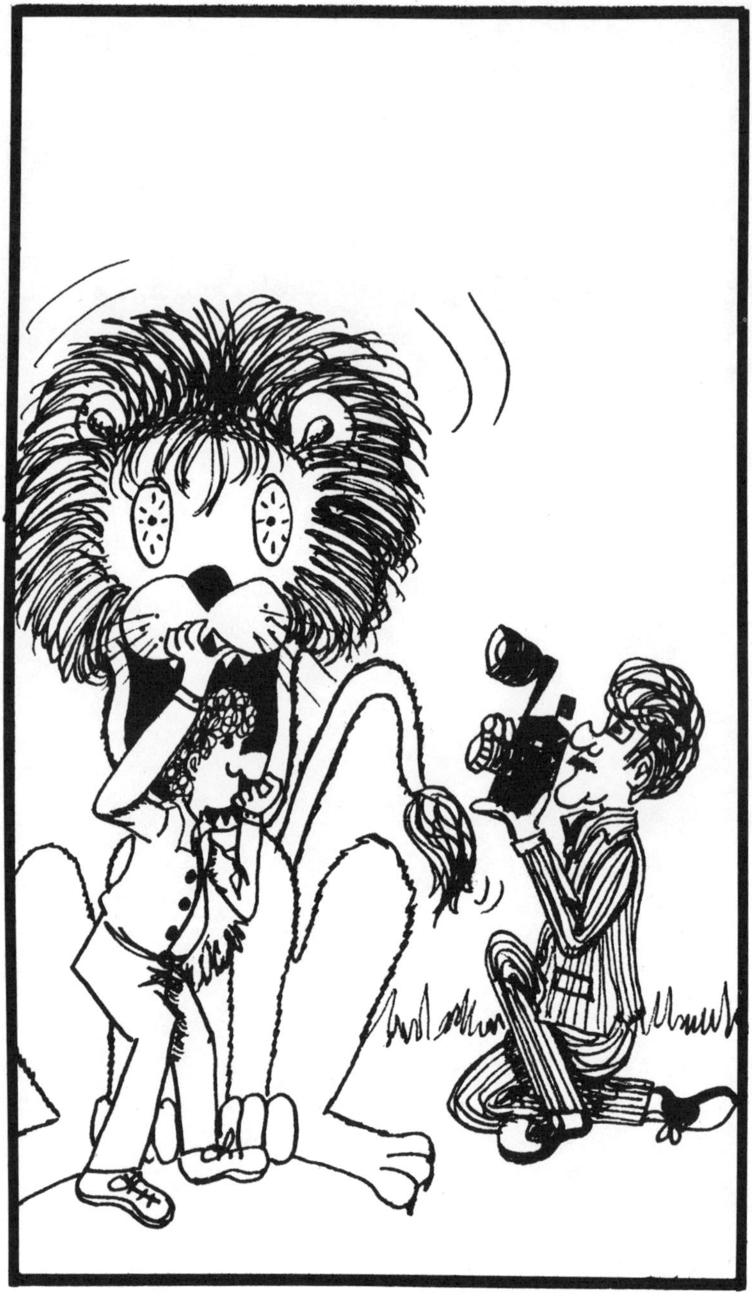

Key # 21 *Report Your Story in Pictures, Too*

. . . "Pictures are for people who can't read the words." The comics writer intended this to be a joke, but there's a measure of truth in it. And there's a great deal of truth in it if you change "can't read" to "don't read." (There really are many people who only glance at a paper.)

There's more truth yet if you stop to think how many news stories really do not—or cannot—give the reader much of a picture. A competent reporter who is a skilled photographer has opportunity to use words *with* pictures to communicate much more completely than with only words or only pictures.

Words *with* pictures, furthermore, give the reporter an opportunity to point out important information. A picture with few or no words can hardly cover a news event. (A news picture, that is. Feature pictures are different.) It usually shows only a who or a what or a where, as, for example, the winner in a yacht race.

For reporting with pictures, call on all your skills as a news writer to produce pictures that help tell the total story, so the reader can actually see the who, what, where, how as he reads.

Anyone can click a camera. It's selectiveness based on sound news judgment that makes the difference.

Picturing the News

We are a visual-minded world. With today's technology, we can see around the world with our own eyes, as it were.

Cameras range from the ultrasophisticated equipment developed for recording data in space to the simplest devices for Mr. Average Citizen to use in picturing the everyday events in family life.

With photography made practical, picture-making came early to journalism. Now the news is told in many ways in pictures, from the television report that offers on-the-spot coverage of situations and action worldwide to the news feature photos that tell more of the story than words can convey. Most reporters, of course, do not try to tell the entire story in pictures, but it can be done.

For school papers the importance of good news photos should not be underestimated. A paper can immediately improve both its appearance and general appeal if it improves its pictures, for readers respond with enthusiasm to pictorial coverage of the news.

"Old News" Possibility

Much of the "old news" on campus, for example, can well be covered in pictures. These might include such events as the cast of a play, the National Honor Society induction, the Future Teachers initiation, the speaker at the Science Club meeting, a demonstration by a visiting teacher.

Also, much that might be rather dull in words can be told in pictures. Certain events are important on the campus, but it is hard to write interesting stories about them. However, a clever reporter with a camera can get glimpses of people in action at those events.

For example: the College Board Examination, the semester tests, the maintenance of the bulletin board by the guidance counselor, the repairing of the public address system, the installation of a new fire alarm, cataloguing of books in the library, new equipment in the woodworking shop, arrival of supplies in the science lab.

It bears repeating that a good way to give a paper life and sparkle is to get more and better news pictures. The question today is not whether to have photographs but how to manage to have them.

That "how" is a two-fold problem: (1) how to get pictures, and (2) how to pay for them.

The Budget Problem

The question of how to pay for pictures is one that every staff has to solve for itself, for no two schools grow out of identical situations. Everyone has to "budge his own budget."

Some staffs are very capable in the matter of budgeting. They know that you can't find seeds to grow a money tree, but that you *can* plant something else, seeds of a different kind.

Those seeds are ideas that you can plant in your school paper, ideas that papers are worthwhile in a school system and that they are important to the individuals in the schools.

You plant those seeds, and you tend them well.

If the student body, the administration, and the community find that the school paper is worthy, together they will help you manage to keep it going financially. They will support your subscription campaign, your advertising, and your miscellaneous money-raising drives, if you sponsor any.

Good Pictures Possible

The first question, however—how to get good pictures—is one that *can* be answered, fully and specifically. The proof of this lies in school papers across the country.

As is generally understood, the sources of good news pictures are the same as the sources of good news stories.

These include events characterized by (1) human interest, (2) drama, (3) the importance of the persons included, (4) immediacy, (5) proximity, and (6) unusualness. (Someone has summarized these as (1) nowness, (2) nearness, (3) newness.)

In addition to these, or rather *with* these, a good news picture must obviously tell a story.

A study of hundreds of school papers shows that while many staffs are following current trends in news photography, many others are still running ineffective news pictures—trite, static, poorly planned, and poorly cropped.

Since printing a poor picture is just as expensive as printing an effective one, all staffs should work at updating their picture coverage.

It is possible for school papers even on modest budgets to have excellent pictures. A school newspaper does not have to be out of date in pictorial coverage of the news.

Examination of a few copies of national magazines that specialize in news photography shows how professional photographers are now reporting the news in pictures. Newspapers, too, of all kinds, are reflecting the contemporary look in pictures.

Concerning this, Irving Lloyd, author of *Creative School Photography,* says: "The old emphasis on perfection has been replaced by the new emphasis on expressions and realism. The very best photographs are not judged as photographs at all, they simply evoke a response from the viewer toward the subject of the picture."

Wilson Hicks, author of *Words and Pictures*, emphasizes the fact that photographers need to increase "their capacity to use the camera mentally as well as mechanically."

He makes this point: "It is the photographer, and not the camera, that takes the picture."

The camera records only what the photographer sees.

Amateurs' Problems

In comments addressed to students interested in news photography, William J. Good, at the University of Arkansas, summarizes thus: "Good pictures are made by photographers who recognize an interesting picture scene when they see it, are able to interpret it through the camera lens, and then have sufficient technical skill to produce a print that will command the attention and gain the understanding of the reader.

"Too many amateur photographers, and professionals for that matter, have never learned the great art of throwing away their technically bad and artistically poor pictures."

Also, some amateur photographers are afflicted with a very stubborn, and extremely unfortunate, disease that Good calls "igottatryititis."

"No matter how far out a photographic idea or technique is, they have to try it," he says. "They try to push films to unrealistic speeds. They use developers in a fantastic manner. And in the process, they produce pictures that are entirely useless. Whenever an editor is unfortunate enough to get a character like that, the best thing to do, generally speaking, is to ease him out as soon and as painlessly as possible.

"Experimentation is fine for the sake of experimentation, when one is sincerely attempting to improve his techniques. But when one is on assignment, there is no substitute for tried and true techniques based on adequate experience."

Humorous Shots Difficult

Humor is the most difficult of all moods to express with the camera, just as it is with the typewriter. Fortunate indeed is a photographer who is able to catch a really humorous but unstaged shot.

Much of our photographic humor must be contrived humor. This is something that very few student photographers are able to arrange.

Key # 21—*Report Your Story in Pictures, Too* 233

If the picture betrays that contrivance entered into the making of it, the picture is a failure. A contrived humor situation cannot successfully be used a second time. No matter how good it is the first time, it is trite if repeated.

Speaking of the oft-quoted phrase that "a picture is worth 10,000 words," Good says: "The truth of that statement depends upon the skill or lack of skill of the person who wrote the words and also of the person who took the picture.

"And as for the quip that 'pictures are for people who can't read,' that's nonsense. Pictures are for people who want to *read more* than can be told adequately in words."

Photo Assignment Card

"How can a serious-minded photographer insure getting a usable picture when a news story breaks?" Good asks.

One help is the assignment card. If the supply of forms used by the staff does not include an assignment card for pictures, the photographer himself should make out a form on a card and either type or duplicate a supply of these for himself.

Though the card can be of any size that is convenient to handle, 3" x 5" seems to be the most popular.

The form on page 234 shows what information is generally included on such an assignment card.

Helps Available

With many good books on photography on the market and with professional photographers willing to help, students have ample opportunity to learn about taking good pictures if they want to make the effort.

It must be remembered that good pictures do not just happen.

You have to work toward good pictures. You have to be "picture-minded," for in photography you are working creatively.

The following suggestions were listed by students in a summer workshop as helpful hints they had picked up in their experience:

1. Composition of the picture is important.
2. In planning for the center of interest, use the "rule of thirds." That is, you can put the center of interest at any point where there is an intersection of lines as in this diagram:
3. You emphasize the center of interest by lines. These lines may

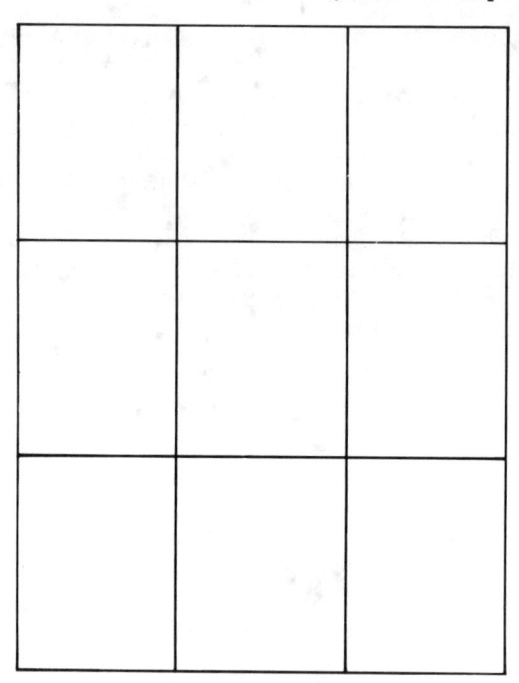

234 The Student Journalist and 21 Keys to News Reporting

be actual lines or implied. That is, there may be something that directs the eye, although no actual line is present—as people looking up toward the sky.
4. Do not cut a picture squarely in two with the horizon.
5. Get close to the subject—close enough to fill the frame with the picture.
6. Take pictures large enough to use effectively.
7. Experiment if you like, but not at the expense of the paper.
8. Go by the book at first. Then as you go along, adapt as you learn.
9. For best possible subjects for news pictures, photograph people, preferably people in action.

SELF-TESTING SUGGESTION

One suggestion that school papers might consider is a quiz in *Creative News Photography* by Rodney Fox and Robert Kerns. They propose the following questions to see whether your publication is achieving the ultimate benefits from modern photographic coverage:

Key # 21—*Report Your Story in Pictures, Too*

```
                PHOTO REQUEST—The High Times
Subject _____

Date _____ Time _____ Deadline _____

Location _____
Comment on picture or angle wanted _____
_____
_____
_____
_____

Person(s) to be included _____
_____

Staff member requesting photo _____
Photographer assigned _____

                                    _____Editor
```

Illustrates Rule of Thirds

1. Do we use enough pictures?
2. Do our pictures really add to the story or do they merely fill space?
3. Do we use pictures large enough to be effective?
4. Are we selecting the best possible available subject matter for our readers?
5. Are our pictures planned, cropped, and organized to make them as effective as possible?
6. What ideas and practices should we add to what we already are doing to improve the quality of our photographic presentations?

A careful study of these items shows that in taking successful news pictures, as in writing successful news stories, there is no place for haphazardness.

They imply forethought, insight, understanding, planning.

The answers can be worked out only by enterprising photographers who bring to their willingness to work a sense of news values and creative imagination.

Avoid Complications

"Keep it simple."

That's the advice of veteran news photographer Allen H. Barnett regarding school photography problems, especially those related to cameras and procedures.

"One reason people fail to get good pictures," he says, "is that they get so involved with various gadgets and complicated techniques that they overlook the basic fact in making good pictures—that it's the enthusiasm of the photographer that really counts."

Expensive cameras, complicated gadgets, and involved processes will not take the place of simple equipment that the photographer knows how to use.

There is no quick way to success in making good pictures.

The photographer approaches every picture with enthusiasm for that one picture and brings all his experience and enthusiasm to bear on it.

To repeat: The secret in taking good pictures is to keep it simple. Learn to take pictures quickly and easily, and enthusiasm will do the rest.

"Keep the controls of the camera simple so you can concentrate on the composition of an interesting picture," Barnett says.

"This is where we want to put all our effort and thinking—into making the picture interesting. The viewer does not care about equipment or procedures. He cares only about what shows up visually on the news page."

It is *the content of the picture* that really counts.

In setting up his picture, the photographer should remember two things:

1. The subject must not look at the camera, unless the picture is specifically posed to show the subject's facial expression.
2. Action is important. Plan so the subjects are doing something. If you do this, the caption and picture will show purpose, compatibility, and action. The words "caption" and "cutline" are used (interchangeably) to refer to words used with a picture to identify, interpret, explain, and supplement the content of the picture.

Consider the Caption

If the photographer merely lines up his subjects and shoots them doing nothing, the caption writer is faced with serious problems. He has nothing to say except the names of the subjects.

Key # 21—Report Your Story in Pictures, Too

Captions should never be merely a statement of what is obvious from the picture itself. Instead, they should explain what the subjects are doing, perhaps when and why.

Captions should not, of course, simply repeat the lead of the accompanying story. And never should they be a display case for trite and weak attempts at humor. As the oft-repeated advice goes: "Write cutlines, not 'cutelines.'"

In almost all cases, the picture has to be a posed picture, giving the photographer some opportunity to use his imagination. At that time he can have in mind what the caption writer is going to be able to say.

Editors should demand, and photographers should supply, all information needed to go with the picture so the cutlines can be complete, meaningful, and written with some imagination.

Both the editor and the photographer have failed if the captions say "Shown here is the winner of . . ." However, if the picture is merely a group of new officers, committee, etc., it is correct to phrase the caption this way: "New officers of the Science Club are James . . ."

Captions are generally put under the picture. In addition, some papers use a heading over the picture or between the picture and the caption.

Some papers, however, run the first few words of the caption in caps or boldface, instead of using a heading. This is called a *rocket lead-in*. Some papers use neither heading nor rocket lead-in, preferring the caption alone.

"GIMMICKS" IMPORTANT

In pictures, as in stories, "gimmicks" are important. To set up your picture, give the subjects something to hold, some object on which they can center their attention or with which they can engage in some action.

"Action in the picture is so important," Barnett says, "that if the subject does not have anything to do, the photographer should 'trick' him into doing something."

For example: In taking a picture of trophy winners Jim and Jean, suggest that Jean straighten Jim's tie. As her attention is centered then on fixing the tie, snap the picture. The caption would then say: "Jean straightens Jim's tie a moment before both go on stage to receive trophies in this year's . . ."

Or perhaps the trophies have already been presented, and both Jim and Jean feel stiff and ill at ease. Suggest that Jim dust off a spot on

Jean's trophy, which might show up in the photo. While he is doing this, snap the picture.

"It is very important for the photographer to keep people's minds off the fact that they are having their pictures made," Barnett says. "In this you are controlled only by the limits of your own mind. The more nimble-witted you are, the quicker you can discover how to help them forget that the camera is there.

"The point to remember is that if you keep the mechanical part of this simple, then you can concentrate on the subjects and how to get the best possible picture of them at that time in that situation."

Cropping Makes a Difference

Once the photographer has a picture, he must—or the editor must—crop the picture so that only the meaning of the shot appears in the paper.

The photographer focuses his attention on one idea, a center of interest. Being mechanical, the camera takes more than this, for it must take in whatever else is in the field. Only by cropping can this "whatever else" be eliminated.

Even with crowds of people, do not hesitate to crop close in order to get the center of interest to the reader. Your guiding question should be only this: What is the heart of the picture?

If you crop to give the reader only this "heart" of the picture, and then enlarge it to fit your space, you increase the impact of the story you are trying to show.

Photographs Record News

Each news picture is a single important occasion. It will not be repeated. If it is captured, it will be captured only by the photographer and the writer of the story.

Therefore, each news picture deserves the photographer's complete attention and the best that he can do. As no two news situations could be exactly the same, no two news pictures will be exactly the same.

The importance of the photographer as a recorder of the news means that he must be ready to go on a moment's notice if a story breaks. He must be ready and his equipment must be ready.

To play on words, we might say that he must be *in readiness.* By this we would mean that he must have ideas himself and must be receptive to ideas of others.

Key # 21—*Report Your Story in Pictures, Too* 239

He must be able to understand what the news event means, be responsive to sudden opportunities, be quick to see how to switch his plans. Like the news writer, the news photographer may discover hidden angles that provide interesting sidebar stories.

The news photographer must not fail, for if he fails, the pictorial coverage of that event is lost forever.

An example: The horrifying pictures of the blazing airliner falling in California—the nation's worst air disaster. This, and the immediate devastation, were recorded by a photographer who just happened to be in the neighborhood to do a feature on a gasoline station. When he heard the explosion as the two planes collided, his being in readiness made it possible for him to respond immediately . . . on the scene, at the moment.

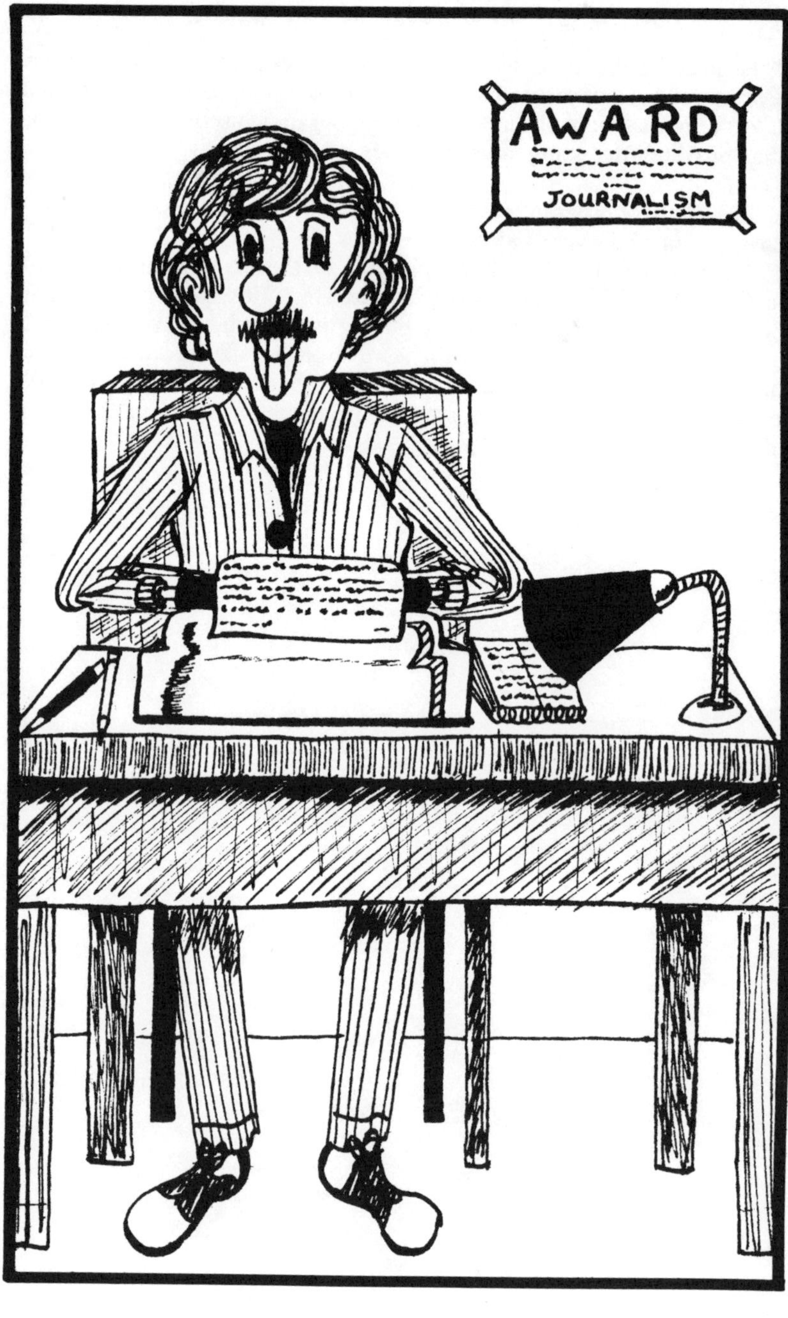
AWARD
JOURNALISM

As is so often true,
    the rules are few.
It's the work that counts
    in large amounts
And care in all that you do.

Associations Offer Aids

Some of the most valuable help for those who are beginning to work on a high school paper or who are taking up journalism for the first time are the publications offered by the various scholastic press associations. These exist at several levels, area, state, and national.

By joining these organizations, the staff becomes eligible for a number of free helps. Other publications can be obtained even by nonmembers. A price list can be obtained upon request.

Many staffs join both their state or area association and one or more national groups. Through publications of these national associations, you can locate names of other groups that you think might have publications that would be helpful to you.

NATIONAL ORGANIZATIONS

Columbia Scholastic Press Association, Box 11 Central Mail Room, Columbia University, New York, NY 10027. Magazine: *School Press Review;* other publications. Columbia Scholastic Press Advisers Association. *Bulletin.*

National Scholastic Press Association, Suite 205, 720 Washington Avenue SE, University of Minnesota, Minneapolis, MN 55414. Magazine: *Scholastic Editor—Graphics/Communication;* other publications. "Bookstore Catalog" available.

Quill and Scroll Society, University of Iowa, Iowa City, IA 52242. Magazine: *Quill and Scroll.*

Future Journalists of America, School of Journalism, University of Oklahoma, Norman, OK 73069.

LB 3620 .P73